AMERICA'S GREATEST ROCK AND ROLL BAND
(*photo by George DuBose*)

TALK ABOUT
THE PASSION

R.E.M.
AN ORAL HISTORY

by
DENISE SULLIVAN

UNDERWOOD-MILLER
CHARLES F. MILLER, PUBLISHER
LANCASTER, PENNSYLVANIA

R.E.M. — Talk About the Passion: An Oral History
ISBN 0-88733-184-X

An Underwood-Miller, Charles F. Miller, Publisher book by
arrangement with the author. No part of this book may be reproduced
in any form or by any electronic or mechanical means including information storage and retrieval stystems without explicit permission from
the author or the author's agent, except by a reviewer who may quote
brief passages. For information address the publisher: Underwood-
Miller, 708 Westover Drive, Lancaster, PA 17601.

All of the statements expressed herein are the opinions of the
individual interviewees whose versions may differ from person-to-
person based on experience and memory.

For Wes, P.S.I.

"It has been my experience, sir, that the normal person enjoys seeing his or her name in print, irrespective of what is said about them . . . Moreover, if you have ever studied psychology, you will know that respectable old gentlemen are by no means averse to having it advertised that they were extremely wild in their youth . . ."

—"Jeeves Takes Charge"
from *The World of Jeeves*
P.G. Wodehouse

"If I'd been happy with the world I'd be selling insurance or teaching English. Fundamentally, the people who change the world are the ones who don't like it. If Bill and Mike were satisfied with life they'd still be in Macon, playing in a boogie band. We're people who, in a lot of ways, wouldn't have fit, and we've managed to change a little corner of our world. We're very . . . I hate to use the word, 'idealistic' . . . more moralistic. Idealism smacks of naivete, and none of us are naive. But our lives are totally morally guided. Not the old morals—church on Sunday, don't drink, shine your shoes—that's bullshit. Mike and I were talking about this the other day, and he said, 'You know, if we were sleazebags we'd have a lot more fun.' I said, 'Yeah, but you have to be stupid to live with it.'"

—Peter Buck to *Details*, February 1993

Table of Contents

THANKS

I wish to thank each interviewee who participated in the book, and those who contributed off the record and led me to some key sources. Special thanks go to my friends Mark Methe and Velena Vego in Atlanta and Athens respectively for accommodations and phone numbers. To Jared and Barrie at the 40 Watt, thanks for always making me feel welcome. Thanks to Jefferson Holt at R.E.M. Athens, LTD. for granting me permission to do everything except interview the band. Thanks to Tim Underwood and Chuck Miller for taking a chance on my idea and putting out the book, and thanks to Paul Williams for introducing me to Tim as well as answering all of my questions. Thanks to Charles Cross for related assistance. Thanks to Neil Feineman for assigning me a story on R.E.M. that provided to be the inspiration for this book. Thanks to Carol LaRusso for editorial suggestions and Larry Brauer for typesetting. Thanks to Kevin Sullivan and Zazu Faure in LA and Lauren Agnelli and Dave Rave in NY for your floor space. Gary Nabors' reference, *Remnants,* was an invaluable source for me and should serve as a companion book for more complete discography information. Thank you Michael Shriver for providing the record sleeves that are reproduced here as well as important bootleg information and catalog numbers. Thanks to Trudy Fisher for photo processing consultation and the slide projector, and to Thessa Mooij for translation from the Dutch. Thanks to all of my friends who listened to me talk about R.E.M. during the gestation period of the book—I quickly realized I was boring everyone around me senseless. A gigantic thank you is saved for my friend Yvette Bozzini who listened to me and encouraged me from the book's inception (as well as informally helped me to edit). Finally, thank you to my husband for helping me through every phase and not minding too much when I listened only to *Fables of the Reconstruction* for about two weeks or when I said, "I dreamt about R.E.M. again last night." Ultimately, I must thank R.E.M. for providing the theme music to the soundtrack of my life for the last thirteen years.

VOICES

KEITH ALTOMARE worked at IRS Records in various promotions positions during R.E.M.'s tenure there. Currently, he is vice-president of sales, Rhino Records, Los Angeles.

GINA ARNOLD is a San Francisco-based rock critic and author of *Route 666: On The Road to Nirvana*.

JARED BAILEY is co-owner and booking agent of the 40 Watt Club and founder of *The Flagpole*, an Athens, GA music magazine.

DANNY BEARD is co-owner of Wax 'n' Facts Records in Atlanta and founder of DB RECS, the label that released the first single by The B-52's as well as records by Pylon, Love Tractor and others.

SEAN BOURNE attended art school in Athens and is an Atlanta-based artist. Through the years he has worked as a crew member for various Atlanta bands and at Wax 'n' Facts.

JOE BOYD started producing records in the Sixties. His credits include The Incredible String Band, Pink Floyd, Fairport Convention and 10,000 Maniacs among others. He produced *Fables of the Reconstruction*, R.E.M.'s third album. He is founder of Hannibal Records, which is distributed by Rykodisc in the U.S.

SARA BROWN first met Peter Buck in the late Seventies in Asheville, NC while he was distributing records through North Georgia and The Carolinas. She lived in Atlanta from 1981-92 and has returned to Asheville to pursue an environmental degree.

KURT COBAIN was the lead singer/songwriter of Nirvana. He was preparing to collaborate with Michael Stipe prior to his suicide in April of 1994.

BILL CODY was a producer on the film *Athens, GA-Inside/Out,* which chronicled the scene in 1986 and featured two performances by R.E.M.

BRIAN CRANE is drummer for the Sugardaddy's, an Athens-based band. He has lived in Athens since 1981.

CURTIS CROWE was the drummer for Pylon and toured with R.E.M. on the Green Tour. He lives in Athens with his wife and two children and works building television and movie location sets.

DIANA J. CROWE attended high school in Macon, GA and the University of Georgia in Athens as did Bill Berry and Mike Mills. She lives in Athens with her husband and two children.

STEPHANIE CHERNIKOWSKI photographed the band in Athens for the Pageantry Tour program. She lives in New York and works as a photographer.

DON DIXON is a producer, songwriter and singer. He co-produced *Murmur* and *Reckoning* with Mitch Easter.

MITCH EASTER is a record producer from Winston-Salem, NC. He produced the first R.E.M. single, the *Chronic Town* ep and co-produced *Murmur* and *Reckoning* with Don Dixon.

GEORGINA FALZARANO is a self-described "road friend" of the band's. She spent the entire Pageantry Tour on the road with R.E.M. in 1976. She works with children on welfare for a non-profit organization in Winnepeg, Manitoba.

KEN FECHTNER has remained friends with Peter Buck since their student days at Emory University in Atlanta. He is currently practicing medicine in San Francisco.

NEIL FEINEMAN is a freelance editor and writer living in Los Angeles.

HOWARD FINSTER is a Georgia-based folk artist who was introduced to wider audiences after painting the cover to R.E.M.'s *Reckoning* and later the Talking Heads' *Little Creatures* album.

BUREN FOWLER was the bass roadie and rhythm guitar player on the Pageantry and Work Tours. He is a guitarist in Drivin' n' Cryin' and lives in Athens with his wife and their son.

GEOFF GANS is an art director and musician. He worked at IRS Records during the *Document* and *Eponymous* periods and co-designed *Eponymous* with Michael Stipe.

MIKE GREEN was a member of The Fans, Peter Buck's one-time favorite Atlanta-based band. He lives and works in Athens, GA.

LAUREN HALL, originally from Georgia, divided her time between Athens and New York from 1980-87 and was Mike Mills' live-in partner. She has since relocated to San Francisco.

JOHN WESLEY HARDING is a folk singer who lives in San Francisco. Peter Buck has helped him out in the studio and onstage.

JACKSON HARING has been a fan of R.E.M. since 1983. "I had the privilege to go on the road with them in a working capacity," as manager of Camper Van Beethoven. Now he manages Cracker.

JONATHAN W. HIBBERT pressed the first R.E.M. seven-inch single on his Hib-Tone label. He is a musician, a lawyer and a woodsman.

KATE INGRAM was part of the Athens party scene that spawned the B-52's and Pylon. She has worked in commercial and college radio and is currently Program Director of a non-commercial college station, KUSF-FM in San Francisco.

JOHN KEANE is a producer/engineer and owner of Keane Recording, LTD. R.E.M. does most of their demo recording and production work with other bands there when they are at home.

VICTOR KRUMMENACHER was bass player in Camper Van Beethoven and Monks of Doom. He toured with Camper Van Beethoven on R.E.M.'s Pageantry Tour. He continues to release records in various guises.

DAVID T. LINDSAY is best known as the controversial music critic at the Atlanta weekly, *Creative Loafing*. He also signs bands and releases them on his Worry-Bird label.

ROBERT LLOYD is a Los Angeles-based journalist and is currently working as an itinerant musician.

LANCE LOUD is a freelance writer and former member of The Mumps. Michael Stipe volunteered to write the liner notes for a reissue of his band's work.

MARK METHE is co-owner of Wuxtry Records in Decatur, GA.

BRUCE MCGUIRE works out of Minneapolis for Warner Brothers Records and has the distinction of having seen R.E.M. perform live on two different islands in the middle of the Mississippi River.

JARID NEFF works for Warner Brothers Records in Atlanta, GA and belongs to the same golf club as Mike Mills' dad.

WOODY NUSS was the first soundman R.E.M. ever hired and the first they fired. He works as a soundman and tour manager based in Los Angeles.

KATHLEEN O'BRIEN threw a birthday party for herself on April 5, 1980 and persuaded R.E.M. to make its live debut there. She lives in Atlanta and is an adminstrator in the restaurant business.

TODD PLOHARSKI is a record collector who works in Athens.

GIL RAY was a drummer in the Mitch Easter-produced band, Game Theory. He currently works in the Bay Area for one of the last existing regional independent record distributors.

LANCE SMITH lived in Athens from 1980-83. Today he is a screenwriter and producer living in Los Angeles.

RUSS TOLMAN toured with R.E.M. as a member of True West. He is a singer/songwriter who splits his time between Los Angeles and Europe.

DAN VALLOR has worked on tour with Robyn Hitchcock, Alex Chilton and Game Theory, among others. He maintained contact with R.E.M. throughout the IRS years.

DAN WALL is co-owner of Wuxtry Records in Athens, GA.

MARC WALLACE is a close friend and confidante of Michael Stipe's and a local business owner in Athens.

DEXTER WEAVER better known as Weaver D, is owner of Weaver D's Fine Foods in Athens, GA. His restaurant's slogan, Automatic for the People, was used as an R.E.M. album title.

ARMISTEAD WELLFORD was bass player in the Athens band Love Tractor. He lives in Athens and continues to perform with Gutterball and The B.L.O.

STEVE WYNN was founder and leader of Dream Syndicate. The band toured with R.E.M. for eight weeks on the Little America tour. He continues to tour and release records with Gutterball and as a solo artist.

DAVID ZWART is a member of the Athens-based, Michael Stipe produced band, The Daisy Group.

START

In many ways, the R.E.M. story is simple: four boys from a small town form a band, show early talent, get some lucky breaks, work hard and eventually succeed, by achieving international fame and glory. But the story of R.E.M. is exceptional for a number of reasons. Not only does the band have an instantly identifiable sound, recognizable the world over, but it has achieved and sustained success on its own terms by following non-traditional methods. And unlike so many of its peers, the band has not fallen prey to musical cliches or differences, drug addiction or mis-management—elements that conspire to create disharmony within the ranks of many working bands.

R.E.M. boldly heralded in the Eighties to the tune of ringing guitars. For the majority of listeners the focal point was enigmatic lead vocalist and lyricist Michael Stipe and the way he slurred his words while he wailed and sang. Peter Buck's contributions, chiming twelve-string and Rickenbacker guitars were the antithesis of the techno-oriented sounds generated from England that dominated the pop music scene. The combination of Mike Mills' melodic bass and Bill Berry's kick drum formed an unusual pattern and people noticed. The R.E.M. sound left critics coining phrases like "jangle-rock," to describe the beautiful mix of acoustic and electric instruments and traditional harmonies set to an up-to-the-minute rock beat. Such a blend hadn't been heard since the Lovin' Spoonful or The Byrds were making records in The Sixties. R.E.M. was more likely to point to The Velvet Underground, Iggy and

The Stooges and Patti Smith as influential and in R.E.M.'s early live performances, those punk rock roots were evident. The debut album, *Murmur,* has been termed "seminal" and frequently shows up in Top Ten and Desert Island Disc lists. The band's arrival also caused the press to proclaim a resurgence in American rock music and a sea of guitar copy bands, some memorable and some not-so, flowed in R.E.M.'s wake. Even into the grunge-infested early Nineties, R.E.M.'s influence can be felt in popular music. Its 1992 release, *Automatic For The People,* has sold in excess of 14 million copies worldwide. Moreover, they have sustained the same four-man line-up; no mean feat in the exhausting, chew-'em-up spit-'em-out world they operate.

Before actually delving into R.E.M.'s beginnings, middle and future, here is some essential background information that may assist the reader: In the late Seventies and early Eighties, Athens, GA. was known for having an especially good "scene." Though there were similar scenes in college towns and cities throughout the U.S., Athens had particularly strong spokespeople and missionaries representing it in the form of The B-52's and later R.E.M. Whether it was the large college campus—University of Georgia—and its attendant art department that drew students from throughout the South, or its classic architecture, cheap rents and proximity to unspoiled countryside, Athens called out to a melange of personalities. The wild, wacky and wonderful all seemed to convene there.

When word got out through underground channels—fanzines, left of the dial public and college radio and word of mouth among night-club-goers and record shoppers—that there were kids in Athens, GA wearing clothes from thrift stores and wigs, dancing on front porches to songs made from chords that beginners could play, it was news! It was the Do-It-Yourself era (thanks to the advent of punk rock in the late Seventies and perhaps also due to the conservative political climate) so you did the best you could to make the same thing happen in your area, if it wasn't happening already.

The B-52's were the first band to "break" out of Athens' art school/party scene, after releasing a seven-inch single on the Atlanta-based independent record label, DB. The label was owned by Danny Beard and was housed under the same roof as his hip record store, Wax 'n' Facts, which (along with Wuxtry Records in Decatur, GA) specialized in independently manufactured and distributed regional seven-inch singles. (DB Records is often confused but has nothing to do with the North Carolina band, The dB's. The band was part of the independent pop scene and its name comes up in the R.E.M. story.)

Strangely, nearby Atlanta did not have as strong a band scene (though The Fans, The Brains, The Swimming Pool Q's and Vietnam had followings) and DB looked to Athens for its acts. The B-52's subsequently signed to a major label, Warner Brothers, in 1979 and the band's quick ascendency found Athens ill-equipped to handle its professional needs so they relocated to New York, a traditional move for a band on the rise. On the way up, The B-52's began to carve a path out of the South, helping to establish a network of friendly faces and nightclub gigs for bands blazing trails from their small hometowns to showcase cities like New York and Los Angeles. R.E.M. expanded the path to include all visible (and not so visible) points in between the major spots.

On the "new music" (as it was termed then) front, The B-52's departure left Athens and the DB label with Pylon, (the band often looked upon as the successor to The "B's"), The Method Actors, Love Tractor and The Side-Effects (often cited but short-lived). Though the aforementioned bands were competent and dearly beloved by their respective fans, they lacked guidance and direction in the form of stable musical line-ups or visionary managers and they finally broke up without making the move to bigger labels or without record contracts at all. In April of 1980, a newly formed R.E.M. became the exception. From the outset, the band found a winning team of a manager, W. Jefferson Holt, and an attorney, Bertis Downs IV, (who serve them to this day). With an initial seven-inch release for Hib-Tone Records under their belts, they scored a record deal with IRS Records, an independent label with major label distribution that had the clout to get the band's records heard outside of the confines of the South and college radio.

With a strong group of professionals-to-be working behind the scenes, R.E.M. never found it necessary to relocate to a larger city or secure high-powered management and till 1992, all four of its members declared permanent residency in Athens. Though not all born and raised there (or in the South for that matter), the members of R.E.M. have called Athens home since their college days in the late Seventies. Lead vocalist and lyricist Michael Stipe was drawn to the University of Georgia's art school and intended to pursue a Fine Arts degree before his bandmates persuaded him to cash it in for fulltime membership in a rock band. Accounts vary on Stipe's upbringing but generally it is agreed he was born in Georgia and raised an army brat, moving from town to town throughout the Southeast, Midwest and even Europe. His high school years were spent in East St. Louis where he sang in a band performing cover songs. Stipe has been successful at hiding those years from the public record, in keeping with his enigmatic stage persona.

Conversely, the band's mouthpiece to the press, guitarist Peter Buck, keeps no secrets. He was born in California and also did his share of moving around till his family finally settled in the Atlanta area. He found himself in Athens chasing down a job in a record store, after stints at odd jobs, vagabonding and studying at Emory University in Atlanta didn't agree with him.

Mike Mills, bassist, was also born in California but grew up in Macon, GA where he met drummer Bill Berry who was born in Duluth, MN, the same town as Bob Dylan. Both Berry and Mills met in Macon and went to high school together, played in other bands together and moved from Macon together to enroll at The University of Georgia in 1980. These similarities and the pair's known enthusiasm for golfing, fishing and spectator sports often evoke people to speak their names in one breath. Nonetheless, many quoted herein believe that this particular rhythm section is the musical muscle behind the band's sound and individually are responsible for some of R.E.M.'s most melodic hooks.

It's clear that R.E.M.'s decision to stay close to home has served them well over the long haul, since The B-52's abandonment of the South left them restless and in search of roots and proper representation throughout its career. (Ironically, The B-52's greatest success came in 1989 with the release of *Cosmic Thing*, a collection of songs recalling the band's late Seventies, Southern halcyon days). By the same token, it would be fair to say R.E.M. has served the tiny community of Athens, GA, more than well in return. The band has regularly donated monies to community organizations, its individual members participate in local elections by campaigning and attending town council meetings, they invest in local businesses and they preserve and restore old buildings by saving them from the wrecking ball.

R.E.M. operates its business and maintains a practice space in a modest, restored building on the main street in downtown Athens. Holt, R.E.M.'s manager since 1980, presides over the headquarters, professionally known as R.E.M./Athens, LTD. R.E.M. is Holt's only client and always has been, so it follows that the non-singing/non-playing North Carolinian is jokingly referred to as "the fifth R.E.M." Holt's inexperience never seemed to deter R.E.M. or others from him and it has been suggested in this book by those acquainted with the young Holt that his initial naiveté may have even been one of the keys to his charm in an otherwise self-obsessed music industry. Attorney-in-residence Downs is generally considered the voice of reason and like Holt, appears to be a lifer. He volunteered his services to the band fresh out of law school and has remained on staff ever since. In R.E.M./Athens, LTD., R.E.M. with Holt and Downs have built an organization that stands for integrity in the music business—an industry that is generally divorced from moral standards. With each careful step, R.E.M. has conducted its business affairs honestly and democratically. All decisions regarding the use of the name, the lyrics, the music, touring, scheduling (and anything else a band decides on) pass through the band at regularly held band meetings. Since Buck's relocation to the Pacific Northwest, band meetings have become less practical, although they are working on solutions.

From its first record contract with IRS Records through the label switch mid-career to the more powerful and visible Warner Brothers Records, the six-man team has kept a steady reign on its slow but ultimately rewarding rise to superstar status in the rock world. From the outside it seems the band has never compromised its ideals for the sake of imagery, or its sound for the sake of fashion. Redefining its own relationship to global politics and thereby setting a standard for other bands to follow is one of its legacies. The Do-It-Yourself ethic which R.E.M./Athens, LTD so staunchly employs has served as a model for bands from Sicily (Flor de Mal) to Seattle (Nirvana) and points in between. Choosing its own producers, album cover artists and video directors are often chores less visionary bands would delegate to its record label. R.E.M. have always kept those decisions close at hand which has consistently worked in its favor.

As a freelance writer, when assigned a piece on a breaking "alternative" act, it would occur to me that some artists wouldn't have an outlet today were it not for the groundwork R.E.M. laid, allowing a new kind of music to be heard. I wanted to tell that story to a generation who live in a time since the floodgates opened wide and welcomed alternative culture at the level of commercial radio, cable television, computer access and the press. In this day of MTV creations, fly-by-nights and overnight successes, the way the story of a rock band (especially one still vital in the culture today), used to develop now qualifies as rock history.

Allowing friends and associates of R.E.M. an opportunity to tell the band's story seemed to me an ideal way to get on the inside track. The band's accessibility to its friends and fans for over fourteen years lent itself nicely to an oral history book. The people interviewed were part of the scene, whether it was in R.E.M.'s hometown of Athens, GA. or in cities and towns across the country where R.E.M. made its presence felt by constant touring. Chances are, you may recognize your own story or someone you know among the quotations as R.E.M. impacted lives everywhere they travelled.

What follows are the thoughts of fellow touring musicians, roadies, producers, industry professionals, ex-partners, college friends and Athens/Atlanta locals. Some of these people witnessed pivotal moments in the young band's career; early recording sessions, first record releases. And some are those who were there observing a more experienced band make major career decisions like switching record labels or learning to cope with new-found notoriety.

The story of a young band freshly signed to a label, as told by onlookers and insiders at the time, resonates with the kind excitement and enthusiasm that only friends can generate when retelling a fable that we now consider a part of history.

I interviewed each person either in their home, on the phone and by fax or in a comfortable coffee shop in Athens, Atlanta, New York, Los Angeles and San Francisco. I found that the closer the person felt to the band, either through friendship or business association, the more revealing their stories were when I had expected the opposite. I attempted to contact a number of sources who declined to be interviewed because I suspect they felt that they may be betraying band members' confidences. Some prospective interviewees sensed from the band that they shouldn't talk to me. I'm afraid those people may have misinterpreted the band's reponse, as I found band and management off the record to be completely ammenable to my project. By pursuing an unauthorized account of the band's history, I feel I am presenting an unadulterated account of its past rather than a pristine, "red-lined" version.

I have been acquainted with R.E.M. and its management since their first trip out West in 1982 when they performed a legendary show at San Francisco's Old Waldorf. Years later, I lived in Atlanta, GA and worked for Warner Brothers Records, gaining a better perspective on the music scene there and its Athens axis. Through the years I developed a number of interesting, mutual acquaintances of the band's and knew they would share their stories with me. In addition, when I got out of bed one morning in late 1992, I remembered a box of press clippings dating back to 1982 that I had stored away and pronounced, "I'm going to write a book about R.E.M." I'd realized I was spending a disproportionate amount of time pondering the band's career when I could have been writing about many other things. But all roads kept leading back to R.E.M. A chance communiqué from Michael Stipe at the time I was deciding to write the book solidified my instinct and an even more coincidental get-together with Peter Buck on the streets of San Francisco sealed the notion. I was writing the book.

Had it not been for R.E.M. helping to shape and pave the road for alternative bands to mass acceptance, the path that their sisters and brothers in bands routinely travel today would be very different indeed. I hope that this book will put that road and those who travelled it during the early eighties into context and contribute towards an appreciation of how R.E.M. unknowingly created a model for anyone with the strength of their own convictions to follow. This book is most significantly about that road, as it reveals the story of a rock band who ultimately achieved international fame and glory in spite of the odds and appears to be living on in the hearts of its fans well into the nineties.

—Denise Sullivan, San Francisco, February 1994

1980

April 5 — Nameless band plays first gig at a party in Athens

April 19 — Koffee Klub, second live appearance

May 6 — First paid gig under name R.E.M. at Tyrone's, Athens. The band played Tyrone's throughout '80-'81.

June 6 — First gig in Atlanta at The Warehouse

July 18 — First gig out of Georgia at The Station, Carrboro, NC

December 6 — Fox Theatre, Atlanta, opening for The Police

December — First recording session at Tyrone's on four-track

EARLY PHOTO SESSION 1981
(*photo by George DuBose*)

1
BEGINNINGS

KEN FECHTNER [friend]: Peter Buck and I met in 1975 at a party at Emory University in Atlanta, GA. It was your average college party at one of the houses. I was going through a Beach Boys phase, dress-wise, wearing Keds surfer sneakers, white jeans and one of those plaid Henley surfer shirts which, in Georgia in 1975 at the height of the Allman Brothers era, was pretty out of place. Over in the corner there was a guy wearing a paisley smoking jacket with a velvet collar and some high-top sneakers, which again, nobody was wearing in Georgia in '75 and I looked at him going, "who's that?" We ended up talking and found out that we liked a lot of the same music so we started going to shows and hanging out together.

KATHLEEN O'BRIEN [Athens scene, early eighties]: I met Pete originally here in Atlanta in 1976. He worked as a record salesman in a little record store called Doo Dah's in Emory Village. It's now a parking lot. I worked at the little restaurant down the way and didn't really know him, except in a professional-neighbor way. He was very eccentric. I was in high school at the time.

MARK METHE [Wuxtry Records, Decatur, GA.]: I heard Peter used to sleep near a window with a string around his wrist so his manager at the record store could come by his apartment and pull on the string in the mornings to wake him up.

KEN FECHTNER: The record store Wax 'n' Facts in the Little Five Points area in Atlanta was probably a big influence in shaping Peter's musical taste. At the time, Little Five Points wasn't that hip and pretty seedy. There was a bar and a deli there. Danny Beard's record store, Wax 'n' Facts, and a used clothing store called Little Egypt were the first two businesses that opened there. Peter was walking through the area one night because you could go down and drink for pretty cheap. After he saw Danny unpacking all these boxes of records, he came back the next day telling everyone "there's going to be a used record store in Little Five Points." That was a big resource because you could buy records there for a dollar. If you didn't know what a record sounded like, you could ask Danny or his partner Harry and they could tell you if it was good or not.

DANNY BEARD [co-owner, Wax 'n' Facts Records, Atlanta and DB RECS]: I'd known Pete for years because he'd been shopping at my store and was working at Doo Dah's, kind of a competing store of mine. Kenny Fechtner was friends with Pete and he was a friend of mine too. I planned a party that the B-52's played at in '78 and Pete and Kenny got me the lounge at Emory to rent.

DIANA J. CROWE [friend]: I went to high school in Macon and Bill Berry had gone to my school the year before we met. We had a lot of mutual friends though, so I went to a lot of parties Bill and Mike Mills were at. When I knew them, they were playing in a band together. They would practice in a little space behind the Paragon Booking Agency offices where Ian Copeland worked. [*Copeland would later form Frontier Booking International (FBI), representing R.E.M., while his brother, Miles, founded IRS Records which signed R.E.M. in 1981.*]. It might have even been a garage. Bill and Mike had an apartment that they shared right next door on Arlington Street. Bill was a very exciting guy to know at the time. If Bill Berry was there, something was happening. I was still in high school and never had seen much of the world. Bill's job at the Paragon Agency was to drive a limo into Atlanta and pick up musicians I'd heard on the radio. To me it was pretty thrilling. We did the typical high school stuff—drank and played a lot of cards.

> "I hated him [Mike Mills] from the first time I saw him 'cause he had that same kind of nerd appeal that he has now, and I was just starting to experiment with drugs and stuff. He was everything I despised: great student, got along with teachers, didn't smoke cigarettes or smoke pot . . ."
>
> —Bill Berry to *Rolling Stone*,
> December 3, 1987

LAUREN HALL [Athens scene, '80-'87]: Mike and Bill are just two boys from Macon, GA. I think that remains with them. They have that smalltown connection.

JARID NEFF [Warner Brothers Records, Atlanta]: You can imagine Mike's dad being a really nice person—I think Mike is the nicest member of the band. I've played golf with Frank Mills a couple of times and asked him what it was like when his kids were growing up, if he had any idea Mike would be musical. He said that Mike and Bill were best friends in school and he gave them the third floor of the house to play in with their bands. He said, "I'd go in the basement away from the noise, but it was nice knowing the kids were home and their friends were hanging around."

WOODY NUSS [soundman]: I don't know much about Michael Stipe's cover band days, but I heard stories that cover band days existed. I know he was a redneck keyboard player in a cover band. Michael has worked very successfully at covering up his East St. Louis background.

KEN FECHTNER: When we first started going to Emory, Peter was trying to play the guitar, but he wasn't very good. He could play Monkees songs, but couldn't jam with the people who were able to play blues, so he got a reputation that he really couldn't play. I think in his sophomore year he was roommates with Alan Skinner from Jacksonville, FL and three of his cousins were there. They were all related to Leonard Skinner—the band Lynyrd Skynyrd was named after him. Alan was supposed to be one of the better guitar players and Peter just couldn't play along.

WOODY NUSS: Peter used to tell people, "I never practice and I never knew how to play," but I knew guys that were in Emory with Peter and they said he used to sit on the lawn and play Grateful Dead songs. Guys that had a dorm above him would hear him practice going, "deedle deedle dee deedle deedle dee." He had an Epiphone with the Grateful Dead logo on the back.

MIKE GREEN [Atlanta band, The Fans]: I don't remember Peter ever coming to see the Fans, but I know now that he liked us.

KEN FECHTNER: The Fans and the Nasty Bucks, featuring Fly Stone and Dan Baird were playing around. One night, I didn't go but it was a big event and Peter went. One of the guys in the Fans needed a ride home and Peter offered to take him. The next day, Peter was so excited that he'd given one of the guys in the Fans a ride. I don't think he had any ideas of playing in a band at that time.

"I figured I'd probably just be at dead-end jobs, going from one to the other, and I kind of hoped I'd marry rich or something. I didn't have a whole lot of things that I could do really, and I figured maybe I'd fall into something if I was lucky. And I actually was lucky enough to fall into this. But this certainly isn't what I saw myself doing, although I would have liked to have thought that I could do this. It was a fantasy I guess, to be in a rock and roll band . . ."   —Peter Buck to *Record*, January-February 1986

KEN FECHTNER: Peter decided he wanted to go to California during the middle of one quarter so he blew off school. I'm pretty sure he failed every course that semester. He got a ride out to California, stayed in San Luis Obispo for five or six months, washing dishes and living in a houseful of Deadheads who apparently irritated him greatly.

When he came back from California, he got a job with a record distributor, basically working as a rack jobber through North Georgia and North Carolina. It was an all-right job, but I think he got tired of it pretty quickly.

SARA BROWN [friend]: I think the record distributor he worked for was called Atlanta Record and Tape Depot. I worked at a record store in Asheville, NC and I would call in our order on Thursday mornings. Peter would start out Friday morning and wind his way up to North Georgia and then to Western North Carolina, dropping off records at stores along the way. He'd spend the night in some cheesy motel and would be almost always at my store when we opened Saturday morning. I helped him unload the records out of an ugly brown Pinto station wagon. I remember conversations that we had, but I don't remember that much about what he looked like except that he had a sort of scruffy shag haircut, and I don't think I would have looked twice at him.

KEN FECHTNER: He was driving to all these little towns with boxes of records in the trunk, stocking shelves. On one trip he finally realized he didn't like it anymore so when he got back to Atlanta he didn't give any notice—just dropped the car off at the parking lot at the warehouse and never went back to work. When he didn't show up for work after a couple of days and they didn't see the car in the lot, they assumed he'd skipped town with their car. They reported him for car theft and he was arrested and taken to jail, so I guess he has an arrest record for grand theft; auto. It's just like Peter. He was tired, he didn't want to do it anymore so he just dropped off the car and left.

SEAN BOURNE [Athens scene, early eighties]: I wasn't one of those people that made Athens famous for being out of control—"Party Out of Bounds," and all that. I just happened to be living there when the party scene started happening. I saw some of the legendary B-52's shows. I had a studio next to where the band Pylon rehearsed. Everybody was an artist. The scene centered around the art school.

ARMISTEAD WELLFORD [Athens band, Love Tractor]: My sister-in-law was in art school at University of Georgia (UOG) and recommended it. I applied on a whim. The one thing I wanted to do was play music, but I figured I'd have to go up to New York to do that. When I got down here to Athens in '78, the B-52's had changed all that just by recording and putting out a single from here. So it was possible to live in Georgia, go to the art school and play music too.

CURTIS CROWE [Athens band, Pylon]: Downstairs from where our apartment was we had studios. We rented them out to art students. Two of the people we rented to were Michael Lachowski [*bassist, Pylon*] and Randy Bewley [*guitarist, Pylon*]. Randy knew Vanessa Briscoe [*vocalist, Pylon*] through work and school so our band Pylon was made up of the art school/party crowd and rock and roll crowd. It was all the same people. When the B-52's left town, someone had to play at the parties, so Pylon was the next in line.

KEN FECHTNER: The art school/party crowd and rock and roll crowd in Athens were a relatively small group of people. Not many people would go to the shows and everybody knew each other. There was a party, and a band would play in somebody's yard or living room. Thirty to fifty people would be there. In Athens you had to make your own fun. Yard sales would turn into a party.

CURTIS CROWE: You had to entertain yourself, so you had to think of something to do. Rock and roll refound itself and everybody started getting excited about it again. It wasn't completely dominated by corporations anymore. It was something individuals could do after all. Part of the fun of it was feeling like we were in a tidewater and that we also belonged to a larger culture. The link, of course, was rock and roll. You'd travel around and meet people and they were all doing the same thing, all over the country and all over the world. It was a real heady time, to feel like you were a member of some sort of revolution. There never was any kind of revolution going on but it felt that way.

KEN FECHTNER: After Peter quit the record distribution job, he went to Wuxtry Records in Decatur, GA looking for work and [*Mark Methe*] offered him a job at the store in Athens. The B-52's had emerged from Athens by then. Peter and I saw them at the Great Southeast Music Hall the first time they played outside of Athens. Pylon was playing around and I think the Method Actors were too. DB RECS, Danny Beard's label, was putting out records. But Peter didn't go to Athens to be in a band. He was out of work, hanging around and his ideal job then was working in a record store.

DAN WALL [Wuxtry Records, Athens, GA.]: Peter came to us to get a job at the Wuxtry in Decatur. We had room at the Athens store so he said fine and he moved here. First he worked at the Baxter Street store and later downtown at the small corner store which is the used-CD shop now. Kids come and take photos of the big store but Peter worked in the small store for two years before the band started in '78-'79.

LANCE SMITH [Athens scene, '80-'83]: America was repressed in the Fifties and exploded in the Sixties, but Athens remained repressed and exploded in the Eighties. I think the B-52's were the ones who rearranged the whole Athens psyche overnight. Fred Schneider [*vocalist, the B-52's*] was wearing a Speedo in public, being openly gay. It was unheard of.

ARMISTEAD WELLFORD: Around that time, "the B's" had just appeared on *Saturday Night Live* for the first time. It was weird because they were such a small thing around town—all the weirdos liked them. It was the anti-hippie thing.

SEAN BOURNE: When Fred Schneider worked at the health food restaurant [*The Bluebird*] he would wear a hard hat with a flashing light and come out with your food—always saying funny, ironic stuff. I never thought he had the potential to be a rock star. The first time I saw them play was like a mystical experience. Mark Methe was there and we were, like, two of five straight people there. I didn't go to sleep that night because the show was such a weird experience. I never had that sense of fascination with R.E.M. but there must have been people that responded that way to them.

ARMISTEAD WELLFORD: I think our attitudes about being in bands and how it could be done was brought on by the B-52's and the fact we were all in art school and the artistic way we had of looking at everything. We were painting, but at the same time music was really important to us. The music was our artistic interpretation of things.

"I don't think it was the scene or the city itself so much as it was the people in that time and place were open to new ideas. The whole punk thing pointed out in Athens that anybody can do it. So lots of people who had training in other types of art things, whether it be painting or poetry, kind of approached rock and roll with a real sideways view.

"That's what Pylon did and came up with something real unique. I think when people do that, approach rock and roll from a non-historical point, it brings out new things. We had about fifteen friends that were in bands that were happening at that time, Method Actors, Pylon, Love Tractor, B-52's and the Side Effects. It was something people did. Nobody thought it was anything real special. No one was trying for fame and fortune. It was something fun that everyone did. I think everyone on my block was in a band basically."

—Peter Buck to *Novus*, January/February 1985

KATHLEEN O'BRIEN: At that time in Athens it was so ripe. The B-52's had already started a scene and there was a space for bands to develop. The climate was right—right after the Seventies. Pete was always hyper and real fired up. He had ambition.

DIANA J. CROWE: Bill moved to Athens about a year before I did. I lost touch with Bill and Mike for a while here. I was actually in college by then and they didn't stay in school very long. They were with a real night crowd and I was trying to run with the night crowd and go to school but couldn't manage both.

KATHLEEN O'BRIEN: When I moved to Athens, Dan Wall was renting a church on Oconee St. and I wanted to move in there because I thought it would be a really cool place to live. Little did I know . . . Dan said he had another friend interested in moving in and I asked who it was. I found out it was Pete. I didn't know he had moved to Athens.

DAN WALL: When Peter moved to Athens he first lived in an apartment on Milledge and then moved out to a house on Oconee. From there he moved into the Church. He lived there for about two weeks before they took it over from me. Peter's brother Ken, Pete and Kathleen moved in.

CURTIS CROWE: All the houses in Athens looked like Munster's houses and they were real cheap. You could get one of these great big houses and put 4-8 people in them and everyone would end up paying $75.00 a month. You could live here for next to nothing which made it a real attractive place to hang out and be someone who is avoiding going into the world and working and all the stuff you have to do later.

KATHLEEN O'BRIEN: While Pete and I were roommates, he struck up a friendship with Michael Stipe. Michael was a customer at Wuxtry where Peter was working. I guess Pete and Michael started to collaborate on their own then.

KEN FECHTNER: Peter thought Vanda and Young [the Easybeats] were terrific songwriters. He listened to the Easybeats, the Troggs, Monkees, Yardbirds. Everybody knows the Velvet Underground now, but nobody did back then.

KATHLEEN O'BRIEN: I had known Bill Berry through the dorm the prior year and had a huge crush on him. Basically I did whatever I could to throw us in the same situation. One night there was a party in the fall of '79. I had gone there with Pete and Michael Stipe was there and Bill Berry was there with Mike Mills. I introduced them at that party because Bill was looking for a band and Bill and Mike were a rhythm section and needed a guitar. Pete and Michael had already started writing songs together. From hanging around listening to them write songs and fool around together, I knew they had some talent. After they were introduced, Bill and Pete decided to have a jam session.

MARK METHE: I traded Peter a guitar for a Stratocaster and he gave me another hundred bucks, besides. I wish I had it back; it was a real nice guitar.

KEN FECHTNER: There was a time when Peter and Michael had one pair of boxer shorts between them. They would trade out.

ARMISTEAD WELLFORD: Michael Stipe, myself, Danny Beard's cousin Bobby and a friend of ours who is now a sculptor in New York all sat at the same table in this art class at UOG and we would just talk about music all day. I was jamming with some people and Michael was just getting together with the other guys in R.E.M. I asked him, now who plays in your band? He said, "Well, there's a guy named Pete and he plays the guitar and he's really great and there's a guy named Bill and he plays the drums and he's really great and there's a guy named Mike and he plays bass and he's really great and I sing and play guitar and I'm really great," but it was said all in fun, in a really positive way.

KATHLEEN O'BRIEN: They practiced for six months or so on covers and then they started writing songs of their own. There was a crowd of us that would just go and listen to them practice all of the time. We'd get in the back of the church and dance and party. Somewhere around that time Bill and I started going out and it became a more personal interest. I really wanted to help Bill succeed.

ARMISTEAD WELLFORD: There was a hole in the wall of the church you could crawl through and you ended up on the altar of the church, which made the perfect stage.

KEN FECHTNER: Peter didn't tell me at first he was in a band. I think he was sort of embarrassed. I stopped by where he was living and they were getting ready for a party and Mills told me they were going to be playing that night. I had to get back to Atlanta so I didn't stay.

KATHLEEN O'BRIEN: My birthday was on April 5. At that point Michael had also moved in so Michael, Pete and Bill were all living in the church and Mike lived off campus somewhere. I kind of coerced them into playing that party because when I first asked them they said no. And then I said, I don't want anything else for my birthday except for you to play at my party. Well, it turned into the party of parties. Once the band was lined up I thought I'd get another band, the Side Effects, to play and then we decided to make it like a club and we got Men in Trees to play. The guys were still fairly reluctant to play. They didn't feel like they were ready to perform. They still wanted to practice and I said no, you have to do this. We got five kegs of beer and 500 people showed up. It was the most phenomenal party ever.

MIKE GREEN: I remember the party at the church and I assumed their songs were covers. I knew they were 50 percent covers [*"Hippy Hippy Shake," "Shakin' All Over," "Stepping Stone," "There She Goes Again," "God Save The Queen," "Secret Agent Man," "Needles and Pins," "California Sun"*] but they sounded like a garage band and everything they played sounded like it *could* be a cover. It was a big deal at the time not necessarily because we thought anybody was going to get famous, but because the party was huge. You couldn't breathe once you got in. Parties were big back then, no doubt because they had free beer. But there was something in the air that night. The two bands were making their debut. I was much more impressed with the Side Effects.

ARMISTEAD WELLFORD: The Side Effects didn't really know how to play, but Kit Schwarz, their guitarist and later our drummer in Love Tractor was so creative. The drummer was the king back then. Curtis Crowe from Pylon and David Gamble from the Method Actors were monstrous drummers so it was cool if you had a band that had a good drummer. No one else in Pylon knew how to play. I think R.E.M. and Love Tractor were the first bands in Athens that knew how to play from the start.

MARK METHE: My main memory about the night R.E.M. played in the church was it was raining. I thought the whole place was going to fall apart and wanted to be outside instead of inside. I had a hooded zip-up sweatshirt with the hood up—which I guess was the look at the time— and several people came up to me thinking I was Danny Beard which always mystified me.

MIKE GREEN: The day after the gig, Curtis Crowe came over to my house to write a review of the show. He was real impressed with them, more so than I was and he went on and on about it in his review.

CURTIS CROWE: That was a real memorable night because at the time, the Side Effects were my favorite local band. They were great. Kind of real dumb surf music. They were a ragged three-piece outfit. You could really definitely dance to it. That night R.E.M. were operating under the name the Twisted Kites.

> "We couldn't think of a name at first. I liked Twisted Kites. Then we thought maybe we should have a name that was real offensive, like Cans of Piss. That was right up there at the top. Then we thought we didn't want to be called something that we couldn't tell our parents or have to mumble. R.E.M. just popped out of the dictionary one night. We needed something that wouldn't typecast us because, hell, we didn't even know what we were gonna do. So R.E.M. was nice—it didn't lock us into anything."
> —Peter Buck to Creem, September 1984

CURTIS CROWE: I remember liking R.E.M. a lot except they were doing a lot of cover songs and at the time the whole art school/party crowd had this thing about cover songs. We were on the "leading edge of a musical revolution" and we thought playing cover songs was taking two steps back and everyone kind of put their nose in the air about that. But they were really good and had a lot of energy about it. I even wrote a review of that show. Mike Green typed it, because I can't type. But I knew something was happening. It just felt like something had happened. It needed to be documented. It was the first and last review I tried to write in my whole life.

KATHLEEN O'BRIEN: Mike Hobbs from Tyrone's, an Athens club, was at the party and he heard them and immediately wanted to book them. They ended up getting their first gig a month later.

KEN FECHTNER: The next time I saw Peter, he told me they got a job opening for the Brains who were from Atlanta. It was the second time R.E.M. played in public, so I went up to see them. Peter was sort of sheepish and embarrassed. Half of the time he would jump around and the other half of the time he would hide behind his amp. He used to have pretty bad stage fright, almost to the point of getting sick.

MARK METHE: The first time they played out in Athens at Tyrone's opening for the Brains, Dan Wall and I videotaped it on this old clunky video equipment—black and white big-ass camera. It was the first time we had ever videoed something in a club, and Dan didn't turn the mic on. We got the video, with one lightbulb in the background—real shadowy. Stipe's face showed up and that's about it. Kate Pierson from the B-52's was there because I remember she operated the camera for part of it.

KEN FECHTNER: They were good. Probably three quarters covers, but good. Cindy Wilson [the B-52's] was there that night and she told Peter

VIDEO STILLS FROM AN EARLY PRACTICE SESSION AT WUXTRY (© Mark Methe and Dan Wall)

she thought they were good and Peter told me, "I can't believe Cindy Wilson thought we were good!" kind of stuttering and excited. They didn't think they'd get that enthusiastic of a response, but it was pretty obvious that night and many subsequent nights that they were better than the band they opened for.

SEAN BOURNE: I had been working with the Brains for a while and they were a well established band; they had a contract with Mercury. I was kind of apprehensive when I heard R.E.M. was opening because I knew from being in the klatch in Athens that there was this weird Athens/Atlanta rivalry thing that Athens had. Atlanta never had it as far as I could tell.

DANNY BEARD: Most of the Atlanta bands didn't go over and play in Athens. They weren't accepted. But there was never any outright battle. Athens always thought they were better. But the Athens bands were accepted here. People recognized they were good.

LANCE SMITH: Even the Athens bands that hated each other would probably gang up on the Atlanta bands. The reviewer from the Atlanta paper came to Athens and totally trashed the Athens scene and said that the only thing good was the Little Tigers. They were my friends and everything, but they were doing mostly covers and fake white reggae.

SEAN BOURNE: That night after R.E.M.'s set Peter came up to me and he was profusely apologetic about how bad they were. He was sorry they took so long to get their stuff off-stage before we could set up the Brains. Apparently he recognized me from seeing me at gigs, and he was always very nice to me, but I didn't even remember their performance because it was very indistinct. I couldn't understand a word that Stipe was singing. There was a lot of energy and everyone was bouncing around, but I didn't ever think they would be anything. I wouldn't say they were a crappy band, but they sounded like one. The newspaper reported on the show and the headline read, "R.E.M. 1, Brains O." The next time they played together they reported "R.E.M. 2, Brains 0" at which point I called up the guy and asked him what was up. He said, "I just don't like Atlanta."

JOHN KEANE [producer/engineer, Keane Recording, LTD.]: I used to go see R.E.M. at Tyrone's sometimes. They used to play for a dollar cover. Back then they were really raw. I didn't really like them that much because I was a musician at the time and had been playing in several bands and was more into seeing musicians who were accomplished. I liked their songs but I thought they were kind of rough.

ARMISTEAD WELLFORD: The Summer of '80 is when Love Tractor formed. It was just two guitars and drums—all instrumental. It was Kit Schwarz and Mark Cline and Mike Richmond. Kit was the guitar player in the Side Effects and really wanted to pursue that so he quit Love Tractor around the time they asked me to join on bass. So then it was two guitars, bass and a drum machine. We did a couple of shows and it went over really well. The first show I did with them, Michael Stipe came up to me and said, "That was a really great show." I said, "I was so nervous" and then felt like I really dropped the ball by analyzing myself so much. He said, "Don't worry about it, you're a star now. Just say, thanks, I had a really good time." He has a really good sense of humor.

KATHLEEN O'BRIEN: Bill started to take a more active interest in the business end of the band. I was the only one with a reliable car and any kind of credit so I took it upon myself to start calling clubs trying to get them opening dates. I thought I wanted to be their manager but Bill was like, "No girlfriend of mine is going to manage this band." He figured they'd find a manager but in the meantime I kept doing the kinds of things a manager does. Basically the business was being run out of our apartment.

WOODY NUSS: I met Paul Scales of Tyrone's through Bill Berry. I was working for a band while I was in high school called Little Tigers and I had a sound system. When I came down to Athens for school in 1980, Little Tigers came through Tyrone's on open mike night, and I started working as a substitute sound guy. Mike Hobbs was supposed to mix sound, but R.E.M. wasn't such a big deal yet and he wanted the night off. I was the fill-in house sound guy at Tyrone's but also had a sound system that I could take out of town so that's why I started working for R.E.M. Bill was the contact. They had a couple of weird gigs and we went and did whatever little shows they had. They had a gig at UOG in the gallery at the art school which was horrible. Then we went to a nearby town in Bill's Ford LTD. We stopped at McDonald's and I felt really self-conscious because I knew Michael was a vegetarian, but the rest of the guys ate whatever. They were trying to convince Michael to leave school that day. One of the other guys, I think it was Bill, had already agreed to leave school and do the band thing full time and they were pressuring Michael to do it. Michael really wanted to be in art school and hang around Jim Herbert, his art teacher at University of Georgia.

> "I kinda had the idea I was pullin' the wool over peoples' eyes, though; mostly I was good at convincing people of things. If they said something was shit I'd go, 'No it's not, it's like this,' and they'd start agreeing. My work was mostly portraiture. I don't like abstracts. I like things to be a little more explained than that."
> —Michael Stipe to XTRA, June 1985

LANCE SMITH: The first time I saw Michael he was walking out of an English class and he was wearing a pair of jeans so completely ripped out, even in the ass, and that was pretty radical for Athens in 1980. His hair was really long in front and short in back and we called it the reverse ponytail.

KATHLEEN O'BRIEN: Bill was always the most serious-minded. When he dropped out of school and made up his mind to be a drummer for this band it was a sink-or-swim situation. If he didn't make it, then what was he going to do? He had the drive to make it work. With Pete it was like, "I like to play guitar anyhow and if we succeed we succeed and if we don't I'll keep playing guitar." I can't really say I know how Michael thinks, but once he'd made a commitment to the band—it wasn't to each other, it was to the entity of the band—that was the cohesion they needed and everything was an equal split.

ARMISTEAD WELLFORD: When Kit Schwarz quit, Bill Berry joined Love Tractor. He wanted to play with us and was real into it. We did some shows with him and it was really great. We sounded like R.E.M. drums with Love Tractor music. There was a time Bill was actually considering staying with us but what happened was Mark Cline, our guitarist, was still in school. Those boys in R.E.M. were ready to go and toss school aside and that was Bill's deciding factor.

KATE INGRAM [Athens scene, late seventies]: A four piece is like a pillar of strength. Each part has to be fairly cognizant of the other and yield when it's right to yield and play their respective roles. R.E.M. seemed to accept each other for what they each really were and had to offer as talent and let each person be himself.

MIKE GREEN: I recognized early that they were like the "digestible-by-frat-boys" version of the Athens sound and they are what turned it into big business. If it hadn't been them it would have been someone else. But I didn't have anything against them for that. They just seemed kind of silly.

CURTIS CROWE: I didn't think they sounded like Pylon. Just because you're from the same town as someone else, people think you sound alike. It probably still happens to this day.

MIKE GREEN: Everybody was stealing from each other. One night when Love Tractor was playing at Tyrone's, someone walked up to me and said, "Pylon sounded pretty good tonight."

ARMISTEAD WELLFORD: No one was *trying* to sound like anyone else. I think the Side Effects wanted to sound like Pylon a little bit but Randy Bewley didn't know how to tune his guitar the right way, so it was impossible to sound exactly like him. There were a couple of bass lines that Love Tractor picked up from the Side Effects and Pylon. I was really influenced by Michael Lachowski's [*Pylon*] minimal style and Kit had his own thing going on. What Pete was doing was really cool, but he was establishing his own thing. R.E.M. had the pop thing working really good. Everyone was trying to have their own thing, but it all somehow related. For some reason, everybody *did* have the Athens sound. Peter once said that everybody here was influenced by everybody else here. It was so close knit and we were all feeding on some kind of energy.

KATE INGRAM: There was a lot of competitive male energy that fueled the Athens music scene and one of the things the bands did to diffuse that energy later on was bring in females [*for example, Oh-OK and Guadalcanal Diary were mixed gender groups*]. Ironically, R.E.M. didn't have a female, but the female energy of the band is very high. Michael has a lot of creative, feminine energy. There was a lot of cross-dressing going on back then and I think that's a symbol of feminine, creative energy manifesting itself.

LANCE SMITH: Love Tractor still respected R.E.M. but were also jealous of them. I think Pylon was like that too because after the B-52's left, Pylon were the godfathers of Athens' bands. The bands that started up after that first generation were the most resentful and it became trendy to be bitchy about R.E.M.

DIANA J. CROWE: There were a few bands around that we knew that if you wanted to dance and really work up a sweat, you'd go to one of their shows. R.E.M. was definitely one of them. The Side Effects and Love Tractor and Pylon were the others.

LAUREN HALL: I met Mike and the rest of the band in 1980. Everyone had a steady girlfriend at first, and we all kind of hung together. We always tried to get in front at shows and let loose and dance. Michael Stipe really fueled that because he would go wild onstage. He'd "let his backbone slip."

KATHLEEN O'BRIEN: I think all of the women who were involved became kind of a group too. We were all very good friends.

DIANA J. CROWE: We did this thing where you would dance the whole way through whether they played one set or two. Then when it was all over, we'd go find some unoccupied pool and all go skinnydipping.

LAUREN HALL: There was this swimming hole called Ball Pump. I only went there a couple of times, but it was really kind of cool. What I miss most about the South is how you can drive out to what seems like the middle of nowhere, traipse through some weeds and find a swimming hole. We would go out there at two or three in the morning and go skinnydippin'. It would be really great because you'd be far enough away from the city and it was dark and so country-southern and very relaxing.

KATE INGRAM: There's something about the climate and nature in Athens that's really calling. To live there is to be a lot more tied to the countryside. It's so cosmopolitan in its intelligence and its sensibility in a certain faction of people, but the nature there spoke to people in the songs and the way they lived their lives.

JARED BAILEY [co-owner, Athens' 40 Watt Club]: I remember seeing R.E.M. at the old 40 Watt here in Athens. It was incredibly crowded and the floor was giving way and I remember Michael jumped out into the crowd. He was one of the first people I ever saw stage dive and a friend of mine and I caught him. He sang the rest of the song while we held him on his back. We felt like we were part of the show.

LANCE SMITH: Being a doorman at the 40 Watt was like the worst job in the world. Ort [*William Carolton, legendary Athens figure*], another doorman from back then, has gone on record saying I was the best doorman in Athens' rock history. It was a tough fucking job. People bitch at you the whole time. People sneaking in and all sorts of shit going on. Every trendy dip shit in Athens that knew six songs and played at a party thought they should just walk into the club because they were rock celebrities. R.E.M. was the only band that was never like that at all. I remember Michael counting out his pennies to get in and I would have let him in free because I liked them a lot. The guy that owned the club told me to let R.E.M. in whenever, but they never came expecting to get in.

KEN FECHTNER: When Peter was still working at Wuxtry Records, the band played one night and there was a party afterward. We were walking home at three a.m. talking about this record and that record and the Monkees came up. Peter said there was a copy of *Head* in the store and I'd never heard it, so we stopped in the store and some guy walked in and started looking through the bins. Peter tried to explain that he worked there but the store wasn't really open and that he should really be on his way. But Peter didn't kick him out or anything—he let him stay until we were done.

That is the quintessential Athens story and Peter story. Afterward he was like, "That was something that I might do, so why not let the guy look at records at 3:00 in the morning."

WOODY NUSS: When Michael cut his hair off, quit the cover band in Athens he was playing with before R.E.M. got together and started hanging out with Jerry Ayers from the band Limbo District, he learned the style of being cool and meek. He started mumbling and letting people figure things out about him instead of answering questions. That was all handed down from the New York art scene that he aspired to. I think he had trouble with the fact that R.E.M. wasn't trendy and he wasn't respected by his art school buddies. Limbo District had more credibility in the art school, and Limbo District sucked! I think Michael's pretense/persona is that you can't tell whether he's changed or not because you could never tell whether he was putting you on in the first place.

KATE INGRAM: R.E.M. are kind of funny people, but their humor is more subtle.

LANCE SMITH: My friend Evan was one of Michael's friend off and on. Michael had a rotating group of friends. The Athens joke at the time was "who is going to be Michael Stipe's new best friend this week?" He'd be with a guy or a girl for two or three weeks all of the time and then you'd never see him with them again. You wouldn't see them even talking again. They wouldn't be on the guest list to shows anymore. I went with Evan over to Michael's place on Barber Street because they traded records. Michael was on his way out and asked me if I could give him a ride to band practice and I said sure. He told us to go on out the back door and he shut it and locked it and the next thing we knew he was crawling out a window because he didn't have a key to his house.

MARK METHE: RIDCO is a place on the road between Atlanta and Athens and they had a sign outside that said, "Bug of the Month: Fleas" or "Cockroaches" or whatever. Whenever R.E.M. would play at 688 Stipe would get up and go, "Bug of the Month: Fleas." Around that time I would see Stipe around a lot and I'd say to him, "bug of the month" and he'd be like, "fuck you" acting like I was insulting him or something for being a bug. It was probably the last thing I ever said to that guy.

KATHLEEN O'BRIEN: R.E.M. met Jefferson Holt on the road and when he came on board, they really needed somebody to do what he was doing. His personality was really the center of the wheel. If they ever had any disagreements, it would be discussed and Jefferson was able to be their friend as well as their manager. He was the one that could be the buffer. That was what they were lacking. Jefferson's personality happened to mesh with their personalities and he became an equal partner too. Instead of him working for them he was working with them and I think that gave him a little more freedom to build the band.

WOODY NUSS: I know there is a story about them going to North Carolina and meeting Jefferson at the record store he ran, but after he moved to Athens he was known as the good guy who ran the door at Tyrone's and those guys trusted him. My impression of why they hooked up with him is that he was the first doorman that didn't rip them off.

KATHLEEN O'BRIEN: I wouldn't say any of them are confrontational people and they decided very early on before they ever started making money that it was going to be a business and they were going to treat it like a business and it was the smartest thing they could have done. If they lost money on shows, it was an equal loss between all of them.

DANNY BEARD: Obviously, Jefferson's effectiveness as a manager has had a lot to do with their success. Good managers are really hard to find. They are usually total assholes. To find someone from here who is a friend, who can stand up to pressure and do the right thing is exceptional. I didn't see anyone else do it. They could have gotten a manager from New York, but they probably wouldn't still be together because the record label would have screwed them over and they'd be hating each other even more than I'm sure they already do. Sure, somebody else could have done the day-to-day thing, but to me what is impressive is that having Jefferson as a manager has allowed them to live in Athens, stand up to their record companies and do the hell what they want to do. The fact that Jefferson has never managed another band is really important. He went through everything with them. If they had gotten some New York guy, he probably would have looked down on the band. I think it took a lot of guts to keep them in Athens. Putting out a single from here first and getting signed by a label was done by the B-52's, but how R.E.M. conducted their business from their hometown was a first.

KATE INGRAM: Jefferson stepped right up and said, "I'm going to do this," and he managed them whereas no other band in Athens had anyone like that. I think he buffered a lot of the difficult decisions and they trusted him to make the contacts and do what was right. Immediately they were put in a place of pretty widespread acceptance in this straight music industry. The B-52's first manager was a Southerner, but she may have not sounded credible. Jefferson was more the picture of what someone at a booking agency or record company could relate to. Even though he was young and seemed naive, he was also charming and intelligent. "The B's" manager might have been charming and intelligent, but they felt really swallowed up and went for more established management in New York. Ultimately, it wasn't a successful liaison for them.

SEAN BOURNE: I remember people referring to Jefferson as "not a real manager," but he stuck to the band's principles. They never sold out and it's as if they cleansed a path for others to follow.

KATHLEEN O'BRIEN: When Jefferson first became the manager, I think I still wanted to manage them because I had invested so much time and energy. . . . Sometimes today I think, do they even remember?

LAUREN HALL: Bertis Downs, R.E.M.'s lawyer, was a good stabilizing person. He helped them understand that they could do what they wanted to do, not what someone else wanted them to do.

KATHLEEN O'BRIEN: Bertis was a loyal fan of theirs, and when he graduated from law school, he offered his services for free to get them going. Bert was another guy whose personality blended well with theirs.

WOODY NUSS: The way the PA was set up at Tyrone's made for really bad recordings. R.E.M. sent Kathleen O'Brien into the basement of the Watt Club to steal Paul Scale's tapes. Paul found her going through his stuff and she made up some story, but everybody knows R.E.M. sent her on a mission to get those tapes back. *Body Count at Tyrone's* [*a well-known bootleg*] is the Fall of 1980 show. They knew *then* they didn't want tapes around. I played a cover of them doing "Hippy Hippy Shake" on my radio show on WUOG in November of 1980 and heard instantly back from them. It came from Kathleen and she said, "we appreciate the sentiment, but when we have something ready to play on the radio, we'll let you know." It was only a two-minute version of "Hippy Hippy Shake." They had taken Jefferson's four-track into

Tyrone's during soundcheck—it has since been bootlegged a million times—and it was shitty. They weren't figuring on it getting played on the radio.

Shortly after that, around Christmas, they got to open for the Police at the Fox Theatre in Atlanta, because of Bill's connections with the Copelands from Macon. [*Ian Copeland had since formed FBI and would represent R.E.M. along with his brother, Stewart, and his band, the Police*] I worked at the Fox as backstage security and runner. R.E.M. had no idea how to behave at a big rock show and they were kind of messing up. Michael invited the audience up on stage at the Fox which you can't do because there's an orchestra pit, and the audience rushed the stage. The band got in huge amounts of trouble. They had no crew, but they brought this guy from Athens down to tune guitars and do stuff. Someone at the Fox described him as a shave-headed speed freak. He was loading out drums through dressing rooms full of people and doing stuff you shouldn't do. They got in trouble from everybody and things were flying around like "You'll never play in this town again." It was great when you consider about three years later they were the biggest thing going and everybody in town was lining up to kiss their asses.

LANCE SMITH: Paul Scales convinced everyone that the Watt Club was going to close and that nobody would have a place to play so he convinced R.E.M. to do a benefit for the club . . . They never played for him again for two years—maybe once.

MARK METHE: [*One of the clubs—not the 40 Watt*] was coke heaven. Have you ever heard of a successful nightclub that wasn't built on cocaine?

LANCE SMITH: Shooting speed in Athens was a big thing to do because needles weren't controlled in Georgia. Guys would walk into the pharmacy downtown after being up for three days and tell the pharmacist they were diabetic and needed a box of needles.

WOODY NUSS: The last gig I did sound for R.E.M. was in Augusta, GA at the New York, New York Disco. Paul Scales had something to do with it. He was the Malcolm McLaren of Athens—lovably corrupt. You knew he was going to rip you off but you could get high with him afterward so no one really worried about it. He wangled this scary gig in Augusta and we didn't know what was going to happen. Everyone was impatient because it took a long time to get set up and it was a terrible sounding room, but a lot of people showed up and R.E.M. made

$600-$700. It was unbelievable to them that they could make that much money so everyone got totally drunk. Their girlfriends had driven down separately—Kathleen O'Brien, Ann Boyles and Lauren Hall—and everyone got really fucked up and couldn't drive home.

LAUREN HALL: That's just one example of the kind of places they were willing to play just so they could play. I wouldn't think of Augusta as a place where I'd want to stay for more than a couple of hours. There's not a whole lot going on there.

WOODY NUSS: Kathleen and Bill ended up leaving in Kathleen's car and I think Lauren and Mike left and the rest of us were standing around in the parking lot going, "Who's driving the car with all the gear home?" Peter said he and Ann were too wasted. The three of us crammed into the front seat. I'd never driven a car that big or one with a trailer and I really didn't want to do it. They said, "We're all drunk so you're doing it." As we got out of Augusta, I missed the entrance ramp to the highway. I didn't know how to turn the thing around, so I backed up so I could get on the highway. Peter looked over his shoulder and said, "You should be careful not to jackknife," and as he said it, the trailer jackknifes and the car wrecks. We made it back to Athens but the next morning the car wouldn't start because the exhaust pipe was crushed in the accident. I called Bill and he said, "We're just sitting around trying to figure out what to do." I offered to give back my pay for the night, but Bill said don't worry about it. I've always said, I worked for R.E.M. till I wrecked Bill Berry's LTD, but in fact, they needed a bigger sound system than mine. So they went and started renting a better PA in town.

KATHLEEN O'BRIEN: I drove them to a show in Atlanta with their equipment and a taxi broadsided me. It totalled my car and dislocated my shoulder but I drove back to Athens that night because they needed their equipment the next day. There were times when everyone did stuff like that. It was a total collaborative effort.

WOODY NUSS: If everybody who says they saw R.E.M. at Tyrone's did, the shows would have had to have taken place at Madison Square Garden. But they were still big shows. By the time they'd done two or three of them, it was *the* thing. At the end of every two months or so, R.E.M. would have both weekend nights and it would sell out. It was a $3 cover and they were making $2000. Nobody was making that much. Those shows were amazing. People would dance unbelievably. The hardcore girl clique—Kathleen O'Brien, Carol

Levy, Leslie Michelle (who was the best dancer that ever lived) and Diana Otto were the cool new wave girls who would dance in front. Kurt Wood was this really tall guy with Eraserhead hair and he was a cool dancer, too. Michael would run down and sing and dance with all these people. Then there was the stuck-up neo-bohemian factor standing toward the back.

KATE INGRAM: The art world had more of an allure to Pylon and the payoff in the rock world was less rewarding to them. They were getting the bookings and the audiences that the B-52's had been offered, though it might have been more difficult for audiences to connect with Pylon. They did everything right, but it didn't gel the way it did with the B-52's or R.E.M.

DANNY BEARD: I saw R.E.M. at the Agora in Atlanta and wasn't knocked out. The only thing I liked was Michael's voice, but the songs weren't that good. Pete couldn't play very well. I saw them a bunch more after that and saw them get better and better. It never came up that DB would put out a single on them, maybe because of that first time I saw them. I told Kenny Fechtner I didn't really like them that night, and maybe he said something to Pete. Actually Bill Berry called me up one time and wanted to ask some questions about putting out records and I said fine. For whatever reason, it never occurred and it never came from their end which is probably how it would have had to happen. I kind of felt like it would have been hard for me to approach them because Pylon wouldn't have liked it and they were my main focus. I was plenty busy with Love Tractor, the Method Actors and Pylon, so I was probably doing too much as it was. But obviously they did the right thing.

KATHLEEN O'BRIEN: I just knew. I had a feeling that these guys were going to make it big and they were going to be millionaires. I knew this in my heart of hearts.

ARMISTEAD WELLFORD: I remember having a dream, before they ever made it, of being at Tyrone's and I was standing by the bar and the Method Actors were playing and they were playing "Radio Free Europe" in my dream. When I woke up, the song was in my head and I thought, man, that's a hit song.

DANNY BEARD: Personally, I felt like the stage had been set in Athens and Atlanta for R.E.M. to do what they wanted and maybe they didn't appreciate it as much as they should have.

The B-52's showed that a bunch of people who weren't musicians could get together and be a band. They also showed what you do and how you make it once you are a band.

ARMISTEAD WELLFORD: I think it was really smart of R.E.M. not to want to be associated with "the B's" as far as not playing shows with them. It would have been easy for them to do, but they chose not to—they always wanted to establish their own thing.

JARED BAILEY: To me it seemed like people treated R.E.M. differently even after their first or second show. I felt differently toward them and I had only briefly met Michael and Peter. Immediately they were local heroes and local gods. You gotta have some reverence for a band that gives you so much fun.

LAUREN HALL: From the very beginning I had one of those gut feelings that they would be successful. I never thought, "they're going to be as big as the Police," or anything like that, I just knew that they were going to be very, very successful. There was such intensity to their shows and everyone in the club would feel it. It just kind of gripped you. It could be a fun escape for a couple of hours.

JARED BAILEY: Nobody knew they were going to be big. They were just a fun dance band who played covers. We were just enjoying it while it lasted.

1981-82

1981
February — Recording session at Bombay Studios, Atlanta

April — Drive-In Studio, Winston-Salem, NC. Tracks for first single recorded with Mitch Easter.

October — Recording session at Drive-In Studio for what will become *Chronic Town* EP

Touring
Gigs throughout Georgia, North Carolina and Tennessee

June 16 — First trip to New York: The Ritz, opening for Gang of Four

First Seven-Inch Single
July — "Radio Free Europe"/"Sitting Still": Produced by Mitch Easter

Awards/Recognition
December — Hib-Tone single tops *Village Voice* Pazz and Jop Critic's Poll as Single of The Year

1982
January — More sessions at Drive-In Studio

May — R.E.M. signs with IRS Records

— More sessions at Drive-In Studio

Touring
First extensive U.S. tour begins in August and continues throughout the year

August 19 — First West Coast appearance: Music Machine, LA

EP and Seven-Inch Singles
August 24 — *Chronic Town* EP, produced by Mitch Easter & R.E.M.

December — *Trouser Press* Flexi Disc, "Wolves, Lower"

Video
"Wolves, Lower"

Awards/Recognition
Chronic Town EP rates in Top Ten of *Village Voice* Pazz and Jop Poll

2

"RADIO FREE EUROPE" SEVEN-INCH SINGLE AND CHRONIC TOWN

"We wanted to be successful, but for me, we were successful the day in 1981 that I didn't have to have a day job."
—Mike Mills to *Pulse!* October 1992

KEN FECHTNER: When they first played in New York, Peter came back raving because he'd gotten to meet The dB's. He met Peter Holsapple of the dBs and he said he liked R.E.M. The rock critic, Lester Bangs, was at the show and that really impressed Peter.

MITCH EASTER [producer, Hib-Tone single, *Chronic Town, Murmur* and *Reckoning*]: I saw a poster with R.E.M.'s name on it and I had a really strong image they were a high-tech band with synths and a drum machine. The first time I ever saw them or heard them was when they came up to North Carolina to record some demos in my studio. We had a mutual friend in Peter Holsapple of The dB's and he told them about the studio I just started. They came up and did a tape of "Radio Free Europe" and "Sitting Still" (which would become the first single) and "White Tornado." Back then I think they had three kinds of songs. They had their "classic R.E.M." songs that were kind of pretty, like "Gardening at Night." Then they had their wilder more disjointed songs—I think of that song "9-9" that ended up on *Murmur*. I think one of the first times they came into my studio they tried to do that song but they didn't have it together. Then they had their funny throw aways like "White Tornado."

JONATHAN W. HIBBERT [Hib-Tone label]: I had a friend at school in Athens whose knowledge of music I trusted. I asked her who the happening band in Athens was and she said there was a group she loved and everybody loved, R.E.M., playing at Tyrone's that night. I went up there to check it out and the place was just going nuts. R.E.M. was making a kind of joyous cacophony.

DANNY BEARD: After a show at the Agora in Atlanta, right before they were doing their single, Johnny Hibbert kind of smugly was sitting outside saying, "I'm putting out a record," but he wouldn't say what band it was. Like I cared.

JONATHAN W. HIBBERT: We got the rough mixes of stuff they had already done at Mitch's Drive In Studio and went back up there for a couple of days to remix and add some vocal parts to "Radio Free Europe" and "Sitting Still." I wanted R.E.M. to sound the way they sounded when I first heard them in Tyrone's. We got the best mix we could at that point and left Mitch's. Later Mitch did another mix on his own of the same stuff and said he thought it was an improvement on the first mix. Peter was the most vocal about wanting to use Mitch's new mix, but I put my foot down and we released the mix I preferred. I was probably the last person ever to override Pete Buck.

MITCH EASTER: This is the way I remember it. They came up here and recorded, then we did some mixes. Then Johnny Hibbert got involved and he wanted to remix it so they came up again and did a mix with him. I didn't think it was so hot so I did one more. I think the one I mailed to them after the sessions turned up on *Dead Letter Office* [1987], the compilation album of unreleased tracks and b-sides. The three mixes are not that different.

TODD PLOHARSKI [record collector]: The quarter-inch mix-down tape of the Hib-Tone single that they got from Mitch sounded like crap.

MITCH EASTER: In my studio back then, I had a good tape machine, a not-so-hot console and no processing equipment. We couldn't mess with stuff the way people were doing it in pop studios. Those were some of the first recordings I'd ever even done, so none of us knew what we were doing in a way.

TODD PLOHARSKI: Jefferson thought it was their reel to reel that was making it sound bad. I had a Nakamichi cassette deck, the best in town at the time. There was no John Keane studios in Athens, there was nothing. So they called me and said we have to see if it is our cassette deck or the reel that sounds bad. They came and put it on my cassette deck and sure enough it didn't sound any better. So then we decided it might be the reel to reel that didn't sound good. We brought the reel to the radio station [WUOG]. Since it isn't the cassette deck, let's put it on the reel to reel there and a good cassette deck there and see if it works. We did it there and it still wasn't that much better, but while we were there, we threw it on cart and played it on the air, months before the single came out. The phones rang immediately. It wasn't the first time R.E.M. had been on the air, it was just the first time [what would ultimately be] the Hib-Tone single got played. It was played all of the time and people would request it every day. We had to put a note on it that said, "no! you can only play this once every three hours" because people would call up and want it played immediately so they could tape it.

KEN FECHTNER: The single came out a little over a year after they started.

TODD PLOHARSKI: Ort bought 50-100 singles when it came out. They made 1000 of the first pressing. 600 went off for promo, the rest went to Wuxtry and some went to New York. It sold quick around here and in New York.

JONATHAN W. HIBBERT: I think we ran six or seven thousand singles altogether.

GIL RAY [musician]: I was in a band called the Happy Eggs and we put out a seven-inch at the same time R.E.M. did. At New World Records in Charlotte, NC where I worked, those were the two kind of "punk" records we sold. We were checking out their record and we were kind of jealous that they had purple on their sleeve and ours was only black and white. Then we listened to it and at first we couldn't understand the production and thought, "what is this?"

SEAN BOURNE: When Danny Beard released the B-52's first single, everyone was having a hard time networking this "new" form of music, the independent single. We had the old Southern rock tag to live down. There were just no avenues for it. There were a few clubs. There was no way for bands to get much action for their singles. At Wax 'n' Facts in

Atlanta, the sales of the R.E.M. Hib-Tone single were steady. There were plenty of local artists that sold more, but there was definitely a real buzz.

DAN VALLOR [acquaintance]: As a follower of the indy-pop underground, I was thrilled by R.E.M. when I first heard them. Their first single had come out around the time of the second dB's album and while I held a lot of bands in higher esteem, I thought R.E.M. was a fine new band.

KATE INGRAM: You couldn't help but get excited that someone that lived in your $70.00 a month building had a record out that was getting played in Boston and New York.

SEAN BOURNE: The first time I heard "Radio Free Europe," I put it on for my ex-wife and she laughed and laughed. She put it on over and over again. There isn't a word you can understand on it.

ARMISTEAD WELLFORD: People liked the single immediately and people were excited for them. They had the ball rolling and everyone wanted to see what their next project was.

STEVE WYNN [Dream Syndicate, toured with R.E.M.]: I was working at the Rhino record store in LA in '81 and I was in charge of buying independent releases and imports. That's the time when a lot of indy singles were coming out so I bought all of them. If I'd heard of something, I'd order five copies. I remember hearing about the R.E.M. single and ordered five. I knew they were from Georgia and I think I read something in New York Rocker and that was it. My friend at another store heard we had the single and was so excited he asked me to hold him a copy. After he said that, I thought I should get a copy too but I took it home and played it and thought it wasn't too great. I brought it back the next day. This was right around the time my band had done our first ep.

GIL RAY: There was this absolute hole in the wall club in Charlotte, NC, the Milestone. I had these friends that said I had to check out the club because it was the first punk rock place in Charlotte. We had this group of friends that liked just about every band that came to the Milestone. It might have had something to do with the Quaaludes we were taking and beer we were drinking but we wanted to have good times. Pylon would play, the Swimming Pool Q's [Atlanta] and this amazing band from Atlanta called Vietnam would come up and play and we loved all those bands. Then the bands from the North like Mission of Burma would start coming down, but we liked the Southern people. They could rock without trying for some reason. They're more real. They grow up in friendly neighborhoods even though they can be frightfully conservative. But I think that made the people in bands work even harder to achieve coolness.

R.E.M. would play at the Milestone and there'd be like 15-20 people in this freezing, fucked up club. It seemed they came up every six weeks or two months. It sounds corny, but I kinda knew something was going to happen with these folks. They weren't that great musically. Well, the rhythm section was. I don't know what it was. I've seen better players, heard better songs. But they were really loose and fun. You could just get up on the stage and dance with them. They were the total party band at the time. They just entertained the hell out of us.

CURTIS CROWE: It was pretty adventurous leaving Athens in a van and touring at that time because the first major stop out of Athens going north was Washington D.C. and that was kind of like the frontier. From there the next stop was New York City. It wasn't an uncommon thing to jump in the van and head to New York City where you could actually play a venue where they wouldn't throw beer bottles at you. The difference between Pylon and R.E.M. is that we [Pylon] were completely unwilling to explore any of these places in between. R.E.M. were just like mercenaries. They would go anywhere and force themselves in. It worked beautifully for them.

JARED BAILEY: If one thing made me appreciate them and realize they were headed for something outside of Athens is that they worked so hard. Constantly playing up and down the east coast, living out of a van. In those years, you didn't think of things like that. The B-52's played a few times in Athens and then moved to New York. You never thought about small bands touring out of here till R.E.M. did.

KATE INGRAM: The B-52's forged a network for future bands to leave Athens. There was a sort of an Athens, New York City axis and I kind of fit into it when I moved to Boston. We used to call it the I-85 Tour. A lot of people from the Athens scene had since relocated to New York to pursue careers in the art world and were willing to open their homes to touring bands from the South. Summer of 1981, R.E.M. was in New York and Pylon was in town and someone was having a party in the Village. When you got to the door, there was a sign with an arrow that said, "Athens." My perception of why people were so willing to help each other once they left Athens was how the hippie movement affected us in Athens and how it was an extension of that. It was a little late, coming in 1973, but there was a hybrid between the hippie sensibility and the Southern sensibility and it had a real charm to it.

DAN WALL: When R.E.M. started going on mini-tours is when Peter had to stop working for us at Wuxtry. He got canned because he couldn't do his job. There was no animosity. We mutually agreed that he would go when it got to be too much.

GIL RAY: I was talking to Peter about the Milestone once and he told me one of the times they played there, the owner didn't have any money to pay them and they didn't have a place to stay that night so he locked them inside the club and let them stay over. Apparently he forgot to lock the beer freezer and the band wiped out his beer in payment. I don't know if I'd want to sleep over in that place.

LANCE SMITH: To understand Athens' music, you have to understand Athens' history. It was always "the Bulldogs," University of Georgia's football team. It was a total Southern intense fucking football town. It was all frats and people into the Bulldogs. When I was in Athens you couldn't be into R.E.M. and into football too. Everything was polarized then. It's not like that now.

DAVID T. LINDSAY [rock critic]: The first time I ever saw them play was when they opened for Bow Wow Wow here in Atlanta at the Biltmore in '81. Michael sang five songs with a broken mic. You can sing one song with a broken mic then either use Mike Mills' mic or ask for another mic. But he continued to sing with a broken mic and that's when I decided they were stupid.

BRIAN CRANE [Athens musician]: I saw them once the second or third month I was in town and went out and bought the record and thought it really sucked compared to them live. Then one night I was at this all night diner and met Peter and Mike Mills and told them I had their record and thought they were great. It turned out Peter was living pretty close to me and so was Bill Berry.

LAUREN HALL: Michael was always at 169 Barber Street because he was such close friends with Lynda Hopper. I lived next door in another house split into three. Peter and Ann lived on one side and I lived on the other side. They used to call it the "street of stars" because a lot of people in bands lived on that street.

BRIAN CRANE: Everyone was living like in a two block area and I used to go down and drive them crazy. "Teach me how to play guitar. . . ." Peter showed me some chords. I went home for Christmas and bought a 12-string Rickenbacker.

KEN FECHTNER: The first time I got a sense that something was happening was over Christmas, I went to New York and I was looking through the *Village Voice* and "Radio Free Europe" was listed as one of the 10 best singles. It was weird and sort of earth-shattering to pick up the *Voice* and see under the best of the year an independent single by R.E.M. I thought, this may really be something. But at the same time, they still weren't massively popular. They were popular in some cities like Atlanta and Chapel Hill, NC but there was a time maybe a little before the ep came out that they played some club in Savannah, GA and two people came, stayed for a song and a half and left. It built slowly. It took them a long time to get a headline slot at the 688 Club in Atlanta.

> *"The thing is, the great reviews and the Top Ten lists didn't change the fact that we were in a '75 Dodge Tradesman lugging all our gear ourselves and still showing up and playing to eight or nine people."* —Jefferson Holt to *Rolling Stone*, December 3, 1987

BRIAN CRANE: The second time I saw R.E.M. at Tyrone's, which was the last time they played there because it burnt right after that, I just thought they were great. I just couldn't believe that four idiots you could talk to on the street could get up on the stage and play like that. They worked as such a unit, it just would take you aback. They were stars from the moment I saw them, just in the way they presented themselves. At the same time, Mike, Pete and Bill are just average guys. Mike and Bill are rednecks from Macon. You could picture them listening to Lynyrd Skynryd, riding around in the car throwing beer cans at road signs. Peter was a rock and roll animal. He knew everything about every record ever recorded and he probably had it. You could ask him any question about any weirdo record and he would know the label it came out on and when it was released.

LAUREN HALL: The one thing I remember most about Tyrone's is that they had video game machines and Mike was addicted to Space Invaders. I'd be there with him and I couldn't get him to do anything but play those video games. But it was a really cool little spot. They used to keep bar tabs for us there because back then nobody had any money. We were all really saddened by Tyrone's demise, but we were really happy that the bar tabs burned with the club.

JARED BAILEY: After Tyrone's burned down, they didn't bother to rebuild. Parking is at a premium in downtown Athens, so they let people park in the space. That's one of the things Michael is involved in these days is historical preservation—trying to prevent old buildings like Tyrone's from being torn down and made into parking lots.

WOODY NUSS: After Tyrone's, R.E.M. was too big for the Watt club, so they started playing at the I&I.

LAUREN HALL: The I&I was kind of a hang out for sorority and fraternity people, so it never really had a cool reputation. The good thing about it was it was huge so we'd get bigger bands coming to town.

KATHLEEN O'BRIEN: Bill had contacts with Miles Copeland at IRS Records through his work [*brother*] Ian Copeland at the Paragon Agency in Macon.

ARMISTEAD WELLFORD: I heard something about them getting a few thousand dollars to put out a record with IRS, which at the time, we didn't know what that really meant. I thought it was great and I told Mike at the time I thought so and he was like, "We don't know what's going to happen." In a way it was a small, big break because IRS ended up being a good label for them. Even though they started off small, they got to spend time in LA, which wasn't something that the B-52's ever did.

KEITH ALTOMARE [IRS Records, college promotion]: I was working for IRS and Jay Boberg, head of A&R at the time, sent me the "Radio Free Europe" single. Jay really liked it and I kind of liked it so at that point we were the only ones there that got into the band. I knew a lot of people working in radio and what they were into and I thought that R.E.M. could be something. It wasn't that the other people at the company didn't like them, but they didn't understand what Michael was saying, therefore they didn't get it.

JONATHAN W. HIBBERT: I tried to make a deal with IRS to buy my stuff out but they wouldn't deal with me directly. They had given R.E.M. a little pocket change to buy me out. Bert Downs drew up a contract so R.E.M could purchase their publishing on the two songs, the metal masters, the artwork and the record. I sold it. I was talked into giving them what they wanted. The only thing I would have done differently is that I wouldn't have given them what they wanted because they weren't grateful and haven't been ever since. I'm not bitter, but I do carry a little bit of disappointment.

KATHLEEN O'BRIEN: I would say R.E.M. was very reputation conscious from the outset. They've always retained intense control from the very first record deal. Johnny Hibbert agreed to the deal but it wasn't good foresight on his part. He had a lot to lose and he lost it.

DANNY BEARD: A key decision for the survival of a band is a choice of record company and they've obviously made good choices. Maybe a different company would have sold more sooner, but it's hard to say. I think as owner of DB, if I had done something different would things have worked out better? If I had hooked up with a major label in 1981 would Pylon have been huge? Probably not. Because it comes down to a willingness to work and that's what R.E.M. had that Pylon didn't have.

MITCH EASTER: After doing the very first sessions, I lobbied really hard with Jefferson one night at a club in Raleigh, NC for them to come back to North Carolina. I really wanted to do more work with them after that first session. They did come back and do *Chronic Town* and I thought that turned out great. I fought to get to do it.

WOODY NUSS: On January 14, 1982, a week after Tyrone's burned, I dragged the PA over to the 40 Watt number three location, the one that was next to the R.E.M. office. They just returned from a short tour and finished mixing and editing what was to become *Chronic Town*. It snowed in Athens that day, and for some reason they decided to play a show. They brought Jason and the Scorchers down from Nashville and in order to build a hype for the Scorchers show, R.E.M. played the night before unannounced and then told everyone to come down the next day for the Scorchers show.

LANCE SMITH: The Scorchers first gig outside of Nashville was in Athens and Jason even said, "We wouldn't be here at all if it wasn't for R.E.M. because when I saw them for the first time they were so great I wanted to be in a band so here I am."

WOODY NUSS: That night, I was sitting out on the hood of the car with Peter and they were going over the sequencing of *Chronic Town*, bitching about how disappointed they were with being in the studio and how tough it was. We were playing a game with him—'What's This Song Called'—because we had all made up titles to the songs based on the lyrics. When he got to "Wolves, Lower" we all started busting up laughing that something could end up being called "Wolves" let alone "comma Lower." Peter was like, "Well, that's what we named it. It's Michael. What can I say? Whatever."

ARMISTEAD WELLFORD: I love Pete's guitar part on "Wolves, Lower." It's just his simple way of playing but if you listen to that stuff, it definitely will bring back memories of that time.

SEAN BOURNE: Suddenly, Athens was the place to be seen, hang and out and be in a band. Which was cool because I would see a lot of shows and there was a really good energy about it. Everybody was real comfortable being there.

ARMISTEAD WELLFORD: You can kind of hear the beginnings of a definitive Athens Sound on *Chronic Town*. Bill can play any kind of beat, but the drum beats on that record were real central to the sound.

DAN VALLOR: Everyone was completely befuddled by the lyrics early on. That was an element of mystery they wanted to maintain. While I think some of the mystery was intentional, a lot of it was Michael's problems with enunciation. Peter once said that once you've talked to Michael enough times you can sit down with the records and understand the words, which is really true, although there was always a lot of sing-songy gibberish thrown in.

> *"The first thing for me is building those walls, coming up with rules—with these turns of phrase—and using them differently, changing them so that old rule doesn't apply anymore and a new rule has taken its place."*   —Michael Stipe to *Musician*,
> September 1985

GIL RAY: I didn't meet them till they played out here in California for the first time. I went up to Michael and said, "You probably don't remember me but . . ." I felt like I had to connect with people from the South any time I saw one. He looked at me like I was crazy, but he remembered the Milestone in Charlotte, NC.

DAN VALLOR: Michael could not have been considered a posturing eccentric at that point. He wasn't so out there that he couldn't fit in with other people, though he definitely had eccentricities that I couldn't fathom anyone faking. He had a tendency to clear his throat constantly. Right into the recorder when he did interviews—clearing his throat and spitting. I've noticed a lot of singers do that, ultimately clearing their throats raw, they worry so much.

KEN FECHTNER: One night I was sleeping over at a friend of mine's in the living room and I woke up to find that Michael had let himself in and was watching me sleep. I asked him what he was doing and he said, "I'm watching you sleep."

DAN VALLOR: Michael behaved normally now and again but he wasn't consistent about it.

MARC WALLACE [friend]: Michael will pull out a toothbrush in the middle of a bar and brush his teeth.

BRIAN CRANE: Michael was cultivating his own thing and he really was cultivating something. The whole image...it worked real well. It was an alluring mystique he was presenting.

DAN VALLOR: Certainly there were intentional ambiguities all over the place. There was also Michael's enunciation but I think he would also just rattle off gibberish to keep people who *could*

MICHAEL STIPE SHAVING AT HOME
(photo by Geoff Gans)

understand him at bay. He used to draw imaginary circles around himself onstage in an apparent attempt to keep other band members and audience members out of his space.

LANCE SMITH: I like the line in "Stumble" about the APT, Athens Party Line. Someone in Athens [*Michael Lachowski, Pylon*] actually had an answering machine at the time and the APT would list where all the parties were outside of going to clubs, since going to parties was the biggest motif in Athens. So many R.E.M. songs are evocative of "The Athens that was." The only song the B-52s did like that was "Deadbeat Club." I think that song captures Athens as well. I can still see those same girls all dancing and sneaking into people's pools.

DANNY BEARD: Immediately when *Chronic Town* came out, we sold a lot at Wax 'n' Facts. We sold a ton because people had been waiting for it.

SEAN BOURNE: After the ep came out, I was more befuddled by people's reaction to it than anything else. I didn't think there was anything on there that was great. I didn't understand it.

BRUCE MCGUIRE [Warner Brothers Records, Minneapolis]: Right at the time *Chronic Town* came out I went back to the store where I bought it and the guy said they had just got more of the Hib-Tone single so I was able to get it like three weeks after I got *Chronic Town*. At that time a new Prince single was as cool as an R.E.M. single, at least in Minneapolis.

LANCE SMITH: You wouldn't believe what it was like when the ep was out. If you walked home from school you could hear it coming from ten different houses on one street. You could not walk anywhere in Athens without hearing that ep.

ROBERT LLOYD [journalist and musician]: I remember that I'd heard the ep and not responded to it but went back to it after the album came out. I just might have thought it was formless. I think it was the production. It sounded so dry.

DAN VALLOR: R.E.M. was excited by nonsense in the recordings, which was always a Mitch Easter trademark. They even put Michael in the alley at Mitch's Drive In Studio and recorded him zipping his pants up and down.

MITCH EASTER: "Wolves, Lower" on *Chronic Town* has some funny noises on it because we did some of the vocals outside. There were a lot of bugs out there. Whenever that "House in order" part comes up, I think you can hear tons of crickets. You don't really hear them, but they are there. Michael just kind of makes voices which you can hear. You can kind of hear him say "wolves" in a spoken voice and the spoken voice will sound different than the sung "wolves."

DANNY BEARD: It probably was frustrating to the other bands here that they were on small labels and R.E.M. was on a bigger label. If they were on a label like R.E.M., maybe they could have gotten more accomplished. But no one ever came for those other bands. I would have been open to listening to some other label or some bigwig saying, "we think we can get more done for Pylon," but it never happened. All these bands were out there on their own and R.E.M. to their credit got Jefferson and Bertis to run their business. Pylon and Love Tractor never found those kind of people.

KATE INGRAM: I think R.E.M. probably always knew they would be successful. They were more directed in wanting to follow the easy road that had been laid out for them. They didn't get so distracted by the twists and turns in it and the places that looked different and strange to them. And in turn they got a real cooperation from people in what they did. There was something else they had that the other bands didn't have and that was early on Jefferson and Bert were part of the band. That took a lot of the weight off of their shoulders.

> *"The first time we ever played San Francisco, I remember it well, because Stiv [Bators] comes out on stage and mumbles, 'Great to be back in Los Angeles' and falls flat offstage. We actually all relocated to Los Angeles for one month in August of '83 and lived in the Oakwood Garden apartments on Barham Boulevard, next to Universal. So we could get to know the record company people and do some gigs. Nobody knew who we were. We were always opening for somebody. We played the Music Machine, Madame Wong's and the Lingerie. Jefferson would take the van into the office to do work all day and it was like five miles to the nearest pay phone. So we'd sit all day and watch TV. We found a liquor store that would deliver beer, sandwiches and cigarettes. So about three o'clock in the afternoon we'd order a case of beer, four sandwiches and a pack of cigs. And that was our stay in LA."*
> —Peter Buck to *Bucketfull of Brains*,
> November 1993

DAN VALLOR: For an entire month, the band holed up in an apartment complex in North Hollywood, doing promotion and an occasional live show. Bill would make solo tapes on a four-track which the band described as sounding like Suicide or Silver Apples, yet Bill had never heard either at that point. They watched TV, drooled over Sissy Spacek movies and spent endless evenings searching for things to keep them occupied. The days were spent at IRS doing interviews, radio station ID's and promotional calls. I was in Los Angeles at the same time. I knew Steve Wynn for some time and introduced him to Peter at a Dream Syndicate radio broadcast. They hit it off pretty well, though I don't know to what extent they maintained contact.

STEVE WYNN: The Dream Syndicate played a live broadcast in August '82 on KPFK in LA. R.E.M. played at the Music Machine that night and they went on at midnight. Our broadcast didn't start until three in the morning so I'm not sure if any of them came to the KPFK show. By the time the Dream Syndicate started touring in summer of '82, R.E.M. had done the same, so I was kind of aware of what they were up to. At that point it wasn't that common to make your own record and do your own tour so you could kind of keep up with all the bands that were doing that. We started having a lot of friends in common.

DAN VALLOR: There was a lot going on in LA during the weeks we were there. Michael and I went to see the Rain Parade one night in East LA. The band and the crowd seemed to all be friends and between sets they all gathered in one corner while Michael and I stood in another. They all seemed puzzled at us strangers—why had we come to see them?

RUSS TOLMAN: [musician] I saw R.E.M. around the time *Chronic Town* came out at Galactica 2000 in Sacramento, a disco that did new wave shows. I always read about how they toured and toured and toured and I used that as a role model for my band, True West. We gotta tour, we gotta tour, we gotta tour. It could have been what broke up our band. It helped that R.E.M. all liked each other.

BUREN FOWLER [R.E.M. road crew and Drivin' n' Cryin' guitarist]: The first time I heard "Box Cars" [*"Carnival of Sorts (Box Cars)"*] I thought that was one of the coolest, hardest rocking songs I'd ever heard. The high-hat was making the whole song rock. At the time, I was in like the worst heavy metal band ever playing AC/DC and Judas Priest covers and I thought R.E.M. were the coolest band in the whole world.

KATHLEEN O'BRIEN: Everywhere they went, the response to them was overwhelming. The four personalities were really intriguing as well as the music.

RUSS TOLMAN: They seemed to be friends and they had their roles. Michael is the artistic guy, Peter is the public relations guy and Mills is just a nice guy and the most professional musician of the lot. Bill Berry is the drummer—what else can you say? I think four members in a band work better than five because you have balance.

KATHLEEN O'BRIEN: All four were polar opposites, yet together they created a unique sound and complemented each other in their creative and business endeavors. For example, Bill was more serious in pursuing his contacts and relentless in getting the exposure they needed. Michael was always more introverted and played the eccentric artist. Peter was eccentric but kind of flamboyant. From the very beginning he started doing most of the interviews because he could talk a blue streak and he's entertaining. Mike Mills is just a truly nice, unassuming person. It was a nice blend of personalities.

KEITH ALTOMARE: We put out *Chronic Town* and it didn't do great, but it did well. Of course the Georgia stations and some of the more together college stations across the country jumped on it, but in conversations with people at college radio, they really didn't know what to make of them.

GINA ARNOLD [rock critic]: I heard R.E.M. through college radio and I bought the record because of the album cover. I loved it immediately and it was totally different than anything I had heard. They were the antithesis to hardcore punk like Black Flag and Circle Jerks and that was what I was into. But just about the time I got into R.E.M. I started working in college radio, so I found out about other bands. I don't know if I would have found out about the other bands as in depth as I did were it not for R.E.M.

KEN FECHTNER: I was at medical school in Augusta and pretty much every time they played in Athens for two years I came up to see them. They were getting better and better. When they started out, they were incredibly prolific songwriters. Every time you'd see them they had new songs and there would be two or three good new songs. Peter got to be a better guitar player. The joke was "they were the band with the lead bass player." Peter couldn't do any of the complicated stuff so Mills' bass sort of carried the melody line. Mike played a high tone, real melodic bass.

MITCH EASTER: They used to spend a fair amount of time at my house when they were recording or if they were playing shows here in North Carolina. The kinds of records they wanted to discuss or got excited about were melodic records from the Sixties. Though we were living in the punk era, they weren't interested in being punkier than thou, they just wanted to be artistes, without it being deliberate.

DAN VALLOR: Whether it was through associations with Mitch Easter and Peter Holsapple and the North Carolina scene or perhaps the New York Rocker scene which included the Bongos and the Individuals, you can assess from the early material that they must have been encouraged at some point to polish up their songwriting. Some of the early songs lasted long enough to make it to vinyl but many more were rightly dumped. "Bodycount" and "Permanant Vacation" and some of the other early material was atrocious.

LANCE SMITH: I liked the song "Bodycount." I think it is the pre-cursor to "Orange Crush." It has the same themes like serve your country and do all this fucked up shit. When R.E.M. played the Nightflight in Savannah, they were the smash hit of the weekend because there wasn't much going on down there. There are a lot of bases around there and a lot of jugheads show up. A fight broke out while R.E.M. was doing "Bodycount" and these guys started yelling "fuck you" and all these other people started screaming at the army guys.

DAN VALLOR: It would behoove them to avoid allowing too many ears to hear the early material. Some of those tapes circulated after the fact. As their popularity rose, somebody leaked them.

MARK METHE: Some hip-pretending weasel from Athens made a bootleg of the cassette I made when R.E.M. rehearsed in the Wuxtry. I duplicated it cheaply on real lo-fi and gave them away to people I deemed to be fans. I never thought someone was going to make a bootleg. Chuck Connolly who worked for us (but lives on some Indian reservation now) drew the cover to the cassette that we named *Slurred*. The cover was the gargyole like on the *Chronic Town* sleeve but as you unfolded it you could see a big stone dick in the gargoyle's hand.

COVER OF SLURRED, THE PRECURSOR OF R.E.M. BOOTLEGS (*drawing by Chuck Connolly*)

LANCE SMITH: There was a show in the Spring of '82 where Jason and the Scorchers opened for R.E.M. at Legion Field and at the end Jason came on holding Michael in his arms singing "Rockville" with him and Michael said, "please throw your money on the stage," and everyone did. There were like 5000-6000 people there and I didn't think they would pick it all up, but they did. Michael and Jason collected all of the money on the stage and walked off.

CURTIS CROWE: R.E.M. used to come to Pylon's shows. I remember seeing them there. As a band, they came to see us up in New York at a show at Hurrah with the Gang of Four. It turned out they slept in their van out on the street somewhere because they didn't have a place to sleep. We didn't even know. They could have stayed in our hotel room.

KEN FECHTNER: Christmas '82 I stopped up in Athens. In front of Belt's Department store there was a big pile of stuff they were throwing out after Christmas. I was walking with Michael and we found some metal grating in the trash that he thought he could use for something so we were digging around in the trash. Months later I ran into a friend and we were trading what we did on Christmas vacation stories. I told her I'd been in Athens and she said, "Yea, I know, I saw y'all digging through the trash but I didn't want to say hello because I thought you would be embarrassed."

WOODY NUSS: After the success of *Chronic Town,* booking agents became interested in sending bands to Athens. The only reason bands would come to Athens before was because Athens bands had gone to New York and made friends. The B-52's made a trail to New York and club bookers there were waiting to kiss anyone's ass if they were from Georgia. The Tractor and Pylon could go there and get an audience. There was also the speed connection. Bands would blaze down to Georgia to get the cheap speed—and that was the reason they would come down. For the Fleshtones and The dB's, it was an added reason to come down South. Plus you could book a mini-tour between Danceteria in New York to City Gardens in Trenton, the 9:30 Club in DC and Club 688 in Atlanta then Athens. You could make enough money to get down and back and all of the agents would work together to make it happen. Whoever came through, they made sure they could get from New York to Athens. The same holds true for the Minneapolis bands— Hüsker Dü and the Replacements. The reason they came down to Athens didn't have to do with jangly guitars. There are records named after the phenomenon—Hüsker Dü's *Land Speed Record* and the Fleshtones *Speed Connection.*

LANCE SMITH: I heard most touring bands came to Athens because of the speed there. If you listen to the way most of those guys played you can tell.

DAN VALLOR: It was a very lively time for new bands in the underground. There were not a lot of bands trying to cash in on the varying scenes.

ARMISTEAD WELLFORD: The freak scene here kind of grew through the Eighties. We also got that yuppie thing too. The natural food restaurants got bigger and things became more success oriented. The club scene got bigger and bigger. It used to be so fun. From then on it was big business.

LANCE SMITH: One example of someone who moved to Athens because of R.E.M. was Matthew Sweet. From what I heard, he saw R.E.M. in Nebraska and decided to move to Athens. Some people [in Athens] have problems with him because he already had a record deal when he moved there and he didn't tell anyone. He relied on the Athens scene's generosity and openness and some of the songs he wrote [with other people] while he was there ended up [uncredited] on his first album.

ARMISTEAD WELLFORD: It was exciting and inspiring to the other bands in town and to the ones that moved there that R.E.M. was taking off. We thought, "they're huge!"

LAUREN HALL: Mike and Bill and I all lived in this one apartment on Barber Street. It was a real dump. It had three rooms. It was $120.00 a month. The front room was our bedroom and the band also practiced in that room. Their drum kit was always set up. Bill lived in the next room. Then there was a kitchen. The bathroom was on the back of it and it was falling off the side of the house. You could literally see outside. I took plastic and covered it up because I had to get up in the morning and take a shower and go to work. They'll probably kill me for saying this but I would try to take a shower and it would be so cold, I can remember standing in the shower crying because I couldn't get a hot bath.

MARK METHE: I had a band in 1982 called Read All Over. We played three gigs all in Athens. One night at the B&L Warehouse we were opening for Love Tractor or the Method Actors. I had to wait around till four in the morning once to get our 20 bucks for playing and I saw Bill Berry come in and cash a check for 200 bucks. I asked him if he thought he could have cashed a check for 200 dollars there at four in the morning two years ago? He looked at me like, "who are you, asshole?"

LOS ANGELES, THE PALACE, JUNE 1983
(photo by Ann Summa courtesy Gans Archive)

1983

January — *Murmur* sessions begin at Reflection Sound Studios, Charlotte, NC

April 12 — *Murmur*, produced by Mitch Easter & Don Dixon. The music and lyrics wed the earthly and ethereal, making R.E.M.'s uniquely Southern, post-punk statement one of the (if not *the*) most important debut records of the decade.

Seven-inch Singles

April 13 — "Radio Free Europe"/"There She Goes Again"

Touring

March-October — They cover the U.S.

November — England for the first time followed by dates in France

December — Home to begin recording the follow-up album

Videos

"Radio Free Europe," directed by Arthur Pierson

Television and Film Appearances

August 18 — First TV appearance: *Live at Five*, New York local news on occasion of opening for the Police at Shea Stadium

October 6 — *Late Night with David Letterman*: "Radio Free Europe" and "So. Central Rain"

Live Wire special on Nickelodeon: Concert and kids chat

"1,000,000" appears in sci-fi film, *Strange Invaders*

Awards/Special Recognition

Murmur named Album of the Year in *Rolling Stone*

Murmur #2 in *Village Voice* Pazz and Jop Critic's Poll

R.E.M. named Best New Artist in *Rolling Stone*

3

MURMUR

SEAN BOURNE: We lived in a brief period of time during the early eighties when no one wanted to co-opt our culture. It's important to let people know about that time. If it wasn't for R.E.M. everything might've sounded like Journey or Boston during the eighties. R.E.M. was a reaction to the reaction to punk. The new wave thing was revitalizing. It opened up new possibilities for everyone, even though they were the same old possibilities. It allowed me to think in terms of having the freedom to do *anything*. It took literally ten years for the mass culture to adopt R.E.M.'s aesthetic. The whole alternative thing has been appropriated, which is fine, that's how things grow and evolve and become accessible in our culture. We can't all sit around in rooms and make great music and not have people hear it. It's a nice ideal, but it's not Western culture.

BRUCE MCGUIRE: I always thought R.E.M.'s sense of community was pretty strange. Everyone who they worked with was their friend. That's kind of a punk ideal, but it's also a hippie thing. I think American rock bands learned as much from punk rockers from England as they did from San Francisco bands of the Sixties.

DANNY BEARD: It was very much an "us versus them" mentality at that time regarding the scene and record labels. They [*the industry*] did everything they could to keep "over-amateurish" music down.

Bands and independent labels pulled together more as a community and were embattled to making it. We weren't going to wait for approval from anyone, we wanted to put out records. Because I worked with the B-52's I felt vindicated when they had success because the industry always said they were never any good. After the B-52's went gold and no A&R people came to Athens I figured they were never going to come to Athens. As far as I know, the first time any A&R person came to Athens was in 1983. Maybe IRS came, but I think R.E.M. was signed out of New York.

KEITH ALTOMARE: What we did with them at IRS was Miles Copeland's [*President of IRS Records*] philosophy. He and Michael Plen [*head of radio promotion at the time*] decided college radio was the way to build them.

BRUCE MCGUIRE: A few people could turn on college radio and hear it, but not very many. Most cities didn't have college radio, contrary to the myth now. There weren't a lot of great stations. Not to sound dumb, but the world was really a smaller place then. The bombardment of cable and CNN and MTV wasn't nearly what it is now. Radio almost doesn't exist at this point. Kids don't listen to it.

KATE INGRAM: I noticed when I was a music director at radio that you would get a record by a new group from England and then a band in Australia would put out a record and sound just like the band from England. They wouldn't have heard them first, it just spontaneously generated. A lot of bands sounded similar, but I think R.E.M. stood out because it was their manifest destiny to become this powerful voice for a generation of people and one of the great things about them was their humility.

STEVE WYNN: The next time I became aware of them, we were on the road before *Murmur* came out. I was at a friend's house in New York and I found out she was a friend of Michael's. I recorded this long rambling tape yelling at Michael for not coming to the KPFK radio show in LA, which it turns out he might have been at anyway. Apparently the tape got to him and he thought it was very funny.

KEITH ALTOMARE: When we put out the records, I don't recall having specific marketing and promotion plans. I only know that when the records came out, they would have to go to number one on college radio. We didn't necessarily know that each record would do it. Because of R.E.M., college radio started to take other bands close to its heart and after *Murmur*, other bands were out there competing for that same slot.

If R.E.M. didn't break tradition by doing different things on each album, we wouldn't have been able to sustain our number one position.

STEVE WYNN: I remember being on tour in April of '83 and our tour manager got an advance tape of *Murmur.* We were on an overnight drive from Minneapolis to Denver and we listened to it. It was raining and it was three in the morning and it was perfect. That was the first time I became a fan of theirs.

BUREN FOWLER: Microwave (Peter's guitar roadie) and I were guitar roadies for Kansas and all I listened to the whole time on the road was *Murmur.* I tried to listen to the tape on the bus and most of the guys on the bus couldn't stand listening to it. The only person on the bus that liked it was Microwave. I kept losing my tape—somebody would either hide it or throw it away. I kept having to buy one every two weeks.

BRUCE MCGUIRE: *1999* by Prince came out at the same time as *Murmur.* In Minneapolis, there were such huge price wars you could get R.E.M. for 4.99 and Prince for 7.99 (double album) so everyone I knew bought them both. The record store brought everyone together. Back then, you couldn't go to Musicland or any chain store and buy R.E.M. They didn't have it. Now, anything that's slightly hip is in every store as long as it's on a big record label. There isn't a sense of community at the record store that there used to be. [*The sense of community is*] different now—it's somewhere I don't know about, because I'm not young enough to know. But we couldn't turn on the television and see R.E.M., that I know for sure.

SEAN BOURNE: I thought they were a really good band by the time *Murmur* came out. I saw a show right after that at the Fox Theatre in Atlanta. They'd already gone up to Foxdom and that surprised me. I was used to other bands eclipsing the bands I worked for, so there wasn't any bitterness because when I saw them, they were really good. They obviously had what it takes.

KEITH ALTOMARE: With *Murmur* I knew that it was better than everything else out there. It's kind of nice to have a record to work that you know is your record. No one was touching it at commercial radio, but they were touching it for me at college so I could really run the show and if the record did well, it was partially due to me. We did so many radio interviews and so many appearances. I virtually had them scheduled to do at least one thing in every market. Even the smallest radio station—if the mailman listened to your show and he was the only person that did—I would try to get R.E.M. in there. R.E.M. was more than willing to go.

KATE INGRAM: The cover of *Murmur* personified R.E.M.'s subtle, vague mysticism that spoke to a lot of people.

KEN FECHTNER: The overall ambience and murkiness of the cover of *Murmur* with the kudzu [*indigenous Southern vine*] summed it up. There was probably a Flannery O'Connor element to what they were doing at the time. I don't think any other band epitomized the Southern experience like they did.

GIL RAY: I don't think unless you're from the South, you can really understand their connection to the South completely. Seeing kudzu on an album cover . . . I could relate. I don't know if they sound too Southern now, but there's something Flannery O'Connor about them.

> *"I think to compare us to Flannery O'Connor or some of the Southern writers would be maybe pushing it a little too far, but it's kind of nice. We've compared ourselves to Carson McCullers or someone. There's a particular slowness to the South that you don't find in the North or the West Coast or in the Midwest. It's just pretty weird."*
> —Michael Stipe to *Melody Maker*,
> April 21, 1984

KATE INGRAM: The songs that they wrote were very universal. They would take Southern imagery and inject it with some of their own charm. If you read William Faulkner, he's a difficult writer, and that might be more like Pylon. But if you read Carson McCullers or Flannery O'Connor, that's really easy Southern reading and I think that's the common universal language R.E.M. used.

LANCE SMITH: I never thought of them as Southern. Bill and Mike are really Southern, but there is nothing Southern about Pete and Michael. Being *really* Southern myself, I thought it seemed like a real marketing ploy that they were representative of a new South. For Pete Buck to speak for the South was kind of a joke.

KEN FECHTNER: Though Peter and Michael moved around a lot in their younger years, during their high school years they were some-place stable and stayed there. Bill and Mike are both *clearly* from Macon.

STEPHANIE CHERNIKOWSKI [photographer]: Michael is Elvis. Peter is Rhett Butler. They are Southern archetypes. Michael's got the sweetness and the love of women that characterizes Elvis and he identifies with him. It's a real Southern boy kind of thing. They're sweet, they're soft-spoken and it does not preclude their ability to go out into the ozone and be wild men.

KEN FECHTNER: Mike Mills is happy-go-lucky and basically oblivious to everything. Give him a beer in his hand and a BBQ in the backyard or a golf game and he's happy.

SEAN BOURNE: I didn't think there was anything Southern about them. Michael is from St. Louis. They spoke about the South the way people who are in awe of it speak of the South. It was kind of like they read Flannery O'Connor and said, "This is too weird." Me being from the South and knowing people like Flannery O'Connor's characters— it's no big deal. It's still fascinating and wonderful, but it's not with a sense of awe that I speak about them. I don't think R.E.M. were about the South as much as they were intrigued by it. "Hey, look at this, look at this weird guy here."

HOWARD FINSTER [Georgia-based folk artist]: Michael Stipe walked up when I was putting that steeple on top of the church over there. Matter of fact, he helped pull it up with a rope. And then they took my water pump and had it welded. I couldn't get nobody to weld it and they took it and had it welded. They give me vitamins and things like that to help my health.

LAUREN HALL: Michael started discovering the folk art resources that were around Athens. Howard Finster was connected to simple living and Georgia and that's what epitomized R.E.M. and smalltown life in rural Georgia. It all had a common thread. Finster is someone who did his art from his soul, not because he wanted to be famous. I don't think he had complex ideas about being an artist, it's just that he was so moved by his religion that he did it out of feeling. Maybe R.E.M. was attracted to him because their music seems to come from a lot of feelings that are inside.

KEN FECHTNER: I went up to Finster's and Michael came up the same day with one of his friends. Michael ended up staying overnight in the church [*focal point of Finster's Paradise Garden*] with no heat in December. Finster and he seemed to really get along. They speak a similar language.

SEAN BOURNE: Finster was definitely a weird guy. And there were other people R.E.M. pointed to who were beautiful examples of human beings. And because they had that sense of fascination and mystery, not about themselves, but about what they were seeing, I think people saw that in them and said, "This is a fascinating and mysterious band," and canonized them. I think people were anxious to build a mythology around them. They had an amazingly devout following.

"If there is anything good about us, it's that we don't feel any need to mythologize ourselves. I'm not going to talk to every single person who bought our albums just to show them I'm a normal guy. But you do try to live your life, to have the business conducted so you're not creating an image for yourself other than what you are."

—Peter Buck to *Musician* July 1984

SEAN BOURNE: They spoke to people in a way they weren't used to hearing. It fascinated me and repulsed me at the same time. But the people that helped make them famous were from around Athens and people even moved there because of them.

HOWARD FINSTER: They made a movie here, [*a video for "Radio Free Europe"*] a little tape, and I had a little part in it down in the little building down there [*points to Garden*]. They designed the program and you just act it out. I thought they did a really good job. They used to come here a lot and they liked the garden and they liked to shoot in the garden so they is my friends. I knew all of them. Since Michael did that film a lot of things have changed. They should come back and do a new film. Maybe a whole movie. Two or three songs in a movie and make it like Hollywood-style and sell it. They give a lot of publicity about the garden to other people you know, and other rock and rolls have come in since them. Like there's rock and rolls as faraway as Australia come here and make a tape of me singin'. I've had other rock and rolls here. I try to get rock and rolls to do more religious songs, you know.

SEAN BOURNE: That's why Finster is popular—because R.E.M. made him famous. R.A. Miller, [*Georgia folk artist featured in R.E.M. videos*] has not fared nearly as well.

KATE INGRAM: I think all of the bands from Athens dealt with specifically Southern themes, but R.E.M. synthesized it in a way that was more universal.

SEAN BOURNE: To be sure, they couldn't have existed without the first wave of the new wave, but they were separate from it in a lot of ways. They were the middle wave, or the second wave of the new wave. It's pointless to try to break it down that far, but everybody has. They came along by themselves and weren't part of any larger movement. They also got to take advantage of a subculture that already existed because the bands that came before them had networked the possibilities. And now people use that part of the second wave subculture that grew as a result of R.E.M.'s popularity as emblems for who they are.

KATE INGRAM: The glitter thing kind of caught on in Atlanta during the Seventies, and you can see vestiges of that in R.E.M. rather than new wave.

BRUCE MCGUIRE: To me, R.E.M. owe a lot more to Patti Smith than to the Clash or the Jam, because they never had that sense of nationalism like those British bands had. There may have been a touch of regionalism to them, but it wasn't stated in words. I suppose a lot of people didn't understand a lot of what they were saying, but they were describing things rather than making political statements.

KATE INGRAM: They had a little bit of a mystique certainly because of the Athens connection. All over the world there were places that had club scenes that enabled a growth to happen and bridged an older generation to the younger people coming out of school and R.E.M. spoke to them. At first they had to affect the new wave contingent and they did that with hands-down grace.

SEAN BOURNE: I think college age is when people want to begin to explore "what it was like to live in an exciting and dangerous time," and they go back to the music of the time to begin exploring it. Sure there were Elvis Costello and the Talking Heads, but they didn't speak about mystery. The Clash sang about social injustice. The B-52's sang about having a good time. R.E.M.—nobody knew what they were speaking about, but they caught all this "stuff," like the kudzu on the cover. "What is this? This isn't something that I know about . . ." Their listeners saw weird, fragmented images of an unfamiliar place. Athens is a pretty weird looking place, even though it's a real beautiful place. The gargoyle on the cover of *Chronic Town* is not a common image in rock and roll unless it's metal or gothic music. They basically gave people that weren't used to seeing things like that something to research. And people responded to it.

ROBERT LLOYD: R.E.M.'s statement was completely personal and real even though we didn't know what it was about. Because of that, it made you want to go further into it and find out about it. Particular obscure lyrics had a resonance to them. Not everybody can write that stuff and make it work. Pere Ubu had that same kind of thing happening.

BRUCE MCGUIRE: I'd read an interview with R.E.M. where they'd mention Flannery O'Connor and I would read one of her books and think, "yea, I can relate to this." They inspired me to find out more about two specific things: Flannery O'Connor and the Velvet Underground. They put out that seven-inch of "Radio Free Europe" on IRS with "There She Goes Again" on the b-side. I'd heard them play it live and never knew what it was, but when I got the single I saw it was a Velvet Underground song. It was the first time I was consciously aware of the Velvet Underground. They made me want to hear more and at that time, those records were hard to find. You couldn't find them until '85 when they all got reissued and then those records were instantly hip, because of R.E.M. and because of no one else. I don't care what anybody else says, they are solely responsible for the revival of the Velvet Underground, as far as I'm concerned. The Velvet Underground should give R.E.M. royalties.

> *"I mean we're not as great as the Velvet Underground or anything, but our records aren't real trendy. They're just records that are approximations of a band working things out. And that's what the Velvet Underground did. It wasn't like they were set in the current trend. They were trying to bring in all of their influences and come up with something uniquely individual."*
>
> —Peter Buck to *New Times*,
> July 24-30, 1985

GINA ARNOLD: I found out about the Velvet Underground and Big Star through R.E.M. I knew about the Velvet Underground, but I listened to them because of R.E.M.

KEITH ALTOMARE: I think R.E.M. did the college thing so well when we started. And unlike other college bands who have one hit single and are off the cool list, R.E.M. was always there.

KEITH ALTOMARE: When we got the demos to *Murmur* and "Catapult" came on I thought Michael was singing "She's a good kind of girl, she's a good kind of girl," during the chorus when he's really saying, "catapult, cat-a-pult." Every time I listened to it from then on I kept hearing and seeing those words from that song. It was really neat because you had great music, but you didn't know what he was saying so everybody tried to interpret things.

GIL RAY: I don't know any of their words. Either Buck or Stipe told Scott Miller in our band the real words to "Radio Free Europe" and every now and then we'd do it as a cover because Scott knew the words. It was a big deal to know the words to any of their songs.

MITCH EASTER: There's some staticky stuff on the beginning of the album version of "Radio Free Europe." We took that static and we keyed it off the bassline so the pulse pattern of the static rhythmically does the same thing that the bass does in the chorus and we figured that was a good subliminal effect.

> *"The first album was a time when a lot of things were changing in our lives and we had a record deal and we were getting to a point where we realized people would listen to us and there's five or six songs where it's not really elucidated on but it's about travel and change and leaving things behind, whether it's 'Pilgrimage' or 'Catapult' or whatever."*
> —Peter Buck to *Jamming*, January 1985

STEPHANIE CHERNIKOWSKI: I think Michael and Peter give voice to each other. Michael's avoidance of writing about love comes out through Peter's fingers. Even though Michael is the lyricist, he's also the mumbler. [*The English press dubbed Michael "Mumbles."*] The music is the real articulation and the early lyrics are almost always subterfuge. I think that's why people feel he is so mysterious. He expresses himself though indirection, as most men do when things are important to them.

LAUREN HALL: People made such a furor about Michael and his mumbling in the beginning. I didn't worry about the titles of the songs or dwell on the lyrics. I didn't try to make a meaning out of it. For me, it wasn't what he was singing, it was the sound of his voice and the whole thing was how it made me feel. It wasn't an intellectual thing for me. It was more about feeling the whole rather than dissecting the parts and trying to figure out what they mean.

DON DIXON: [producer] At the time, Michael was particularly self-conscious about the lyrics. He would pull out a match book that would have something on it and that's what he was taking his words from. It wasn't like he was organized. We protected Michael a lot in terms of allowing him to feel completely free in the studio. We gave him his own space that no one could see in. He could turn the lights on and off, he could lay down on the floor and sing if he wanted to. He could do anything he wanted to and that probably gave him a certain freedom and a kind of confidence that a lot of producers don't understand. Mitch and I understood that, coming from the artist-side.

> *"I feel that once the words are on a record they're public property. They're everyone's to try on and button up and see how they will fit. If they're a little bit too big, then stuff some Kleenex in the toes."* —Michael Stipe to *Musician,*
> September 1985

KEITH ALTOMARE: That line from "Sitting Still"—"Up to par and Katie bar the kitchen door but not me in." What does that *mean?*

SEAN BOURNE: What was the big deal? God knows in the Stooges and MC-5 there is plenty of unintelligible stuff. Michael sounded really alien and cool. Everything seemed like it was mixed together in a blender and they waited to see what would fall out. It was in parts recognizable and in parts unintelligible.

LANCE SMITH: The song "We Walk" is about Dory Duke. I can still remember the first day we saw Dory and Michael hanging out, he was walking and she was walking five steps behind him and it seemed so weird. When I first met her she was a hippie but she reinvented herself. A lot of people reinvented themselves in Athens.

MITCH EASTER: "We Walk" was a problematic song. We had a hard time getting it to work. We had to do some funny stuff to get the basic track to work.

GIL RAY: Mitch told us about pool balls going backwards or some trick like that which makes him Mitch.

MITCH EASTER: It was a little song—almost too little. Somehow the pool balls just made sense. It was just a case of a microphone picking up the sound of the band playing pool and we thought, "We can use this."

DON DIXON: I think the thing that appealed to us was that they weren't afraid to let us put noises around them. Our contribution was definitely in that we left the bulk of the playing and the essential heart of what they were doing alone and helped make it more interesting by adding "sound art." We didn't believe in telling them to play one little part 50,000 times, we were into the more spontaneous aspects of playing and Michael's singing. His singing had a certain noise quality anyway, but there was definitely melody there.

BUREN FOWLER: Peter Buck plays guitar totally different than most people. He plays with really heavy strings and it's really impossible to bend the strings and play solos. He plays a lot of half chords and he uses a really thin pick and strums really fast with his right hand whereas most people do most of the work with their left hand, he does most of the work with his right hand. When I got *Murmur* I learned to play just like that.

MITCH EASTER: Those bits in between songs on *Murmur* would be taken from when the band would be getting ready to do a take of one of their songs. They might go into a little fiddly thing just before we started recording. We would take those things and edit the tape to make something out of it. So what you hear isn't exactly what they played, but what they started off as a little micro-jam.

DON DIXON: That's part of the freshness of the way R.E.M. sounded. It wasn't just guitar music with nice chords and piano accompaniment, it was jangling guitar with a whole substrata of funny sounds underneath it—to make it more interesting to us. Mitch's and my goal was kind of to flip things in without the band realizing it. If they accepted it great. We'd look at each other, give a little wink and continue.

ROBERT LLOYD: I really got them the first time I saw them play LA on the *Murmur* tour. The thing that struck me most were their harmonies and the vocal interplay on songs like "Pilgrimage." The fact that they were playing almost in the dark helped make it feel personal and private. They had a real presence and I was just captivated.

KEITH ALTOMARE: You might have to call your book "Talk About The Passion," because that's what I've just done for the last hour.

SEAN BOURNE: The first song of theirs I thought was really good was "Shakin' Through." I started hearing that they could actually write songs. Hearing their record made me a fan rather than seeing their live shows. But later on, I thought they got really great live.

DON DIXON: I really love that song, "Pilgrimage." I think that may be the first song we cut for *Murmur*.

KEITH ALTOMARE: When they would do "Catapult" live, there's a bridge in the middle, and I don't even know what he is saying but at various shows Michael would mumble different things. If you would be at more than one show, it would be different words. He might know the phone book in the town they were in or he would throw in whatever he was reading. He liked my name and he would scream it during the bridge. The first time it happened in Milwaukee I was in the audience and I heard, "Altomare, Altomare, Altomare." I'm going whoa, this is really neat. They played in Shea Stadium opening for Joan Jett and the Police and it was their first big show. Thousands of people were there and Michael sang "Altomare" in the bridge. It was so touching. It really showed they were conscious of their people and their fans.

STEVE WYNN: They were very different from the other stuff that was around. Most of the music at the time was very amateurish or very slick and power-poppy. R.E.M. sounded amateurish, but they had a lot of imagination. For a first album, *Murmur* seemed very sophisticated. It had a lot to do with Mitch Easter's production—adding weird sounds and things.

MITCH EASTER: I think Don Dixon would agree that we were fascinated with records and the process of making them was mysterious. It used to be something that wasn't written about, so I never knew what was going on. These days it's easier to read about the record-making process. Whenever I could hear some clue on a record like the sound of footsteps or a voice from an engineer, I always wondered what was going on in that studio and tried to picture it. Whenever we just by chance got little moments like that on our tape, if we put it on the album, it would make it so much more of an experience for the listener. You know the audience is all going to get different impressions, but I like the thought that *Murmur* was kind of like a little documentary instead of just a bunch of songs. It created an image about what must have been going on and what it looked like.

KEITH ALTOMARE: *Murmur* went to number one on the college charts and that's when it clicked in. People realized that maybe this was something special.

DANNY BEARD: After *Murmur* came out and R.E.M. were getting great reviews in *Rolling Stone* magazine, they said to *Rolling Stone* that they would never open for the B-52's. They put it in such a way that implied they were better than them. At least that's the way I took it. They probably just meant that they didn't want to play giant stadiums, but it didn't come across that way. And then Pete said to *Music,* a magazine in Atlanta, that Steve May of the 688 Club was a prick. So I wrote a letter in saying that

Steve May was into music and had really served the Atlanta community. I guess there were some problems between him and R.E.M. I also said that the B-52's had supported the whole local band scene and there probably wouldn't be an R.E.M. if it wasn't for the B-52's. I think Bill was pissed off about it. I had the feeling their attitude was they were too big for Georgia. They were a little like, "Athens is small potatoes," and after that small controversy, they didn't really show that side anymore.

LANCE SMITH: As soon as they started getting written up, I knew enough about them from the guys in Love Tractor that I knew they had begun to reinvent themselves in the press. The real story doesn't matter and they were brilliant at playing along with it. They were being touted as a Southern band. Well, ok, it doesn't seem that way to me, but if you don't come up with an angle like that for the media, they'll come up with something for you.

ROBERT LLOYD: I've seen myself referred to in print as one of the first to write about them but I came on a little late, around the time of *Murmur.* I guess I was writing more passionately about them and that's what people remembered.

LANCE SMITH: The end result, is that the South has come out looking better because of R.E.M. For years, people would find out I lived in Athens and they would be in awe and ask a lot of questions about what it was like.

WOODY NUSS: Michael has said some stuff that was amazing. I remember sitting on the porch on Barber Street in 1983 and Mills had just bought that acrylic lucite bass that sucked and would never stay in tune. Michael said, "that's Mike's new bass. We really like it. He used to have one of those violin-shaped basses like that guy in the Beatles, what was his name . . ." and my friend goes, "You mean, Paul McCartney. You don't know who Paul McCartney is?" Michael wanted to create the illusion that he didn't know who Paul McCartney was. He was putting people on very early.

KATE INGRAM: Michael very early on took on the personality of R.E.M. thereby personifying them, leaving the other members free to just get on with their lives. He was the fulcrum for that.

DANNY BEARD: One night in '83 I was at the Agora in Atlanta at someone's party. I remember the night because Kenny Fechtner got his car stolen because he parked where I told him to park. Michael was sitting there and it had just become news that Pylon was going to break up and he was visibly shaken. Not crying but he was seriously sad about it.

KEITH ALTOMARE: R.E.M. was just happy to get out there and play. Virtually anything we wanted to do at the label, we did. One of the things I did was set them up on the BBC College Concert Hour. I knew a guy there and I told him I had a really cool band for him. I got approval from them and we were going to tape at City Gardens in Trenton, NJ. They got there and there were maybe 30-40 people in the audience. I had a mic draped over the middle of the floor so whenever the band finished a song, I got the people to stand over this mic and hoot and holler to make it seem like it was happening. It was those kind of things that got us out there.

DAN VALLOR: In San Francisco they did a show with the Renegades and Let's Active at the Old Waldorf. When I arrived at the club, Michael asked me to drive him over to their hotel—he'd forgotten his glasses. As we drove back to the York Hotel, he was going on about Eartha Kitt performing that night in the Plush Room at the hotel. He slathered praise on Eartha Kitt, saying he wished he could sing. He was convinced that he had no voice and Eartha Kitt was where it was at. We arrived back at the club just in time for their set, having missed an apparently fiery performance by Let's Active.

GIL RAY: One of the most bizarre things I'd ever seen on stage happened at that show. Peter joined Let's Active for an encore and the speaker cone in his amp ignited. I didn't know they could do that. There was this ring of fire through the grill cloth. All these roadies were frantically hitting it with towels to put out the fire.

MITCH EASTER: That was one of those classic showbiz moments. That fire coming out of the amp really got the kids going!

GINA ARNOLD: I was really excited the first time I saw them. I didn't know what they looked like, except from the pictures on the ep. Michael had really long curly hair and was all over the stage dancing. He was really impassioned and that was rare then. Bands tried to be impassive then and were into techo and black clothing and had clipped short hair and would stare gloomily at the crowd and try to be mechanized.

DON DIXON: At the time, the cool thing was drum machines, things like the Thompson Twins—gross kind of stuff when you go back and listen to it now. Most people thought it was cutting edge and cool. What we were doing was spitting in the face of all that kind of mechanized stuff that was going on.

GINA ARNOLD: Michael was really different because he was wearing loose sloppy clothing that wasn't black and had long hippie hair which was appallingly weird, but he was really great looking so we didn't care. Basically, he danced for the entire set and we found that to be enchanting. I don't remember the rest of the band.

GIL RAY: They always looked cool without trying. I'd see a torn up sweater on Michael and it looked one way and I'd try to get one and people would ask, "why are you wearing that torn up sweater?"

RUSS TOLMAN: One night I passed out in a spare room in Peter's house and woke up to find myself in the room he kept his clothes. I was sleeping among a thousand of those ruffled shirts and a thousand of those vests that he wore. He must have had one for every day of the year.

GINA ARNOLD: The Dream Syndicate to me was more conscious of style than R.E.M. Being kind of a hippie and not caring what you looked like I associated more with the Dream Syndicate than R.E.M. I always thought the people that went to see the Dream Syndicate were kind of hippies. But somehow the R.E.M. thing and the Dream Syndicate thing merged into an actual new style.

"THEY ALWAYS LOOKED COOL WITHOUT TRYING"
(*photo by George DuBose*)

KATE INGRAM: All of the people from Athens were masters of style. Somehow by the way they dressed and what they exuded, they personified their image. There was a conformity to it, but they all did it somehow differently. R.E.M. were really the masters of it. You may think R.E.M. wore kind of nondescript clothing, but if you really examined it, it was very descript in its subtlety along with the stage persona they would bring to a performance. That was a result of the art background that was so prevalent in Athens. Everything was well-executed.

RUSS TOLMAN: All of them in their own way were clothes horses. Bill had his own clothes thing going on. Mike was Mr. jeans and T-shirt and tennis shoes. Either they were wearing their stage clothes all the time, or they didn't have such a thing as stage clothes. They wore what they wore. But they weren't posing, they were really being themselves and that set a precedent for the way "alternative" bands began to dress.

GINA ARNOLD: In San Francisco, you stared at the show. People tried to look as cool as possible and as English as possible. Michael didn't look any of those things. He didn't look English, he didn't look glum. He just looked flesh and blood and it was really neat.

STEVE WYNN: I saw them live for the first time at the Kabuki in San Francisco with the Neats and Let's Active. When we were recording *Medicine Show* in San Francisco, I pretty much met any band who came to town because I would go to their shows and hang out with them whether they were friends or people I didn't know. When R.E.M. played that Kabuki show, Dan Vallor hooked me up with Peter and we all took a very drunken drive to the top of Twin Peaks, listened to music and ended up hanging out till five in the morning somewhere by Ghirardelli Square, screaming and singing as the sun was coming up. That was my first meeting with Peter and is very similar to many meetings I've since had with Peter.

BRUCE MCGUIRE: Everybody has their own path in life, but at that time, a lot of people's path's converged. I remember weird, really good conversations I would have with people after R.E.M. shows. I don't think I'm jaded or romanticizing the times, but today when I go to shows, it just isn't like that because my peers aren't there with me. I talked to Bob Mould [*Hüsker Dü, Sugar*] forever one night after an R.E.M. show in St. Paul. I talked to Paul Westerberg [*the Replacements*] a long time. These were just people I knew at the time and they are really good memories of those times.

KEITH ALTOMARE: R.E.M. went out, met anybody, did anything, hung out and made friends during the show and after the show. You'd have the groupies, but the guys thought they were cool too. They were the easiest band I ever promoted because they were self-promoters.

LANCE SMITH: I saw Michael at the Beverly Theatre in LA in '83. R.E.M. would usually pretend they didn't know who I was unless I was with Love Tractor. But Michael said to me, "it's the guy from the 40 Watt," and I said something like, "Beverly Hills is a long way from the Watt Club on Clayton Street," and he said something like, "hey, it's a nice theatre." He wouldn't go along with the flow at all. For a guy who is supposed to have a great sense of humor, when he chooses *not* to engage he's able to put on quite an act.

MITCH EASTER: I think the fans back then thought Michael did nothing but brood from dawn to dusk, but that wasn't the case. There was a microphone at the studio that Michael used to call "Angela Davis." It was the funniest thing in the world because it looked like her. It had this big round windscreen on it that was this big, black fluffy thing. It was just brilliant for him to mention that because nobody had been thinking of her for quite a while.

WOODY NUSS: By '83 there was weird jealousy that came from other bands in Athens, like "we're going to be the next R.E.M." kind of pressure. I remember Barry from Dreams So Real so pissed off at Mark Cline [*Love Tractor*]. He said to him, "*We're* the next band out of here," because everybody thought Love Tractor was on that path.

ARMISTEAD WELLFORD: When Love Tractor first went on the road we would tell stories about the people and the parties in Athens but later when people would ask us about R.E.M. in particular, we learned to say, "We know them—kind of." Bill told me that they plugged us in the press every chance they got but I told him sorry, but if we mention R.E.M. the articles about us might as well have the headline "Love Tractor Knows R.E.M."

KATE INGRAM: One thing about Love Tractor is they tried really hard. They tried to follow in the mold of R.E.M. It was almost turning into a formula—not so much in the music but more in the style of how to be a band.

ARMISTEAD WELLFORD: We thought of them as hugely successful, but they didn't see any money for a long time. They had a machine going and had something to work toward. But they were all living in their same apartments.

WOODY NUSS: Bill and Mike and Chris Edwards, their soundman at the time, lived in the same duplex as me on Barber Street next to Pylon's big house.

ARMISTEAD WELLFORD: The summer of the year *Murmur* came out, Bill bought his girlfriend a tape player and I thought, man he's got the money to buy that? That's cool! At times, R.E.M.'s success overshadowing ours did hurt Love Tractor. I kind of wish we could have gone out on the road with them in the eighties, but I guess it would have left the impression that the Athens thing was incestuous. We were different enough from them, but we always had to deal with their shadow. Instead of riding on their coattails, we did the opposite. With Love Tractor it was like squeezing water from a rock every time we wanted to make another record and every step R.E.M. took was greater and greater. But I didn't want any kind of career thing to get in the way of our friendships.

LANCE SMITH: In about '83 the frat boys started showing up at the R.E.M. gigs. I heard stories of Michael walking by the SAE frat house [*when the band first started*] and they started fucking with him and chased him down and beat him up. So it was weird seeing these guys in polo shirts who had probably beat him up a few years before yelling, "Michael!" Then you'd get the sorority girls dressed in their new wave outfits. They didn't have anything right. They didn't have the thrift store look that was Athens. They looked really goofy with weird eye-makeup or mousse in their hair or sunglasses. We figured it was completely over once the fraternities and sororities began playing new wave.

KATHLEEN O'BRIEN: R.E.M. was much more rock-and-roll-oriented than the other bands in town. Everything was a dance thing and a party. The same people would come out and there was a real camaraderie among the fans and the band. By '84 when they would come home after touring, people they'd met on the road would begin visiting from out of town. Things had changed a lot and people were starting to notice.

ON TOUR, 1984
(© *Ebet Roberts 1992*)

1984

December '83-January '84 — *Reckoning* recording, Reflection Sound Studios, Charlotte, NC

April 14 — *Reckoning*, produced by Mitch Easter & Don Dixon. Album spine reads, "File Under Water." Artist Howard Finster and Stipe collaborate on the album sleeve. The album is a solid follow-up with no hint of a sophomore slump and further cements the band's reputation in the guitar-rock pantheon.

Seven-inch Singles

March — "So. Central Rain (I'm Sorry)"/"King of the Road"

August — "Don't Go Back to Rockville"/"Catapult"(live)

Videos

"So. Central Rain (I'm Sorry)," directed by Howard Libov

"Left of Reckoning" (An over-long film by Jim Herbert to accompany almost all of the album's songs, compiled for commercial release on *R.E.M. Succumbs*)

Touring

Europe in the beginning of the year followed by Little America Tour Parts I-IV till October

November 5 — First Trip to Japan, Waseda University Tokyo, followed by dates in Europe till end of year

Television and Film Appearances

"Windout" appears in film *Bachelor Party* and on soundtrack

Rock of the '80s for Showtime — three songs recorded at The Palace in Hollywood: "Radio Free Europe," "Little America" and "Sitting Still"

Entertainment Tonight small feature

Solid Gold Hits: Performance of "So. Central Rain (I'm Sorry)"

IRS' *The Cutting Edge* series on MTV: Acoustic renditions of "Rockville," "Time After Time," "Femme Fatal," "Louie, Louie," "Smoking in the Boy's Room," "Driver 8" and "Wendell Gee"

Rock Influences for MTV — *Folk Rock*: Roger McGuinn jams with R.E.M. on "So You Wanna Be a Rock and Roll Star"

Select Guest Appearances

Peter Buck plays guitar on "I Will Dare," from the Replacements *Let It Be*

Michael Stipe contributes vocals to "Hot Nights in Georgia," on Jason and the Scorchers' debut, *Fervor*

AUTOGRAPH SIGNING, STRAWBERRY RECORDS, BOSTON, JULY 1984
(*photo by Georgina Falzarano*)

4
RECKONING

"We've always kind of said that on the ladder of important things, being in a rock and roll band is probably the lowest rung, but when you think about being Secretary of State to the United States of America, it isn't much sillier. And if Peter was Secretary of State, I wouldn't be here today."
— Michael Stipe to *New Musical Express*,
April 21, 1984

JOHN KEANE: The first I time I recorded R.E.M. was in '84. I'd been running an eight-track studio in my house and was using it to record demos for the band I was in and other bands around Athens. There weren't any other studios in town at that time. I worked with Love Tractor and Dreams So Real— every band in town that made any kind of money would come in to record demos. I'd done a few records and was just getting started and wasn't a very accomplished engineer. One day Jefferson called me up and said that they wanted to come in and do a demo. They came in and recorded a song called "Romance." It was supposed to be used in a movie. They recut it later maybe with Scott Litt and then it got used on a soundtrack [*Made In Heaven*].

LANCE SMITH: I saw the Hindu Love Gods, R.E.M. without Michael, a couple of times with Brian Cook [*Time Toy*] as the lead singer. He used to come onstage with R.E.M. at the I & I and do "Rock and Roll Nurse" with Michael and "Narrator."

GINA ARNOLD: I think the Hindu Love Gods taught us that R.E.M. doesn't have a prayer without Michael. On the other hand, he could make solo records forever.

ROBERT LLOYD: I don't think I'd be interested in hearing a solo record from any of them. It's been true of most of the really great bands. It would probably be in a different league than what they can do together.

DON DIXON: Individually, none of them had particularly outstanding features but as a collective unit it was truly interesting. They were coming up with something completely different. Their limitations created interesting music. The fact that none of them were "hotdog" players, they just did what they did well was part of the beauty of the art school approach they brought to the band. You didn't have to be the local guitar screecher to write a good song.

In hindsight it would be easy to overstate this, but there is no question that Mitch and I both saw something in them or we never would have done it. We thought there was a good yin and yang thing going on among the members of the band. It was the special quality that they had combined—a lot of "fire."

JOHN KEANE: They called me up and said they wanted to bring Warren Zevon into the studio to record some demos. They wanted to record an album with him and they needed some demos first for whatever record company it was they were pitching it to [*Virgin*]. As you could imagine, that was pretty exciting for me because basically I just had a bunch of equipment sitting in a room. I hadn't gotten very far along in the studio business. I was a little in awe of it. They came in and recorded four or five songs with Zevon and while they were doing that, they recorded the Hindu Love Gods single, "Gonna Have A Good Time Tonight" and "Narrator." The whole Hindu Love Gods session took about fifteen minutes. I think it's a kind of studio world record: Shortest Time Ever Spent on a Recording. Brian Cook came in and sang it one time through and that was it. That was the first thing I recorded that came out on a major label on vinyl.

KEITH ALTOMARE: After the first record when they were preparing the next record, Jefferson told Jay Boberg at IRS he was worried about college radio and R.E.M. because "Keith likes the band too much." It was very weird. I don't know what that means. I don't know if it was true or not. Maybe he thought I was so close I couldn't work it objectively. That's the polite way I took it.

BRIAN CRANE: Even though *Reckoning* came out after *Murmur,* a lot of the songs were old songs—songs they wrote before *Murmur* but didn't fit in because *Murmur* was a single, linear thought process.

GEORGINA FALZARANO: I never struggled with the lyrics. That tends to be something that males do more. For me it was often the quality and texture of Michael's voice. I talked to him about that and told him he should keep doing that—not to bother with pointed lyrics so much because there were people he was reaching the other way too. He is intrigued by how certain sounds affect the brain.

KATHLEEN O'BRIEN: I could usually understand the lyrics. It wasn't such a problem, but a lot of times I would see them written down in rough draft. I think they were more stream of consciousness rather than particular instances. Some of them were basically poetry. They didn't have a narrative or story going on and they weren't supposed to. I knew ["(Don't Go Back to)] Rockville" was about a girl named Ingrid from Rockville, MD. She was fast friends with everyone in the band and that song was a little tribute to her. But that was one of the few songs with intelligible lyrics.

LANCE SMITH: Ingrid had moved to Athens from Rockville, MD and lived there awhile and she was going to go back there. I think that was one of the few that Mills wrote the lyrics to. The idea behind the song was "don't go back to your dippy home town because it's such a drag and everyone's going to put you down." I think a big part of the Athens scene was that a lot of the people in it were the nerdy people that always got beat up in high school so when they started having something of their own they became super snobby. Unless you were in a band it was like, "who the fuck are you?"

DAN VALLOR: Mills had written a bunch of songs in college before the band was around. The songwriting is credited to everybody but there are all sorts of stories about who wrote what. I've been told Bill Berry wrote "Radio Free Europe" and Mills wrote "(Don't Go Back To)Rockville" before the band was formed.

> *"With Reckoning, there's a whole lot of weirdness about lost love or lost friends because we've had a couple of suicides and car wrecks and stuff like that which happened to close friends. And communication—there are a number of songs about communication."*
> —Peter Buck to *Jamming*, January 1985

WOODY NUSS: "Camera" is obviously [*about Michael's friend*] Carol Levy.

LANCE SMITH: Michael's house was 15 feet of weeds and grass, and when you looked out the window it was like looking out into a jungle, it was so green. I remember the first time I heard the song "Camera" (which he wrote about Carol Levy, his friend who died in a car accident). The line about the "green light room" jumped out at me because I knew exactly what room he was talking about. That's all that room was—just weeds in front of you and the afternoon sun coming through and this blinding green glare.

HOWARD FINSTER: I did that album cover [*Reckoning*] setting there [*points to other room*] and they set there and watch me do it. When I done that album cover I tried to get 'em to tell me how they wanted me to do it and they wouldn't do it, I just done it myself there with them watching me. They wanted serpents on it so I made them cloud serpents. It was only a 10 or 15 minute job and they liked it so they used it. I made another one for them with all four of their pictures on it and they didn't use it. I used to have it here, somewhere. There's one of them there [*points to Little America Tour issue bandanna*]. I don't know what they done with that. Made cushions out of it I believe.

STEVE WYNN: I thought *Reckoning* was really similar to *Murmur* and at the time preferred *Murmur*. I felt like our band was cool by branching out on our second record. But people thought we'd "sold out." If we had made *Days of Wine and Roses* Part Two, I thought that would be selling out. So at the time, I still thought of R.E.M. and the Dream Syndicate as equals. But during the tour we went on with them, the gap became very clear. We were definitely staying in the cult arena and they were escalating hugely during the course of that tour.

KEITH ALTOMARE: I don't recall the record label having any promotion schemes that were dramatically different than what we were doing with other bands. I recall with the "So. Central Rain" video we did a big publicity thing because Michael refused to lip-synch to the record. He did his vocal live during the video shoot. We did major publicity to promote the fact that we had this really cool band that was breaking tradition by not lip-synching.

SEAN BOURNE: The "So. Central Rain" single had a picture of somebody holding a boat and I think it's Bill Berry but I'm not sure. Some guy was in the store [*Wax'n'Facts*] and says, "that's his brother who built that boat." The fans know all these stories about the band that you'd have to be in their hip pocket to know about much less care about. It's not that import-ant. The fans just have to con-sume the mystery. They want to make the band's lives more cred-ible. More than any other band I know of from that time, people had to do that. They pulled the whole alternative scene with them through that progression. There was no precedent except rock and roll itself.

KEN FECHTNER: Around the time of the second album, Peter and I were at Popeye's Fried Chicken in Athens. We were sitting down to eat dirty rice and chicken and some college kid came up and asked him for an autograph. I was like, "huh?" and Peter was a little embarrassed.

GINA ARNOLD: I sort of looked up and noticed that fans of the band and others were starting to adopt the R.E.M.-look around 1984.

DAN VALLOR: As R.E.M. gained popularity, a glut of imitators swarmed into the scene, swallowing up a large portion of the underground.

DON DIXON: I think most of the bands trying to be like R.E.M. have missed the fact that they actually wrote songs and they aren't just droning guitar riffs, there are great melodies under there.

ROBERT LLOYD: I don't think their influence on other bands was that good—Indistinct chords, mumbling vocals and lyrics that were hard to uncoil. Most of those other bands were boring. I can't think of anyone they influenced that I like. I think Nirvana is heavily influenced by R.E.M. and I like them, but it's well after the fact.

KURT COBAIN [Nirvana]: I was heavily into pop, I really liked R.E.M., and I was into all kinds of old Sixties stuff (*Rolling Stone,* January 27, 1994).

GINA ARNOLD: Morrissey of the Smiths and Michael Stipe were similar. There was the Paisley Underground in LA and its East Coast equivalent and similar things going on in England, like Robyn Hitchcock. It was clearly in the air. Somebody was going to do it.

ROBERT LLOYD: One of the things about the hip music of the mid-Seventies to the Eighties was that it was specifically about something. The thing about R.E.M. was that they were a tonic to the overly explicit stuff. You didn't know what it was about. New Wave wore its subject matters on its sleeve. Punk too. They quickly established a menu of subjects that was too clear. There was nothing clear about R.E.M. At the beginning it felt like pure feeling. They practically played in the dark. You couldn't understand what Michael was singing, but it didn't mean you didn't know what the songs were about. It just felt great at the time. It was what the time required. R.E.M. didn't grab the public immediately. By the time they grabbed the public, they were already being more explicit.

KEN FECHTNER: Peter and Jefferson had been sharing an apartment. They gave that up and Peter moved in with his brother Kenny to his small apartment. There was an entry foyer which was about eight feet long and five or six feet wide and that's where Peter lived for six or eight months. He just put a mattress down and between tours lived in the hallway of his brother's apartment. This was at a point where people might've thought he was a rock star, but he was just a guy living in his brother's hall.

STEVE WYNN: Between the tape mail with Michael and meeting Peter, by the time the Dream Syndicate album, *Medicine Show,* came out we figured that the R.E.M. tour would be the best tour to get on. But they didn't want us. They wanted Jason and the Scorchers. I think they actually liked the band, but *Medicine Show* had already gotten the reputation as "what the hell is this band trying to do" so they might have felt that too. I'm not sure, because R.E.M. actually seemed to like the record.

We got the tour, and near the beginning, we played Boise, ID. *Reckoning* was a top forty album right away but even so, it was the only show of the tour we played in a club. The headlines in the paper said "New Wave Comes to Boise." The place was packed, but I know R.E.M. was unhappy that night because at the end of the show Peter took his beautiful Rickenbacker which I think he'd had for a long time and threw it into the ceiling and smashed it. I don't know what it was all about. Maybe it was just tour wig-out. Maybe it reminded the band too much of what things had been like just a year before.

KEITH ALTOMARE: In the Midwest there were three girls, one black and two white, and they were everywhere. We were in Chicago and they were there. We'd be in Lawrence, KS and they were there, we'd be in Madison, WI and they were there. We'd be in Minneapolis and they were there. It took them at least six or seven shows to say to me, "well, who *are* you?" And I was like, "who are *you?*"

I think they slept with some of these girls, but they handled it really well. I think they really dug the fact that people were really into them. And they were so natural about it. They all got bigger egos—who wouldn't? But they were such homefolks from Athens. They would say things like, "Come down and visit us," and people would take them up on it! They had a fanatical following. It was Grateful Dead-like.

DON DIXON: We always felt they were more like the Grateful Dead than people realized. The fan frenzy was existent even at the small level they were at.

BRUCE MCGUIRE: When they played here for *Reckoning*, they did a Velvet Underground song and Steve Wynn sang it because Dream Syndicate opened that night. Paul Westerberg [*the Replacements*] came out and sang with them for an encore and they did "Color Me Impressed," the Replacements song. That was pretty cool.

STEVE WYNN: There were no nights when the places were half-full or the audiences didn't "get" them for seven straight weeks. They were playing great and had been on the road constantly. There were a lot of people coming out and they were playing really great shows. They were playing a few songs that hadn't been recorded yet, and they were really good. They connected with the audience really well. That's when I thought "these guys are going to be huge."

KEITH ALTOMARE: In Minnesota, KDWB was presenting a show but they weren't playing the record. But KQRS was, so we snuck a dj from KQRS onstage with R.E.M.'s approval at a KDWB show. It was those sort of things that could have been dangerous as far as severing ties with people but it really worked in R.E.M.'s favor.

STEVE WYNN: We played Buffalo on that tour in a big club, about a 1,000 seater. This was maybe 3-4 weeks into the tour. We were getting a little weary and everyone was pretty heavily into partying. We were getting that mid-tour exhaustion. I think for whatever reason, R.E.M. had some attitude about that show—whether it was the vibe they got when they went on stage or something about the club—but they played all covers; "Medicine Show," "Every Word Means No" by Let's Active, "Tusk," by Fleetwood Mac. I think that's something they would have done a half year before and not thought anything of it. After the show, some kids came up to me in the parking lot and said, "Do you know those guys?" and I said, "Yea." "Well tell them we hate their guts and they ripped us off and we're really angry at them." That night it occurred to me and I think they realized it too—the stakes were bigger. They were no longer playing to the hip people in town who will get the jokes. But they wanted to see if they could get away with it one last time.

KEITH ALTOMARE: I remember coming out of the New York office with Buck to visit WNYU and IRS was so cheap I couldn't take a cab. I was embarrassed and I told him, "Look, we gotta take the subway," and he's like, "Cool." They were just really good people.

DAN VALLOR: On tour Michael was eating garlic by the clove constantly. He told me it was purifying his blood. I think the band was a little disturbed by the massive amounts of garlic he ate.

DON DIXON: He was worried about his health after the long bouts of touring and a friend had gotten him on this garlic thing. He was eating cloves of garlics like apples. We had to de-garlic the microphone after [*the* Reckoning *session*]. That mic had its own little room for a while. We had to air it out. It was one of my favorite mics. I think it's being used to mic a bass drum now.

STEVE WYNN: Very quickly into the tour we were all hanging out together. There was no element of "this is your area this is our area and stay away" or that sort of thing.

LANCE SMITH: R.E.M. would take a lot of requests and usually if it was their friends asking for it they would play it.

KEITH ALTOMARE: I felt like they were my friends. I really did. I felt closest to Mills and Buck. I only approached Michael when I wanted to have a good talk. If we sat down and had a good talk, he would look me straight in the eye and focus his attention on me and what I was saying which is an amazing talent to have.

STEVE WYNN: At the end of the tour, I didn't want to be around our guitarist Karl [Precoda] anymore, so I think that's why I started hanging out with Peter. We were a band that was falling apart. The music we were doing at that point wasn't what fans of R.E.M. wanted to hear.

BRUCE MCGUIRE: The crowd hated Dream Syndicate. Almost every time I saw Dream Syndicate [*open for R.E.M.*] they were playing under adverse conditions.

STEVE WYNN: We had a keyboard player named Tommy Zvoncheck who was a Holiday Inn player from New Jersey and really into album-oriented rock. He did that tour with us, watched them every night, and said, "I just don't get it." I'm sure everyone gets it now but at that time, someone with his background couldn't see why a band like that could sell out 3000-4000 tickets in advance.

GINA ARNOLD: I never wanted to meet any of the other bands I liked, like the Clash or the Cramps, because I was totally in awe of them. They were like scary huge rock stars and there was no sense that you could kind of be friends with them or know them. I didn't know R.E.M.; they weren't my friends. But I felt very personal toward them. I knew nothing about them personally, but their music touched me so deeply that I felt like it was mine. And I mean that in the best way possible way.

LAUREN HALL: When they started to get a more national following they would come into contact with celebrities and better known fellow musicians. I always found it endearing that Mike would be so excited about meeting these people. He would call me up and say, "Guess who I met tonight . . ." I always thought, the success hasn't gone to his head. He didn't realize that he was approaching their level of notoriety or was maybe even peers with some of these people.

KEN FECHTNER: The thing that really impressed me was once Peter was in LA and got Van Dyke Parks' autograph for me. He was sorta the same way—really impressed that he'd met Van Dyke Parks. [Parks is a songwriter and arranger notable for his collaborations with the Beach Boys.]

LANCE SMITH: At the Greek Theatre in LA in 1984 they brought Warren Zevon out on stage thinking it would be a big treat for the audience and all these kids from Beverly High had no idea who he was. I think R.E.M. had lost touch with who their audience was.

DAVID T. LINDSAY: In 1984, the LA Weekly interviewed Johnny Rotten and they asked him what he thought of R.E.M. and he said, "I hate hippies. The Sex Pistols were supposed to end all that." I think he hit the nail on the head. What they brought back that punk had gotten rid of was political awareness which I don't see as a positive in rock and roll—I see it as a negative. This whole idea of following the band and treating them like they are superstars was what punk was against.

GINA ARNOLD: R.E.M. made us interested in America instead of England. They de-exoticized punk. In the Summer of '84 when R.E.M. played here, I remember Siouxsie and the Banshees also played that summer and so did Echo and the Bunnymen. I remember not going to see Siouxsie and the Banshees and prior to that moment, not caring about them. I thought, "these people are old farts and I'm so sick of this stupid, black gothic eyeshadow up to her eyebrows, kind of Bauhaus, dumb English poser, white-skinned Vampira kind of thing." It struck me as completely outre. And that thought was really tied up with the thought that "R.E.M. is *it*, and you should be a hippie now and not be a stupid English poser."

ROBERT LLOYD: R.E.M. was more like a punk band than some of the punk bands. A lot of punk and new wave was very formal music. It was about mannerisms and style and saying the expected thing which was, "I hate . . ." If you listen to that stuff now it sounds dated. Look at the way people dressed! It's all so corny and these were the people supposedly breaking the bonds of something. It didn't matter what R.E.M. looked like. They all looked different. And they were singing about personal things. R.E.M. didn't have any of the cliches that were infecting music. Their music was private and personal and immediate and real. In a way they were more like the first wave of punk bands like Television and Pere Ubu and Patti Smith. They were so far out there, there wasn't anything that they were copying. They weren't thinking in any kind of commercial terms. R.E.M. was styleless. As mannered as it was, it was still about four guys getting up and playing music.

STEVE WYNN: Any tour has tension, but you knew they were all together. These were the same four guys that had started out together and I really admired that.

GINA ARNOLD: I was at the college radio station, doing my show the day the new Elvis Costello record came in and I was reading the new issue of *Record* magazine with Prince on the cover. It had an interview with R.E.M. and Pete Buck said something like, "All the best records in my collection are from 1983, and they're all American" followed by a long, long list of bands. So I decided for my show that day I would play all the bands on the list and I said over the air, "This is all American day. All we are playing is American music on independent labels, anything that Pete Buck suggested, anything that you listeners want and no Elvis Costello." Basically, it wasn't just an American day, but has been an American life ever since that day. I don't think I've ever played that Elvis Costello record. Not just because Pete Buck said it, but because I had the opportunity to play all those records for myself, and he was right.

*"I like to think it makes a difference when somebody listens to
R.E.M., just as it makes a difference to me when I listen to The
dBs, Jason and the Scorchers, the Minutemen or any number of
contemporary bands. These bands may eventually appeal to a
larger audience that responds differently, but I think people would
be missing the point if they listened to this music in an entirely su-
perficial way. . . . I don't know if any or all of these bands will eventually be famous, rich or even remembered but as a movement
they're inspiring kids to pick up instruments and work in ways
that aren't prescribed. I talk to kids all the time who are excited by
bands like R.E.M. because, first of all, they like our music; but
mostly because we show that you don't have to knuckle under to
the dictates of the music business to be successful. They're excited
by the fact that what we've done is possible . . ."*
—Peter Buck penned article in *Record,*
October 1984

DAN VALLOR: Peter said that the singer in the Dream Academy [*Nick
Laird-Clowes*] told him that he and Johnny Marr of the Smiths were his
favorite guitarists. That struck Peter as embarrassing company, as with
most of us at the time, there was no great love for the Smiths in the
American indy scene.

*"People used to ask me if I was influenced by Johnny Marr and
that used to piss me off so much that I said really nasty things
about the Smiths—but I do like the Smiths. When I came over to
England people asked 'Are you influenced by the Smiths?' and I
was like, 'Fuck you! I've had two records out before the Smiths
even started.'"*   —Peter Buck to *Bucketfull of Brains,*
December 1987

STEVE WYNN: It wasn't until well into the *Reckoning* tour that I
thought of them as a superstar kind of band.

KEN FECHTNER: Peter never discussed with me what it felt like being
in the public eye. Sometimes he would say, "I can't believe this is
happening." His ambition was to put out a single and he'd done what
he set out to do.

WOODY NUSS: There's a story about the first time they went to Japan.
The promoters there are very literal about what's in the contract so there
was "Budweiser beer in a can" in the dressing room. Everyone thought

it was a little funny, since the label said Seattle on it. It turned out the Japanese promoter had sent for it from the States which probably cost them way more money than necessary. The whole point of Bud being in the rider is that it is the cheapest beer around in the States, and they never wanted clubs to have to go to any trouble.

> *"Sun. Dreamt Boyd at beach. Woke 6, walked around short bldgs here. Dreamt I had to write a song and sing with Julio Iglesias. Woke up with a sore throat. Bridge and water, temple flea market plastic food in windows, ROCK N ROCK stores, sickly sweet smell, young hipster types in bright colors everywhere sweeping sidewalks, courtesy. Glass bricks, stark Bauhausian concrete pigeon-English signs, everyone bowing. Armor chest, finally ate, Jap. pumpkin, crackers, some weird fishcake blue wall, old man in wooden clothes. . ."*
> —Michael Stipe's Japanese tour diary, *Matter*,
> April/May 1985

GINA ARNOLD: In 1983-84 rock and roll became such a growth industry that it started to hit the mainstream media more and maybe that's why the Athens scene was made into such an event.

LAUREN HALL: It's interesting that there was a scene in Seattle at the beginning of the Nineties, very similar to what there was in Athens at the beginning of the Eighties. It would be interesting to try to compare the two and spot the similarities and difference.

> *"I would have loved to have been in Seattle two years ago. You can tell it's like Athens was. Before you know you've got a scene, it's a pretty great scene."* —Peter Buck to *Pulse!* October 1992

GINA ARNOLD: R.E.M.'s region was really strong and they made us look toward their region. I felt very romantic about the South, Georgia, kudzu, a small college town and an alternative band in the small town—all those things struck me powerfully. It turned my attention away from the New York City thing. Before that, I looked to New York City as the arbiter of cool. If you were really cool, you went there. I think by that time, New York City was becoming uncool. It was becoming way too dangerous and way too expensive and it wasn't only R.E.M. that chose not to go there. Economically, it was becoming a trend to stay in your hometown, and R.E.M. was symptomatic of that. Through them I saw the beauty of small town life, the beauty of America and the beauty of regionalism.

LAUREN HALL: You don't expect anything like what happened in Athens to happen there. It's a teeny tiny town. It's amazing it did.

ARMISTEAD WELLFORD: Bill and I once counted up 35 Athens bands in 1984. We thought, "already there's 35 bands!" There must be hundreds today. When we all started out there were five bands doing "new music."

GINA ARNOLD: The media applies so much to other scenes and not their own. I think that people that work within a scene support their own scene and no one band is going to tell you to look to your own scene to find what's happening. Why there are really good scenes in Minneapolis, Athens, Austin and Seattle and not in various other places is one of those mysteries. Cheap rents seem to help. Bad weather seems to help, but that's not enough. I think the whole scene thing comes down to individuals who are highly motivated, organized and creative. Each scene that has happened has had an individual who was absolutely a focal point. In Athens it was a band.

BRUCE MCGUIRE: Here in Minneapolis, the Replacements inspired me to check out R.E.M. instead of the other way around.

GINA ARNOLD: Peter Buck was an eloquent spokesperson for his scene. More eloquent than other people might be. He loved his scene and he told everybody about it and we fell. Some people might not have seen the beauty in it and he did, but again the time was right, and if he was somebody else he might have moved to New York like The dB'S did. I didn't see the dB'S going around celebrating Winston-Salem, NC till long after the scene was done. But that was the thing to do at the time. So in a way, it was a great creative leap on Peter Buck's part not to do that. But he ran into the right people at the right time.

STEPHANIE CHERNIKOWSKI: It's odd that Peter is the most articulate in terms of interviews. The guitarist usually can't talk. I guess it's because he is an incredible collector and reader.

STEVE WYNN: Peter has always turned me on to bands before they were well known. Bands like Sonic Youth and Hüsker Dü. I think you can hear both of those bands in R.E.M. It's obvious they were listening to cool stuff and new stuff that maybe you didn't even know about yet. That's always the sign of a cool band. That's what the Beatles did. It's what the Stones and Dylan did.

ROBERT LLOYD: You could say the same thing about the Liverpool scene that people might say about Athens. And they probably did:

"These other guys are so much better. Why not them?" But it was a combination of things. The Beatles were good looking, they put on the suits, they were four distinct characters that combined in a certain way. It was the right people at the right time. There are a million choices and some people are going to make more of the right choices for the time. For the Beatles or R.E.M. it wasn't about saying, "let's be in a band and get famous," it was more about "let's do this because this is what we feel like doing." There's a certain exhilaration in watching a band behave that way. I don't think R.E.M. have ever lost their way in that sense.

STEVE WYNN: Mike's parents showed up on our later club tours in Atlanta. I'd heard that they try to learn all they can about the other bands that play with R.E.M.

GIL RAY: R.E.M. talking about The dB'S made me want to listen to dB'S records. Mitch Easter spun off millions of bands for me to listen to after he produced the first R.E.M. records. Some of us would start buying records if they were produced by Mitch or if they were from the South. In more cases than not, it would be a great record.

MITCH EASTER: The more people that are talking about you, the more famous you are. At the time, I was just lucky to get my name on my own records and other people's records which made me look like "The Dude—this guy is everywhere." That was great at the time. R.E.M. has been a band that attracted good will and their fans really like them. Any association you have with those guys, a little bit of it rubs off. In effect, they got Let's Active our record deal with IRS. Not by going in and negotiating on our behalf, but by talking about us. The first show Let's Active ever played was opening for R.E.M. They just helped us a lot.

BRUCE MCGUIRE: Pylon's *Chomp* was the first record I bought because R.E.M. was into it and I didn't like it. There were others that were part of that scene that came later like the Swimming Pool Q's and Oh-OK and I thought those bands were terrible. But the band that I thought that was great that I never would have heard were it not for R.E.M. was Let's Active. For a lot of R.E.M. fans Mitch Easter's band Let's Active was a good band for a long time.

MITCH EASTER: No one ever believes me when I say this, but R.E.M. going on to use other producers was just fine with me. It was the thing to do. Either way it would have been fine with me. All I really wanted to do was the follow up to the single, and I did that. By the time we had done the two albums, it made sense for them to move on. Plus, I was pretty busy at the time. My band was playing a lot and I didn't want to feel like I was hanging on someone's coattails.

DON DIXON: It was definitely time for them to find out what other people were like. There was only so far we could go and they needed to be moving in a forward direction. I'm not sure we could have done that for them.

MITCH EASTER: If they had the slightest inclination to work with someone else, I thought that they should do it. I hope they didn't think that I didn't care, but I didn't want to act crushed, because I wasn't crushed. They hadn't worked with anyone else much. They wanted to check out the wide world and they wanted to do the sessions with Joe Boyd. I thought it was a real hip choice and I thought it made sense.

1985

March — Recording of *Fables of the Reconstruction* at Livingston Studios, London

June 10 — *Fables of the Reconstruction*, produced by Joe Boyd. Choosing Boyd (known primarily for his work with Fairport Convention and Richard Thompson) indicated a conscious shift in direction. The result was an album with a folkier sound and a distinct Southern theme—from title to cover art to content.

Seven-inch Singles

March — "Tighten Up," *Bucketfull of Brains* Flexi Disc

June — "Can't Get There From Here"/"Bandwagon"

September — "Driver 8"/"Crazy"

Touring

April/May — Pre-Construction tour of U.S. college campuses

July-September — Reconstruction Tour Parts I-IV

Videos

"Can't Get There From Here," directed by Stipe/Aguar Video Prod./Hart

"Driver 8," directed by James Herbert/Stipe

"Life and How to Live It" and "Feeling Gravitys Pull" (Both videos were cobbled together from *Reckoning* period live footage taken by Jim Herbert and Jackie Slayton)

Television and Film Appearances

Entertainment Tonight profile on transition to bigger venues

Select Guest Appearances

Peter Buck plays guitar on "Windout" and "When The Night Falls" on the Fleshtones' live album, *Speed Connection II*

Michael Stipe contributes lead vocals to "Omaha," "Clustering Train" and "Boy(Go)" on *Visions of Excess* by the Golden Palominos and tours with them as a vocalist

Awards and Recognition

Fables of the Reconstruction named Album of the Year at the CMJ (*College Media Journal*) New Music Awards. Band performed at the show off-camera.

5

FABLES OF THE RECONSTRUCTION

KEN FECHTNER: In '85, Peter was thrilled to buy his first house. I think the bigger thrill was when he put in a pool. That was like the ultimate success. Within about a year and a half he went from living in his brother's hall to having a house with a pool.

SARA BROWN: Kenny Fechtner and I went to a party at Peter's house one night and we were watching *Lolita*. Peter and I started talking about Peter Sellers' movies. I mentioned my favorite one was *Being There* because it was filmed in my hometown, Asheville, NC. He said, "Oh, Asheville. I used to deliver records to some stores there." I asked him if he remembered delivering records to the store I worked at and all of a sudden we looked at each other, like, "I remember you." We realized we probably never would have thought about each other ever again had we not made that connection. He said I was the missing link from that point in his life because he had never run into anyone from that job since then.

LANCE SMITH: I heard stories that all those guys did around 1984-85 was snort coke and play darts. I figured, if they were rich enough not to do speed, then why not?

KEN FECHTNER: In February they did a show in Atlanta at a converted A&P [*the Moonshadow*] and Joe Boyd was there. I knew of him from all of the Fairport Convention records, so I was kind of like, "Oh, maybe something *is* happening."

JOE BOYD [producer, *Fables of the Reconstruction*]: Up until a few days before I went to Athens, my combined schedule of the Mary Margaret O'Hara and 10,000 Maniacs projects had meant I had to turn down R.E.M. Then Mary Margaret O'Hara went funny and postponed everything so I rang Jefferson and he said, "Come on down." We did an afternoon of song demos in a garage studio in Athens and I thought the songs were great. We went out to dinner, had a few drinks and I saw them play in Atlanta the following night. We agreed to start work a few weeks later in London.

KEN FECHTNER: I sensed something was going on, because they went to England to record their album. They had previously only been to Charlotte, NC.

"I found myself surrounded a whole lot when we were writing these songs by fables and nursery rhymes and Uncle Remus and old tales. The idea of stories being passed down and becoming a tradition and having those stories become as much a part of a way of living or a particular area that you live in as the religion or the trees or the weather, I like the connection between that and the South."   —Michael Stipe to *Record*, July 1985

JOE BOYD: The songs were all written before the trip to London. I didn't know the band at all before the sessions so it was hard for me to judge whether their moods were out of character. I thought they were just fine and very easy to get along with. They were less into "getting sounds" on their instruments (drum tunings, amp settings, etc.) than others I had worked with, which caused a few problems. I thought their previous albums were pretty dark, so the darkness didn't surprise or disturb me. It rained a lot, which did tend to bring them down, and the studio was a long depressing drive from where they were staying. Michael got into London, going out a lot to visit galleries, bookshops and vegetarian restaurants all over the underground, but the others just went back and forth and played a lot of pool.

STEPHANIE CHERNIKOWSKI: They've always disclaimed *Fables* and I think it's one of the most profoundly beautiful records ever. It has a consistency of mood that is pure Southern Gothic with its genuine sensibility. It was the meeting of people that come from the same traditions and I recognized it because I have a Southern Gothic streak in me. Their music is dark and brooding and shadowy.

*"I had a miserable time making that album. We were all miserable
and mean to each other. If there ever was a point in our career
where we thought we were sick to death of each other, that was it.
We had just got off an eight and a half month tour, we rehearsed
for eight or nine days and wrote these fifteen songs, been home for
a week and half—the first time in a year. We flew over to London
and it rained all the time, it's winter, it's snowing. We didn't have
enough money to rent cars and shit so we had to take the tube and
there's nothing wrong with that but we were a mile from the tube
station so I had to carry my guitar in the snow to the tube. I had
to stand up the whole way then walk a mile to the studio. I wasn't
sleeping, I slept about an hour a night and I drank all the time. If
I didn't feel bad anyway, that was enough to make me feel
crummy. That record just reflects that perfectly, it's a misery
album in a lot of ways—but I like it, the songwriting's great, it's
one of our stronger albums as far as songwriting."*
—Peter Buck to Bucketfull of Brains,
December 1987

DANNY BEARD: They did some really great stuff on *Fables of the Reconstruction,* even though they say they hate it. For ballads and slow songs,
it has some of the best. That's when they got really good. There were
songs that were making lyrical sense. Pete did some great stuff on that
record that was more psychedelic and less "tweedly." He came alive as
a guitarist.

CURTIS CROWE: When R.E.M. recorded the [*Pylon*] song, "Crazy," they
were in the studio but they didn't know all the words. They couldn't
understand them on the record so they tried calling Vanessa Briscoe. They
couldn't reach her so they ended up just having to make them up, which
was fine. I think that's how music ought to be. I really dug the concept
that they couldn't figure out the words so they just made their own up.

STEVE WYNN: Around the time *Fables* came out, I thought it was their
best album to date. I talked to Peter about it and he said he didn't like
it. I like when bands try to destroy what they are all about and try to
build it back up again. I think *Fables* was great for that.

JOE BOYD: I was disappointed in the album myself. I never felt the mix
was right and viewed it as a failure. Part of that was due to the
excessively egalitarian group—no one wanted themselves "turned up"
in the mix, so it all sounded a bit flat and one-dimensional to me. But I

was never comfortable with the speakers in the studio and felt badly that I never got a sound I was totally happy with.

> *"Everything works . . . all together. I always hated the idea of having the vocal way above the music. On 'Old Man Kensey' the vocal's way out there—but that's the only way it could be handled. On some songs, like 'Kohoutek,' I can't imagine the vocal being loud. That's a real swirling one."* —Michael Stipe to *Musician*,
> September 1985

JOE BOYD: I was pleased with the tracks involving extra musicians, [*"Feeling Gravitys Pull," "Wendell Gee," "Can't Get There From Here," "Old Man Kensey"*] where I felt I made a genuine contribution, but the band tracks didn't sound as good as I wanted them to. I was very relieved when the reviews were good and it doubled the previous record's sales figures. I didn't blame the group for disliking the record and saying so—I kind of agreed with them. I am pleased that more and more people seem to like *Fables*, including some of the group.

BRUCE MCGUIRE: Before *Fables of the Reconstruction* came out they did a small college tour called the Pre-Construction Tour. I saw them in Madison, WI in an agriculture barn. Dirt floor. Unbelievable. The Neats opened for them. Mills and Stipe came out and sang with them on the last song and they did "Sweet Emotion" by Aerosmith. It was totally great. Then R.E.M. did a mind-blowing set. It was all new stuff, because the record wasn't out yet. They opened with "Feeling Gravitys Pull," and they came onstage to the sound of train whistles and train lights blinking. That was very cool. I dug that completely.

GEORGINA FALZARANO [road friend]: The Stock Pavilion show in Madison, WI is a great live tape. They talk about having pigs under their feet. That was the first time I heard them play that song, "Theme from Two Steps Onward" [*unreleased*].

RUSS TOLMAN: My band, True West, had played at the 40 Watt in 1985. A couple of weeks later, R.E.M. called us to open some dates on their tour. Robyn Hitchcock who was supposed to be their opening act on the Reconstruction Tour got sick. I think the fact that Peter had seen us and liked us and Bertis Downs was a big fan of ours led them to call us up and ask us on the tour during July and August of 1985. We immediately said yes. We had only played in clubs and we were all fans of R.E.M. so it was our chance to play in bigger places and it was exciting. On tour with them it got kind of old because I knew every night they were going to open with "Feeling Gravitys Pull."

DANNY BEARD: By the time *Fables* came out, they were so popular that we knew we would sell a hundred copies in the first day in the Athens store, Wax Jr. Facts. They weren't on that level in Atlanta yet.

RUSS TOLMAN: The first night of the tour we were in Portland, OR and before the show Peter and I were in the dressing room having a beer. Peter's always in his Mr. friendly-guy mode and I don't think he opens up much. And I certainly don't, even though I had opportunities. I don't think once during the whole tour I ever opened up and treated them just like guys because I was in too much awe of them.

ROBERT LLOYD: There is a certain power in collecting records by a band who is still obscure and R.E.M. could no longer be considered obscure. I saw them in Paris in '85 and it was the first time I realized that they might not be "my" band anymore. The balcony was filled with American college students who were obnoxious.

RUSS TOLMAN: Peter's grandparents came to the show at the Greek Theatre in LA and they asked him if he was playing with the first band because they saw me and I guess from faraway they thought he *was* me.

LANCE SMITH: Chris Edwards, their tour manager at the time, worked at the I&I. Everyone from the I&I could get into the Watt Club but I could never get into the I&I. In '85 R.E.M. played Savannah, GA and one of my cousins went to the backstage area and said, "My cousin said I could come backstage," and they said, "Who's your cousin?" Security was like, "I don't know that guy." Chris was there and he let my cousin in. I couldn't believe my cousin did that, I was so embarrassed.

RUSS TOLMAN: Their road crew were really nice people. Everything came off well and was well organized. As an opening band they made sure we were taken care of. Unlike a lot of bands who pick on the opening act, they went out of their way. Their sound man mixed us and we only needed to tip him. I had a feeling their guys would have been nice even if we hadn't paid them. One of the things I really like about them is that they are a hometown, family operation. They've had their road crew for years and that's nice.

DAVID T. LINDSAY: The best show R.E.M. ever gave was when they played with Jason and the Scorchers and the Minutemen in Atlanta. It was like all three bands were competing with each other and all of the bands were in top form. It was the only time I ever liked R.E.M. They didn't have any stage props or any of that stuff.

RUSS TOLMAN: In a club you can be a little more spontaneous. In a big place you have to remember it's an act. You have to make big movements. I imagine R.E.M. had figured this out a few years before.

KEN FECHTNER: I think "Can't Get There From Here" was the first song that really got any notice.

> *"I was thinking of sounding like Mahalia Jackson. I tried to do as many different voices on the album as possible. On ['Can't Get There From Here'] I can pick five different voices. I had to show them how to do that [jazz squeal at the end] I said, 'I want you to sound like Louis Armstrong,' They didn't understand. I had to use my mouth and go 'Waaah Waaaah-Waah' and they thought I meant his trumpet sound. What I really meant was his voice! They were really confused."* —Michael Stipe to *Tasty World* #7

SEAN BOURNE: There are probably lots of R.E.M. jokes. Maybe not. I know one. It's not very funny, but it's probably emblematic of how little humor there is in the R.E.M. world. Knock knock. Who's there? Windy. Windy Who? Windy world is a monster.

JACKSON HARING [rock manager]: I had a photo of myself sitting on the porch of Wendell Gee's Used Cars. I lost it in a fire, but it was my most treasured R.E.M. memento because *Fables* turned out to be my favorite album of theirs. The production is rich and the songs are beautiful. It was the first R.E.M. record I discovered on my own instead of being turned on to by other people.

GINA ARNOLD: "Come on aboard, I promise you we won't hurt the horse," ["*Bandwagon*"]—Michael always insinuated that was a sarcastic line and I thought, no, it's not. He didn't know what he was saying maybe. But if I hadn't felt that I was welcome on that horse, I wouldn't have been there ever. Their attitude of welcomingness was always there and it was in their music too. They just exuded it.

ROBERT LLOYD: I interviewed Michael during *Fables* and it must have been a period when he was forthcoming because even by then he was known as someone who wouldn't talk. The first time I interviewed Peter, Michael sat in a corner, kind of mysteriously. I don't know how much of that is put on and how much isn't.

GEORGINA FALZARANO: When I met up with the band on the *Fables* tour, I noticed Michael was opening up to people more. He had just come out of his "moody artistic phase." Previously, he would do things like turn his back on the audience and do the show that way. But he'd started to do a lot more reading and he started to realize the power the band and his lyrics could have. He became concerned about how he could use the power and how easily it could also be abused. He wanted to be careful not to abuse it.

BRUCE MCGUIRE: I met Michael Stipe in '85. It's directly because of Michael that I got turned on to Howard Finster. If any one thing has completely blown me away it was Howard Finster. I've become a Finster fanatic. I've been to his place seven or eight times. I have 17 Finster paintings. I thought the *Reckoning* cover was really cool and then there was a Talking Heads cover for *Little Creatures*. I asked Michael about Howard. He told me all about him. I was completely blown away by Michael's stories of Finster. And he in turn admitted how completely inspirational Howard was to him. Howard had been painting for nine years when I met him and he'd done 5000 paintings. Now he's almost at 30,000 so that means he did about 23,000 [*pieces of artwork*] in the last eight years.

WATCHING MICHAEL WATCHING REV. HOWARD FINSTER AT WORK IN HIS PARADISE GARDEN STUDIO (*photo by Georgina Falzarano*)

GEORGINA FALZARANO: I went up to Howard Finster's with Michael in the days when you could stay the night and watch him work in his studio. Watching Michael watching Howard is something I will never forget. Watching Michael's admiration for him was touching. I'll always remember it.

RUSS TOLMAN: Michael Stipe pretty much kept to himself. He and our lead singer kind of became friends. Michael would always have different food than everyone else. He was more into doing his thing and the other guys were more like regular guys. I think Mills is the most genuine of them. He's the guy that always says hi to anyone.

STEPHANIE CHERNIKOWSKI: Mike is the rock star who sees it as part of his job description to love women. He's the one that will get in a cab with you and grope your knee.

ROBERT LLOYD: I guess *Fables* was when things really changed for them. I saw them in Irvine and the guy next to me peed in his cup. There were a lot of rowdy people there and it felt like it didn't go with R.E.M. That happens with any band you like. You don't want to wish them obscurity.

RUSS TOLMAN: In Fresno, CA one of the guys' [*from True West*] wife was there and she said to Peter, "You're sort of the Peter Townshend of the band, aren't you?" Peter flipped out. He left very soon after that.

JOE BOYD: They are a totally unique group in their attitude, intelligence, organization, management, and their unwillingness to be intimidated by the music business. Plus of course, their talent and originality. I have total respect for them and if the cliche about people deserving success is ever true, it is with them. They are very nice guys and I am proud to have had a role in their career.

RUSS TOLMAN: R.E.M. were very much a band that worked real hard to become successful. They were a very professional group that went out and did their job every night. As a business unit I think they always had things down. They said their tours broke even, but they made money from the merchandising.

KEITH ALTOMARE: I remember the days when R.E.M. didn't want to do T-shirts because they didn't want to take advantage of their fan. If they ever did a T-shirt they said they would only do one style. I really thought it was humorous because at one point they had like 32 different designs.

RUSS TOLMAN: By the time we were playing with them, the profile of the R.E.M. fan had been established—the neo-hippie; arty college kids.

VICTOR KRUMMENACHER [Camper Van Beethoven, toured with R.E.M.]: When I saw R.E.M. play in Santa Cruz, CA was the first time I met them. Afterwards, we went backstage and gave them our first record, *Telephone Free Landslide Victory* [*Camper Van Beethoven*]. We were pretty surprised to hear from them a few days after we saw them. Michael called our lead singer, David Lowery, from a phone booth in the desert to say how much he liked the record. We thought it was a prank. A phone booth in the desert? After many calls to the R.E.M. office and getting shrugged off, Jefferson finally acknowledged that yes, Michael was into the band and that we should talk about touring together in the future.

GEORGINA FALZARANO: The Barrymore's show in Ottawa was legendary. I was three feet in front of Peter at that show and I had to duck every time he swung his guitar. It was a great show. They walked into the place and were like, "We're playing a bar?!" They all got drunk and went onstage and did the show. It was exactly the right thing to do.

KEN FECHTNER: There started being a lot of people around who wanted to meet the band. I would go see them occasionally, but mainly because I was friends with Peter. I still hung around with him a lot and Mills some and occasionally with Bill but it wasn't the same going to see the shows. It got really big. They were in theatres, you needed passes and in a way I felt I was intruding. It wasn't my place to be there anymore. That's a common complaint of anyone who is a fan of a band when they are small. "Unless you saw the B-52's play in a living room in Athens, you never saw the B-52's," that kind of thing. Not that it is the band's fault, but it has to become a business. They became aware that they had an obligation to give a decent performance to their audience. They used to play songs not on the set list, start it, realize they didn't know it and the whole thing would fall apart. If you've got a tour manager and you're charging people 10 or 15 dollars for a ticket it's not fair to your audience to give that kind of presentation.

BRUCE MCGUIRE: The people hanging around them before and after shows were other bands and friends of theirs from elsewhere. There always seemed to be some people around that weren't in the music scene but in the art scene or old college friends.

JOE BOYD: I remained friends with them, particularly the Michaels and I consider the experience of having worked with them a good one overall. The only uncomfortable moment for me while working with them was long after the project was done. At the College Media Journal (CMJ) Awards at the Beacon Theatre in New York when they got an award for Album of the Year, they thanked everyone under the sun from the podium except me!

STEVE WYNN: I think beginning to deal with fame was a hard thing during *Fables*—the growing pains that come from no longer being a cult band, being able to travel around and have fun. All of a sudden, the stakes were much bigger.

RUSS TOLMAN: Unfortunately, R.E.M.'s benevolent act of taking us on the road didn't help us in the long term because we broke up shortly after that tour. It was a culmination of a lot of things.

GINA ARNOLD: There was a vast difference back then between the alternative/indy world and the mainstream world. There was no point of contact, and R.E.M. became the point of contact late in the Eighties. Now, it's all mushed up and there's Alternative Nation on MTV. But in 1985, MTV wasn't a viable route for a band like R.E.M. or anybody. It was so different then.

JEFFERSON, I THINK WE'RE IN LITTLE AMERICA, WY
(photo by Georgina Falzarano)

1986

April — Recording begins for *Lifes Rich Pageant* at Belmont Mall Studio, Belmont, IN

July 30 — *Lifes Rich Pageant*, produced by Don Gehman. For the first time, R.E.M. moves into topical or political songs: "Fall on Me" (in part about acid rain), "Cuyahoga" (the dying river), "Flowers of Guatemala" (U.S. intervention in Central America) and a general call to arms in "Begin the Begin" and "I Believe."

Seven-inch Singles

June — *The Bob* Flexi Disc—"Femme Fatale"

August 18 — "Fall on Me"/"Rotary 10"

November 3 — "Superman"/"White Tornado"

Touring

September-November — Pageantry Tour

Video

"Fall On Me," directed by Stipe. Includes some lyrics and band does not appear

Pageantry promo video

Compilations

May — "Ages of You" on *Live for Life*, benefitting Children's Cancer Fund

Select Guest Appearances

Peter Buck plays guitar on "The Party" from the debut by *The Dream Academy*

Television and Film Appearances

"Driver 8" on car radio in "A Very Happy Ending," an episode of *Alfred Hitchcock Presents*

"Romance," re-recorded for the soundtrack to *Made in Heaven*

Awards and Recognition

Creem Magazine Reader's Poll: *Lifes Rich Pageant* named Album of the Year, "Fall on Me" Single of the Year and R.E.M. Band of the Year

6

LIFES RICH PAGEANT

DAN WALL: Later on after R.E.M. had three albums out, Pete "guest clerked" at Wuxtry for about a year. He came back to work because he is a record nut and he wanted to be around a source of records. I guess you could call him a record nerd. The store did better when he was in there, but he was too well-known by then. It got to be too much for him. Everybody was bugging him. He would tell people, "My boss wants me in here to sell stuff, not to talk about the band." I was amazed that he still called me boss even when he was making lots more money than I ever had.

BRIAN CRANE: Mills started taking bands into the studio helping them with their tapes [*Kilkenney Cats, Waxing Poetics*].

JOHN KEANE: In '86 I bought the sixteen-track recorder and started doing more records for people like Dog Gone, Jefferson's record label. Jefferson's band, the Vibrating Egg, is a funny record. If you were there during the making of it, it's even funnier. He was so nervous. He was getting ready to do the eight-minute version of "Whiter Shade of Pale" and he had to down about a quart of Jack Daniels just to get the nerve to go in there and sing that.

DAN WALL: Almost everyone who's ever worked for us at Wuxtry besides Peter is a musician. Kate Pierson from the B-52's worked here, members of Love Tractor, Guadalcanal Diary, Porn Orchard, the Woggles. It's because we hire townies rather than students and most of the townies are musicians.

JOHN KEANE: All four of them have brought people in and produced stuff for them. All of them have different styles. Bill Berry and Mike Mills tend to get more into arrangements—taking the songs apart and putting them back together. They get more specific about certain parts they want to hear and more involved actually playing on the recordings. Peter is more of a laissez-faire producer. He basically just brings bands into the studio and lets them do their thing, helps them make decisions and solve arguments about whether to do this or that. He keeps the bands from getting bogged down in lack of objectivity about their music. Michael is more of an idea kind of guy, less technical. Usually, he'll go out and find someone he likes, bring them into the studio and act as a cheerleader. He tries to make them feel good and keep them relaxed and not really mess with the nuts and bolts of the music too much.

BRUCE MCGUIRE: I have never liked anything any of the members of R.E.M. have done outside of the band. Not at all. I can even name several that are disastrous, like virtually every record any of those guys produced. But I went and checked out an awful lot of those bands. Ooh boy. I don't have any of those records in my collection anymore.

> *"I think I now write songs well enough that I would want to write and produce for other artists. I could see myself in the artier fields, maybe photography, or the other visual arts, 'cause I have a flair for that. It is something I've thought about because here I am on my twenty-eighth birthday, my hair is falling out, and I can't see myself being bald and playing drums onstage. The hair in the shower drain every morning does concern me."*
> —Bill Berry to *SPIN*, October 1986

GEOFF GANS [art director and musician]: I was introduced to Michael in 1986 by Michael Meister who owned Texas Records. I didn't know that much about R.E.M. I liked some of their records but I wasn't a fanatic. So many people thought that R.E.M. could do no wrong and got into the idol worship. But I related to Michael like a human being. I would ask him point blank about lyrics, stuff you weren't "supposed" to ask and he would answer very straightforwardly.

At the time, Michael was touring as a vocalist with the Golden Palominos. He said it was hard for him on the West Coast because he didn't know anyone and everyone else in the band had friends around so he was kind of on his own. That made me believe he was very humble and almost quiet—which was what his public persona was like at the time.

KEN FECHTNER: Peter is really hyper and has a lot of energy. On the road, he wouldn't sleep for days and he'd get wound really tight. He was given a prescription for some Halcion by a physician. He hadn't taken one yet. We went to see Hüsker Dü in Atlanta in 1986 and when we got home, he couldn't go to sleep so he took one. It didn't tire him enough to go to sleep so he took a second one. He was still up when I went to sleep but when I got up in the morning, he was asleep on the couch with his neck backwards over the arm of the couch. A lamp was shining six inches from his face. His mouth was wide open and that day's newspaper was neatly shredded into one inch strips and tossed all over my living room. When he got up I asked him what he did last night and he said he didn't do anything. I said *somebody* had shredded that newspaper but he had no recollection of it. For some reason he felt the need to shred that newspaper and how he slept that way for eight hours I'll never understand, but apparently some people have amnesia when they take Halcion.

STEPHANIE CHERNIKOWSKI: Peter suffers through photography. Bill and Mike were indifferent. Michael was the control freak. I had to pass his scrutiny to get the job of shooting the Pageantry Tour program. I worked most closely with him on the editing. He's got a wonderful eye. He was extremely apologetic about what he didn't like and he was overprotective of Peter—"I don't think Peter would like this shot," things like that.

SOMEWHERE ON THE ROAD, PAGEANTRY TOUR
(*photo by Georgina Falzarano*)

GIL RAY: The sex appeal of Stipe kills me. From all of the sexes. He's got the most beautiful eyes. But almost everyone I know wants him to grow his hair again.

STEPHANIE CHERNIKOWSKI: I don't use stylists, hairdos or makeup in my photos. I use rice powder on the cheekbones, mascara and lighting. When I wanted to put mascara on Michael, he said, "Stephanie, look at my eyelashes." He's got the richest, thickest longest eyelashes I've ever seen on any human. They're like spiders or something. He was right, he didn't need it. Michael is much more self conscious than the others, but unjustifiably. When he got the contacts he said, "you make me look so handsome. I look like Wham!" He wasn't vain. He didn't think he was attractive, much less handsome.

GEOFF GANS: I never understood why Michael would say things like, "Of course I don't drink" or "I don't smoke" or "I don't have electricity in my house" or "I don't watch TV."

STEPHANIE CHERNIKOWSKI: Michael didn't have a phone while I was there. He barely had a refrigerator. He was into minimal electricity.

> *"I can't have refrigerators in my house because of the sound they make. It just drives me nuts that that thing operates without me turning it on and off. It just goes. I can't take that."*
> —Michael Stipe to *Musician*, January 1988

GEOFF GANS: He would play it to the hilt and no one ever called him on it. But what is the big deal? It obviously wasn't true. A lot of people took him for about 80 percent of what he was. I guess you can chalk it up to rock and roll. That's what you do. You create a persona and do your thing.

STEPHANIE CHERNIKOWSKI: They function in two pairs. Michael and Peter and Bill and Mike.

DIANA J. CROWE: Eventually, Mike and Bill and I fell back into the same group. When I got reconnected to Bill was really after he got married to Mari. Mari and I have become pretty good friends.

**A MOMENTO OF
BILL & MARI'S WEDDING**

LANCE SMITH: Bill is the only one that I liked as a person. I found that he was the most genuine.

MARC WALLACE: Of anybody that I've ever met, Michael's a true artist. It's just something that he has all the way around. It's not just aesthetically or musically it's all the way around. He has that touch.

STEPHANIE CHERNIKOWSKI: We'd had some intense days of shooting while they were working on the songs for *Lifes Rich Pageant*. One day they had just finished writing a song and were really excited about it. I got to see the way they work together.

JOHN KEANE: R.E.M. has a kind of unique way of working in that Mike, Bill and Peter tend to write the music parts of the songs and put them in some kind of form on tape without Michael, then they'll give him the tape. Usually with bands it happens the other way around. The first time I realized that's the way they were doing things was when they came in with Don Gehman and I think it was a revelation for Don also. They came in with Gehman for a week and they were kind of trying him out to see if they were going to get along with him. They demoed all the songs they had up to that point for the album. Don was a really nice guy. He actually stuck around after the session and helped me straighten out some wiring problems I had in the studio.

BUREN FOWLER: Microwave and Curtis Goodman who worked for R.E.M. were trying to hire me to work for them. Basically they said if there was ever a need to get another person, they wanted me. I think R.E.M. was a little wary of having a frustrated guitar player as a roadie. It wasn't immediately decided so I left town. I went to Louisville, KY to visit my girlfriend's parents. The two things I was really into were R.E.M. and *Master of Puppets* by Metallica. Metallica was playing in town so I called a friend of mine who was working for them. He said they had an opening—they needed a guitar roadie starting next week. I went to the show and I went backstage to talk to their road manager. I got to talking to Kirk Hammett [*lead guitarist, Metallica*] for a minute on their bus and he said, "So you'd like to go to work for us," and I'm like, "Yea." And he said, "I heard you might be getting a job with R.E.M." and I was like, "Well I don't know, it's not official." He showed me his two R.E.M. tapes and said, "They're the new band I'm totally into right now."

I couldn't believe it. I thought he was joking but it was true, he was really into R.E.M. So he said, "if you can get a job with R.E.M., maybe you should try to hold out for that." As it turned out, five weeks later they had that bus wreck in Europe [*Metallica bassist Cliff Burton died in the crash*].

KEN FECHTNER: Peter was really excited about the song "Superman." [*The song featured Mike Mills on lead vocals for the first time. The song was originally recorded by the Clique.*]

VICTOR KRUMMENACHER: I thought "Underneath the Bunker" was at once a nod to Camper Van Beethoven and a rip-off. In a certain way it was a little more sophisticated than what we were doing because it had a tango feel, and we were still back at the two-step. But I definitely felt like it was a nod of some sort even though I got outright denial of that from them. I always felt like it was some kind of indication that they were listening to what we were doing. How could it not be? [*The song is an instrumental, left unlisted on the sleeve but appears between "Hyena" and "The Flowers of Guatemala" and definitely sounds like Camper Van Beethoven.*]

JOE BOYD: I like the most recent albums better than the first ones after *Fables*. I thought they went to another extreme—much cleaner, more "radio ready," voice out front (which Michael absolutely forbade on *Fables*), hint of a drum machine or sequencer here and there on *Lifes Rich Pageant*. I didn't really like it that much, but you can't argue with the success it had.

GIL RAY: After Mitch quit producing them, I kind of started liking their records less and less. They turned more into real musicians and the remembrances of them as a party dance band is what I liked best. They started doing more ballads.

BUREN FOWLER: Jefferson came into where I was working and asked me to step outside. He said, "they want to know if you can play bass because Mike wants to play keyboards." I borrowed Mike's bass and stayed up all night learning all the bass parts to *Lifes Rich Pageant*.

> "I like a simple bass pattern. I like to hear that kick drum and bass drum lock in. But that wouldn't work for our group. We all have these odd styles that for some reason plug in and work. There's no reason they should, but they do."
> —Bill Berry to *Musician*, January 1988

BUREN FOWLER: I went to R.E.M.'s practice the next day and Jefferson told me to talk to Peter. It wasn't great timing to talk to Peter because his father was really sick and was in the hospital and he'd just broken up with his girlfriend. We were playing ping-pong, and he was telling me how he hated ping-pong. He said, "So, we hear you can play bass." And I was like "Yea." And he said, "Well, I don't know, we kind of like the way Mike plays bass." I was letting him win at ping-pong and he says, "Can you play guitar? We might need someone to play rhythm guitar." I said, "Cool, I can do that." "Okay," he said, "Let's learn some songs." We put down the ping-pong paddles and went to work.

DAVID T. LINDSAY: I got a phone call from Jefferson once telling me the band didn't want to do a video for IRS. The trade-off they'd made was they would do an interview record instead of a video and Peter decided of all the rock writers in America, he wanted me to interview the band—will I do it? Jefferson asked me if I needed to think about it and I said no, if it gives me a chance to ask them some questions I want to ask and if it's not edited, then sure, I'd be glad to do it. Jefferson said Peter would be really happy and he would tell the band I agreed. He called me back in a week and told me the label said, okay, but they would have to fly the band and me out to LA to record it and deduct the expenses from R.E.M.'s royalties. Michael said there was no way they would waste that kind of money so he would make the video for them. The video he did was "Fall On Me," and I think it was the best video they ever did. He went out to a rock quarry and turned himself upside down and filmed.

MARC WALLACE: Michael takes complete control of the band's video work. He picks who is going to direct it and the rest of the band give him the power to do what he wants creatively.

STEPHANIE CHERNIKOWSKI: I can't stress enough that it was due to Michael's editing that the program for the Pageantry tour turned out as it did. The four individual shots were his choices and I think they are inspired. I think he is incredibly underestimated visually.

ROBERT LLOYD: If they were an English band, they would have been lionized then they would have been dumped on and people would forget them, but that didn't happened to them. I imagine there's been some backlash through the years, but I haven't followed it.

GINA ARNOLD: Tom Carson's *Village Voice* review of *Lifes Rich Pageant* decided to backlash on them. One of the things he implied that really offended me was that they were Reaganistic because they recalled the nostalgia of a perfect America and their whole glamorization of the Small-town South was a real Reagan kind of thing. I thought that was a simplistic argument and that he didn't understand the music at all. R.E.M. weren't alienated, and that was his criticism. It seems kind of funny to me in retrospect that they weren't more alienated, given what was going on in the world. There *was* something kind of user-friendly about them so I understand his argument though I don't agree with it.

> Sure, the band's ideals are sincere, however limited by what they're used for. But all those ideals are couched in tendentious appeals to a cloudily glorious past (even their hopes for the future are nostalgic), an uncritical preference for sentiment over thought, and a wishful confusion of cultural might-have-beens with historical truth (if something can't be mythicized, it doesn't exist for them). This is the emotional syntax of Reaganism, pure and simple. It's lulling and delusive in much the same way: seduced by the mood, you lose the ability to relate it back to whatever purpose it serves, whether for the president (paying thugs to blow up children) or the pop band (???beats me). They end up furthering the atmosphere that produces what their messages attack—and it's clear, for the band and their listener alike, which resonates more.
>
> —Tom Carson, from "Sandbox Supermen,"
> *Village Voice*, September 2, 1986

BRUCE MCGUIRE: R.E.M. is an easy target. It's pretty tough not to jab R.E.M. because they've always left themselves open. They've never tried to hide anything. They've always been pretty normal so they're easy to pick on. Then there are people like critics that like to cause trouble and stir stuff up to get attention.

GEORGINA FALZARANO: I think the reason I was accepted on the road so much is that Michael was totally intrigued with the fact that I was a teacher. He asked a lot of questions about what that was like. He talked about the power of being in front of a group of people, being able to manipulate them that way and how to control those impulses and use them productively. I told him, you can't just throw things in front of people and you can't tell them but you can suggest. That will make them pause and want to learn about things a little more. That's what I strive for as a teacher and I see an element of that in his work. I think he gives people ideas to think about and suggestions. He was thinking about all of these concepts preceding *Lifes Rich Pageant*.

JACKSON HARING: R.E.M. was a whole cloth to cut whatever meaning you wanted from. To have that kind of power is incredible, yet at the same time, I was so impressed that Michael realized it was kind of a cop-out not to say anything —he had this power, he should wield it and he did. On the first three records, you could attach whatever meaning you wanted to the songs. Michael was still in the "Mumbles" stage. I've spent many an evening listening to people expound on the profundity of R.E.M. and I'm sure if the band were flies on the wall they would laugh their silly heads off.

GEORGINA FALZARANO: Michael is extremely serious about what he does and the idea of realizing his potential. I think he realized early on that the band was going to make it and, as chief lyricist, he realized the importance of what he was doing. He wanted to make sure that he used his experience well.

VICTOR KRUMMENACHER: I was really impressed with Michael a lot on the Pageantry tour because the commentary that he was making onstage (even though it was oblique as usual), would be interpreted as pointed by anyone who had left-leaning political tendencies. I was just beginning to read about and understand the Iran-Contra affair, so I was pleasantly surprised that they would be political about that onstage. It was really intense. He would do this rap [*"I Believe"*] and recite the Pledge of Allegiance. At the end of it he would mimic blowing his head off.

GEORGINA FALZARANO: At the end of "I Believe" after the line "I'm so young, I'm so god damned young," onstage Michael would say "and I'm a Republican."

VICTOR KRUMMENACHER: They probably haven't done anything as pointed as "The Flowers of Guatemala" since then.

> *"If you want to talk about politics or your love life or social problems or what it's like to live in 1983, then you should do it somewhere other than on stage."*
> —Michael Stipe to *Record*, July 1983

GEORGINA FALZARANO: There were pros and cons to Michael beginning to address issues in his songs. Michael used his voice as an instrument rather than a tool for expressing ideas so when he changed and concentrated more on the words, I was skeptical. But I liked the messages he was trying to get across. They were subtly raised and not too leading. I liked that.

"There are brief explanations on the back of Lifes Rich Pageant's sleeve that I think make the songs mean more. Like 'Cuyahoga' is an Indian word for a river in Ohio so polluted they had to burn part of it off. And 'Fall on Me' is about acid rain. Sometime people will send Michael what they think the lyrics are in the hope that he'll tell them what they are. One time, a guy thought one of the lines in 'Sitting Still' is 'We will gather throw up beer.' Sometimes Michael will change the lyrics to what people thought they were."

—Bill Berry to *SPIN*, October 1986

JACKSON HARING: People made them into something greater than they really were. Not that what they were doing wasn't wonderful, but being in the public eye amplified what they were doing in a way. People heard Michael saying stuff that they wanted him to say.

VICTOR KRUMMENACHER: They seemed really edgy doing those songs from the album. I know Peter was uncomfortable with it and not pleased about it. He's much more a balladeer.

GEORGINA FALZARANO: When I was on the *Pageantry* tour, I saw a lot of people backstage with Michael and at that point they would get into some fairly intense political discussions. He was starting to attract more politically aware audiences by virtue of some of the places they were playing, like college campuses.

BUREN FOWLER: I started working for R.E.M. on the tour for *Lifes Rich Pageant*. They hired me to be Mike Mills' bass roadie. At the time they were going to hire a keyboard player and somebody to play rhythm guitar. They tried out some guy from New York and he didn't really work so I was at rehearsal one day and Jefferson told me they were having trouble finding a rhythm guitar player and I told him, I can play guitar. I guess he talked to the band about it and they decided to give it a try. I learned five songs, they played a show two nights later and I played acoustic twelve-string. I guess it worked out okay because Jefferson told me the next day, "You're going to do both jobs." I could hardly believe it because R.E.M. was one of my favorite bands.

DAVID ZWART [Athens musician]: The first show I decided it wasn't happening for me anymore was on the Pageantry tour. It was filled with frat guys. It was like seeing Skynyrd or something. It wasn't the same.

*"There are a lot of people who like bands when they're smaller—
and I'm one of them. I really love the Replacements, but I don't go
see them now. I saw them in front of twenty people fifty times,
and the same with Hüsker Dü. The last time I went to see Hüsker
Dü, I was like, 800 people back and getting elbowed in the gut by
a fat guy with a leather jacket. So whenever people say, 'You're
just too big, I don't enjoy going to your shows,' I say, 'That's fine.'*
—Peter Buck to *Rolling Stone*, April 20, 1989

GEORGINA FALZARANO: At that point all of their airplay was on alternative stations. It certainly wasn't mainstream radio.

BUREN FOWLER: The first show we played in Birmingham, AL I played five songs on Peter's acoustic twelve-string and my left hand hurt so bad, I couldn't make my hand move off the chords. Peter's guitar was so hard to play, but he likes it that way.

*"Peter does a lot of low, open chord strumming. The range of our
instruments all overlap. Bill's got a low voice and Michael has a bari-
tone that can go up real high and Peter uses real heavy strings and
the low end of his range just about coincides with the high end of
mine. So you do get a lot of overlapping and flowing together. I
would be bored to tears playing a regular flat bass, like basses were
until recently. I almost never play with the kick drum. We tried it
once or twice and it sounded terrible: a lot of the rhythm went away."*
—Mike Mills to *Musician*, January 1988

BRUCE MCGUIRE: I went to a few shows in a row on the Pageantry Tour. I snuck into the show at the Grand Old Opry in Nashville. It was very cool.

GEORGINA FALZARANO: I started off in Nashville, four days into the tour. I met up with Bill backstage at the Grand Old Opry and got escorted in. The original plan was to stay on for a few weeks to see how it went but I stayed on the whole tour. It was an incredible experience.

SARA BROWN: Kenny Fechtner and I went to see them at the Grand Old Opry and Peter was introducing me to everyone in the crew. You know how he exaggerates? It started out he'd known me for eight years. By that show, he was telling people he'd known me for ten years. By later that tour, he was telling people we'd known each other for fifteen years which would have made me eight years old when I was working at the record store in Asheville.

JACKSON HARING: The crew, Geoff Trump, Chris Edwards, Microwave, Curtis Goodman and Buren Fowler were all really, really nice people.

BUREN FOWLER: I played "Fall On Me," "Flowers of Guatemala," "I Believe," "Cuyahoga," and I learned a bunch of other songs in case they did them. They played with a set list, but everything changed a lot.

BRUCE MCGUIRE: The show at the Saenger Theater in New Orleans was awesome. Jackson, MS I don't even think I went to the show. I slept in the hotel room I was so exhausted. I definitely remember Mudd Island, Memphis. There's always that Mudd Island poster in psychedelic poster books. I can't imagine there are many people that have seen R.E.M. on two different islands in the middle of the Mississippi River. But I saw them on Navy Island near St. Paul as well. After that show they went to some little bar and jammed. Some band was playing and R.E.M. used their equipment and played. There were maybe 20 people there.

BUREN FOWLER: That was a really cool time for R.E.M. because they were doing really big general admission shows and a lot of bands had stopped doing general admission. It can make a concert really intense because people would fight their way to the front and you would have to fight your way just to keep your place. It could get scary. There were a lot of nights I would tune the bass, go out and play two songs, go get some guy or girl that would get thrown out of the pit, take them back, make a drink, tune a bass, go play a song, go carry some kid off the stage. It was really intense. Like one night we heard something crack and we thought it was the barricade and it turned out it was a girl's arm. It's not a lot of fun to watch that night after night.

> *"I will never, ever, ever, ever play another general-admission show, ever. Ever. And I will never, ever, ever play a place that's bigger than the place we played tonight, ever. Did I put enough evers in there?"*
> —Peter Buck to *Rolling Stone*, December 3, 1987

GEOFF GANS: It seemed like Michael and the other guys were in two different camps. I didn't even meet the rest of them till a year and a half later. But Michael and I immediately hit it off, talking about art and other things.

JACKSON HARING: At the shows you'd see what people from Athens coined followers of Michael: the Distiples. They were usually pretty, henna-haired, Chinese peasant-shoe-wearing girls. Camper Van Beethoven were probably a little easier to get to because we didn't have the pressures that R.E.M. had so a lot of these people became our friends. Next time we went to their town, we would drop in on them. R.E.M. seemed to be a catalyst for a lot of people meeting each other.

BRUCE MCGUIRE: I remember spending an evening in Memphis with Michael trying to find this cartoonist, Bob X. That was before the real explosion of underground cartoonists happened and comic books were just coming back into vogue.

STEPHANIE CHERNIKOWSKI: Michael in no way tried to hide anything about who he was from me. I'm reminded of a line by Virginia Woolf about every person being thousands of people. On the first day I met Michael he struck me as incredibly down to earth. Michael is the flower child and the elusive stage persona in moments. He's also one of the most physical people I've ever met. He's very connected to the earth for someone who is an aesthete.

WOODY NUSS: I toured with Guadalcanal Diary on R.E.M.'s 1986 tour in the West. Camper Van Beethoven did a leg, Fetchin' Bones did a leg and I think Let's Active did too. We did the Southwestern and Southern Amphitheaters. One of the best R.E.M. shows I've ever seen was in the rain in Mesa, AZ at the County Bowl. They didn't care that it was raining. They were doing a lot of songs that would be on *Document*. It was a really good tour, they were playing really well and all of the shows were sold out in nice amphitheaters. It was good to see them like that. I would see their homecoming shows at the Fox in Atlanta or University of Georgia in Athens and the shows were always kind of fucked up. They were hugely plagued by technical problems. I saw them in Piedmont Park in Atlanta and the PA cut off. At Six Flags in Atlanta the PA shut down. Plus they had a knack for hiring shitty soundmen. Guys always had excuses. They had so many bad-sounding shows, so to see them sound good was great. I didn't see them good again till they got the guy who did the *Green* World Tour [*Bruce Neese*].

GINA ARNOLD: In 1986 R.E.M. played the Greek Theatre in Berkeley and it threatened to rain all day. At 6:00 it started to pour and they weren't going to go on till 8:00. At 7:00 the band came on and said, "we can't play, we'll be electrocuted to death. We know you've been sitting here and it's such a drag but we're sorry." They played two nights later at the Oakland Coliseum. We were more bummed out that they were going to play the bigger Coliseum than we were about being soaking wet. We couldn't believe they could play a place that big, because they weren't that big then.

JACKSON HARING: It was a big thing for Camper Van Beethoven to be invited to see the show in Berkeley as guests of the band and to go backstage. No matter how insouciant and iconoclastic Camper was, we were still awed by R.E.M.'s incredible artistry and commercial success and we tried to relate to them on that level, instead of being snotty ass kids. "Ew, isn't it gross, but isn't it kind of attractive too," were the feelings we were dealing with. After the show at the Greek got rained out, our agent started to deal with their agent to sort out which leg of the tour we would go on as an opening act because Guadalcanal Diary, Fetchin Bones and the Feelies were also doing dates.

BRUCE MCGUIRE: A lot of bands got a big boost from R.E.M. Camper Van Beethoven was one of those bands. But some bands were along for the ride, like The dBs, the Neats and Fetchin' Bones and it didn't work.

JACKSON HARING: Going on tour with R.E.M. lent the band a certain prestige. But did it help us? Did it help the Feelies, Fetchin' Bones and Guadalcanal Diary? No, no, no and no.

VICTOR KRUMMENACHER: It's interesting to think whether touring with them helped us or not. When we went back to the Midwest in '87 and the areas we toured with them, it was quiet in some places, like Iowa City. I remember David Lowery saying, "we came here with R.E.M. and it didn't seem to help." I think he thought that erroneously. In places like Lincoln, NE it helped and certain college towns it helped. We were on a small label and it was hard to buy our records, so it's hard to judge. But when we went to a major label, those areas that we'd played with R.E.M. did turn out to be our strongest places.

JACKSON HARING: I was impressed with the venues R.E.M. were playing. The modern ones sucked and the older ones were incredible. It was such a pleasure to be playing in a rooms like that. I think that's where I got my first taste of the "roar of the greasepaint, the smell of the crowd" kind of stuff. Other than that, the tour was hours of boredom punctuated by moments of sheer terror.

GINA ARNOLD: I've seen R.E.M. in the little teeniest places and the biggest places possible and they are always good. I never felt they were better in a club and that it didn't translate to bigger places. They always managed to fill up whatever space they were in.

"In the old days, if I was gone for a year it meant I ate nothing but cheese sandwiches or the deli tray and slept on the floor of someone's house or in the van, or even worse, in a bed with Mike Mills. The one time you were alone was in the shower, and maybe not then: there'd be someone shaving. Five years of that and everyone was really worn out. The lack of privacy was mind-boggling."
—Peter Buck to *Q Magazine*, October 1992

GEORGINA FALZARANO: Michael was getting a little claustrophobic on the bus, so he used to ride with us a lot. Around Portland, OR, a month or so into the tour, Michael intentionally missed the bus and told the crew he would be hanging with us. Since the next day was Seattle, WA, it was fairly close so it worked out okay. Then he just kept on doing it. After three or four weeks on the road, people can get on each other's nerves a little bit, and especially with the entire band and friends on board, it got to be a bit much. The drives were long. I think he bottomed out on people. The record was getting a lot of attention and I think it had just made the charts. It was getting to be where he would come into a hotel lobby after a show and people would be waiting to take photos. He doesn't like that. Being away from the band allowed him to travel a little more incognito. By the time we got to Seattle, they had their weekly band meeting and decided that I could have a hard pass [*laminate*] for the rest of the tour. That made life very, very easy.

VICTOR KRUMMENACHER: Our manager's partner used to work for the management company that managed R.E.O. Speedwagon so we brought volumes of R.E.O. Speedwagon backstage passes and guitar picks on tour with us and terrorized R.E.M. by leaving them on their amp cases and everywhere else all of the time. Finally we were told in no uncertain terms that the band did not think the joke was funny anymore and that we should stop.

GEORGINA FALZARANO: Michael decided he was going to ride with me from Seattle, WA to Boulder, CO. It's a very long drive and the band was worried because it was so far. Bill pulled me aside and said, "There isn't anyone else we would trust him with. What will you do if something happens?" I thought like what, if the van breaks down, and he said, "What will you do?" I said, "Rent a car and get Michael to the venue?" Bill said, "Yes! Don't let him go on his own. You must make sure he gets there."

GEOFF GANS: Michael wore a Downey Mildew shirt onstage at a Universal Amphitheatre show in LA and then shortly after he told

Rolling Stone the bands to watch are Hetch Hetchy and Downey Mildew. Michael was into Downey Mildew in a generally enthusiastic way because his friend Michael Meister managed them. I don't think he ever came and saw them, but there was genuine interest. At the time, it was more about an attitude of camaraderie. If he could mention something to help someone out he would and it almost didn't matter how he really felt about it. That attitude kind of prevailed at the time. When you think about it, there is always someone Michael's trying to help out.

SARA BROWN: It was by sort of coincidence that I ended up in LA when they were playing there. Peter told me around what time to call the hotel and to use the alias he registers under. I called and asked for him and started laughing so hard when I said the name that the girl that answered the phone started laughing. We were laughing so hard we couldn't speak and finally I said, "That's not his real name" and she said, "I hope not!"

GEOFF GANS: It was strange that the band wasn't spending any time together. I heard what the band used to say about the people that hung out with Michael—they were sycophants. Michael always had weird guys hanging around. Michael Meister and I would drive him to and from gigs just so Michael could come and go as he pleased.

KEITH ALTOMARE: Chicago is probably one of the best R.E.M. markets because WXRT, the big station there, picked up on it. The first time I think R.E.M. sold out a 5000-6000 seater was the Aragon. The first time they ever played a huge stadium was there.

GIL RAY: I quit seeing them once they started playing the Hoover Domes except one time in Cleveland. We [*Game Theory*] were playing at some club and R.E.M. was playing with Richard Thompson in some huge place. Turning people on to Richard Thompson . . . who would have thought.

JACKSON HARING: I became fans of the people that influenced Peter, like Richard Thompson and Roger McGuinn of the Byrds. I know Peter is self-effacing and believes it's kismet that got him where he's at—he's incredibly humble. But his guitar playing is incredible.

VICTOR KRUMMENACHER: I think it was Peter's special request that if there was a point they could link up, they would put Richard Thompson on as an opener. We got a gig somewhere else that night. Peter has this huge Richard Thompson fixation and really wanted him to play.

GIL RAY: Our gig in Cleveland that night ended up being a post-R.E.M. party. After their show they came to see us but as usual they got there right after we finished. It seems like every time we played in Athens or Atlanta, Peter and/or Mike would come to the show but would show up right after our set.

VICTOR KRUMMENACHER: We were leaving the gig in Kansas City and we ended up catching a ride on R.E.M.'s bus. We got bogged down by a bunch of fans so Peter and I bailed on the bus and got in a car. People kept surrounding the bus and Bill got caught in the crowd and mistaken for Peter. Peter and I were sitting in a car watching this happen while all these girls swarmed around Bill yelling, "Peter, Peter, Peter, do you have a guitar pick?" Someone from our band threw him a guitar pick that said R.E.O. Speedwagon on it. So Bill was handing out guitar picks saying he was in R.E.O. Speedwagon and nobody seemed to notice because they thought he was Peter Buck anyway.

GEORGINA FALZARANO: When it came up that I might quit my job and go on the road for awhile, I let R.E.M. know and they said, "Hey that's no problem, anyone can do what they want." I ended up never paying for one show and when my van broke down on the last week of the tour, I left it in Athens and rode in their bus.

> *"This year we're more up, more confident. We had a great tour*
> *and we're writing good songs. The new LP is a show of strength,*
> *a middle finger to the business. It's like, you guys think we're*
> *some dumb art-hippies from Georgia, huh? Well, you can put us*
> *in a gross aural contest with Huey Lewis or whatever else is on*
> *the radio this week and we're gonna come out fine."*
> —Peter Buck to *Music Connection Magazine,*
> September 29-October 12, 1986

SARA BROWN: Any time I would go anywhere with Peter there was always a crowd around him. We went to see 10,000 Maniacs and Squeeze at the Fox in Atlanta because Peter wanted to see his friend Andy Metcalfe playing with Squeeze. We waited in line for our tickets and the whole time people were bugging him and then after the show we were waiting for Andy and people were bothering Peter the whole time. He was completely gracious, but finally he threw up his hands and said, "let's get out of here." As we were leaving some little cretinous guy yelled, "Michael Stipe! R.E.M.!" I remember saying something like, "I don't know how you deal with this." I never saw him lose it. He was always real polite.

JARED BAILEY: I moved away from Athens for a while, and when I came back in '86 R.E.M. were already international stars of sorts. That's when it really sunk in that there *was* something magical going on. I've seen a lot of bands and always felt there was something especially magical about R.E.M.'s shows.

KATE INGRAM: I guess you could say it was magical the way they began to evolve. Other bands might deflect that type of energy because they are fearful of it or they have ambivalence toward it. Their success wasn't without a formula, but I think the formula came by organic means. As the formula for what people liked began to get feedback, R.E.M. wasn't afraid of the power that it gave. Somehow in their stability of their line-up and in their creative work they had a confidence that wasn't very shakable. They knew when to retreat and they knew when it was time to work. But it was perfectly ok for R.E.M. to become famous.

LAUREN HALL: It wasn't a calculated plan to become successful. I think they had fun doing it, they loved it and to my knowledge they didn't plan their career steps. It built like a snowball effect. And everything they did along the way was something they wanted to do.

STEPHANIE CHERNIKOWSKI: Walking around Athens, Michael was approached by a fan who was awestruck. Michael was really unable to deal with it. It threw him. He's most likely to go into "the ethereal Michael" in that kind of situation and his friends have to ground him. People approach him as if he's Jesus and he's not. He's a wonderful man, but he ain't Jesus.

KATE INGRAM: KUSF [*University of San Francisco's radio station*] received a gold record for *Lifes Rich Pageant*. It was a thank you for all the work that preceded that record. College radio kind of turns out its successes and disavows them. But R.E.M. didn't have a hang-up about becoming successful so college radio's fickle manueverings kind of played into R.E.M.'s success. As I would watch each R.E.M. record get released, people at college radio would play them some. No one hated them or anything, but at the same time, almost no one [*at college radio*] wanted to identify with R.E.M. because it was too big and too scary and now belonged to a world they had already decided they didn't want to be a part of.

STEPHANIE CHERNIKOWSKI: I think from the Pageantry Tour, they went more pro. They hide more now. My shots were honest. To have money lavished on me as much as they did as well as the pleasure of working with them was incredible. They had total integrity and they were totally generous.

I was very fortunate to be the one that captured them at that moment when they had discovered what they wanted to project and that was a stroke of luck.

DAN WALL: R.E.M. has helped elect the present government in town, knocked the good old boy network out and put in a liberal woman. They've helped with the historical preservation of the town and advocated and practiced recycling early on.

MARC WALLACE: Michael's got so many things going on and is involved in so many organizations that I hear of a new one all of the time. He doesn't pound it into you what he does.

DEXTER WEAVER [coined the phrase "Automatic For The People"]: R.E.M. have been customers of Weaver D's Fine Foods since day one when I opened in '86. A lot of them used to come down here in their fancy cars and a lot of the staff members from the office would come. One year the staff gave me some of their T-shirts for Christmas. Back then R.E.M. was sort of Greek to me. I didn't know exactly who they was. They have a low profile that they carry and keep. Nobody would know they were real big stars. Back in '86 I don't think *Out of Time* was out so they weren't that big then. But they were great supporters of the business. And even now they are great supporters of everything that goes on in Athens whether it be new businesses or government or fundraisers. They are there.

CURTIS CROWE: They were directly responsible for my income for a couple of years just doing carpentry work for them. That house [*points to Jefferson's house*] over there got rebuilt.

LANCE SMITH: I think they own more of Athens than the Japanese own LA.

JARED BAILEY: They began to have an influence on local politics, especially Michael. They give money directly to different charities, perform for different charities and help raise awareness by speaking out about things, even locally. I think the town would still be similar if it weren't for them. It's still a college town. There'd still be bands coming out of it, it just wouldn't be as world renowned.

1987-88

1987

Document sessions at Sound Emporium, Nashville

February — *Athens,GA-Inside/Out* film and soundtrack

April — *Dead Letter Office*: Compilation of b-sides

August — *Document*, produced by Scott Litt & R.E.M. This time the spine reads "File Under Fire," due to multiple references to it on the album. The final release for IRS yielded the band's first top ten hit, "The One I Love," and was the beginning of a long liaison with producer Litt.

Seven-inch Singles

August — "The One I Love"/"Maps and Legends" (live)

Twelve-inch Singles

September — "The One I Love"/"The One I Love" (live)/ "Maps and Legends" (live). Recorded at McCabe's.

Videos

"The One I Love," directed by Robert Longo

Television and Film Appearances

Michael Stipe makes his acting debut in a short film, *Arena Brains*, by artist Robert Longo

Select Guest Appearances

Berry/Buck/Mills contribute the instrumental tracks to *Sentimental Hygiene* by Warren Zevon and Stipe adds vocals to "Bad Karma"

Stipe and Natalie Merchant sing "A Campfire Song" from *In My Tribe*, 10,000 Maniacs

Peter Buck appears on Robyn Hitchcock's *Globe of Frogs*

1988

Seven-inch Singles

January — "Its the End of the World As We know It (and I Feel Fine)"/"Last Date"

December — "Parade of the Wooden Soldiers"/"See No Evil" (fan club only)

Twelve-inch Singles

March — "Finest Worksong"(lengthy club mix)/"Finest Worksong" (other mix)/"Time After Time" etc. (live)

Videos

"Its The End of The World As We Know It (And I Feel Fine)," directed by James Herbert

"Finest Worksong," directed by Michael Stipe

June — *R.E.M. Succumbs*: Video compilation plus James Herbert's short film, *Left of Reckoning*

Television and Film Appearances

Athens, GA-Inside/Out feature film: Performances of "(All I've Got To Do Is) Dream" and "Swan Swan H"

Select Guest Appearances

Michael Stipe adds vocals, instruments and produces *Drum* by Hugo Largo

Touring

Work Tour, September through November

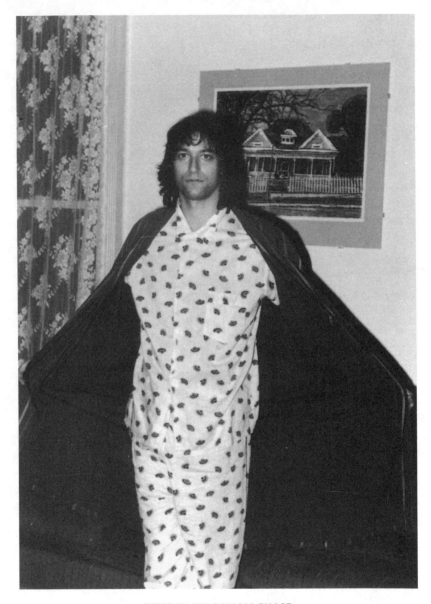

PETER IN HIS PAJAMA-PHASE
(*photo by Georgina Falzarano*)

7

DOCUMENT

LANCE SMITH: I met Bill Cody who produced *Athens,GA-Inside/Out* while he was working on post production. I couldn't believe he would attempt to make a movie about that scene. First of all the Flat Duo Jets did not belong in the movie. They were musical carpetbaggers who moved there 'cause it was a scene. By that time the scene was jaded and pretentious and people were trying to cash in on it. It seemed like what it must have been like in San Francisco after the Dead and the Jefferson Airplane and Quicksilver had their success and then all these people moved there trying to be in bands. All of a sudden it wasn't as genuine anymore. The film was presented as "Athens—a community of friends," and I thought he really missed the point. People say the Seattle bands are all friends but it wasn't like that in Athens at all. Athens is much too bitchy for that.

BILL CODY [producer, *Athens, GA-Inside/Out*]: I wanted to remake a movie by Errol Morris called *Vernon, Florida*. Basically, the premise was to make a film about strange people in the South and to do it with music. The most eligible town at the time was Athens.

ARMISTEAD WELLFORD: The greatest time here was from '77-'81. That was when you would have liked to have had a camera rolling. Everyone was so young and everything was really new and different. Most of the bands that made it into the film aren't around anymore. They just clicked on a camera and those bands happened to be there. They never even talked about the Side Effects.

LANCE SMITH: I asked someone that lived in Athens at the time what Peter's problem was, wearing his pajamas in that movie. He said that was his new thing, wearing pajamas the whole time.

ARMISTEAD WELLFORD: When Pete says in that movie, "I realized you didn't have to be like Styx or Journey to be in a band," it's so funny. That's the perfect description of what it was really about in the early days. No one ever wanted to play lead guitar. It was a silly thing. Lead was over.

BILL CODY: Initially, R.E.M. agreed to be interviewed in the film, but did not want to be in the film. Then it was going to be Michael and Peter playing and eventually we got all four of them. I think Michael was interested in what we were doing. He was pretty excited about not only being involved in the making of a film, but I got the impression he was excited about some of the concepts we wanted to use. It was based on an art concept that if you throw a lot of ideas in, almost like a collage, you will get a better perception of the whole. He seemed to understand what we were doing much more so than anybody else. We were doing strange interviews that didn't seem to have any linear concept. In film at the time, you didn't see a lot of people being interviewed on camera while the interviewer was off camera. I liked what Erroll Morris was doing in his films in that you would see the people talking and then the way the interviews were put together made his statement. That's what we were trying to do.

LANCE SMITH: Love Tractor was pretty pissed about that movie because I think the only reason they agreed to be in it was if R.E.M. weren't in it then they went ahead and put R.E.M. in it. Everybody thought the guy who made the movie was a pretty out-there guy anyway.

ARMISTEAD WELLFORD: They approached us to be in the film first. I guess they were Love Tractor fans. But I don't remember being disappointed that R.E.M. was in it. R.E.M. wasn't into the idea at first, so when they decided to be in it I guess it made it into a bigger film for the filmmakers. R.E.M. would *have* to be in it. There's no way they could make a movie here and not have R.E.M. in it!

BILL CODY: I am proud of the way that film turned out. I don't know too much about the reactions people in Athens had. I heard people weren't happy about it. I certainly hope it's not true, but there isn't much I can do about that. The film does real well as a cult film. I've gotten positive reactions from people myself. Some people have actually had parties and shown it where they've memorized lines and recited them.

LANCE SMITH: By the time *Athens, GA-Inside/Out* came out, Athens had fallen in on itself. The second generation of Athens bands found out about the scene from reading about it in the New York Rocker. They thought they should be playing to Chapel Hill in front of 2000 people too. The third generation of bands was even lamer than the second.

BRIAN CRANE: There was really a lot of tension and I kind of disliked all the attention that was focused on Athens. Probably a lot of the reason the type of music that comes out of here and the amount of music that comes out of here is because people don't judge what you do. They just try to accept it. When you get a lot of outside attention focused on it, that stops happening and people start deciding who is better than who and it leads to a lot of bullshit that I don't really like.

ARMISTEAD WELLFORD: The B-52's inspired the first generation of Athens bands to get out there and do it but other people were feeling that way about R.E.M. for sure.

> *"In a way, the success we've had has left this horrid taint over bands in town because you can't ignore that we're getting recognition. But with these new bands, I would hope that their priorities would be to get together and create a sound that really moves them, and the rest would follow later."*
> —Michael Stipe to *XTRA*, June 1985

JARED BAILEY: Athens certainly wouldn't have the worldwide reputation that it has if it weren't for R.E.M. We're still having bands signed from here to major labels to this day.

BUREN FOWLER: Curtis Goodman, who worked for R.E.M. for a long time, knew he had cancer. About halfway through the Pageantry tour, he started getting sick and he needed to do something about it. When the tour was over, Curtis was going through chemotherapy, so I kind of started working for the band when we were off the road too. When you work for a band, there's always something to do. In March we went to Nashville to begin recording *Document*.

WOODY NUSS: When they were in Nashville making the first record with Scott Litt, I was on tour with Love Tractor and we all went to breakfast. Mark Cline [*Love Tractor*] said something like, "Has Tammy Wynette come by to visit y'all in the studio?" and Michael was like, "She and George Jones were recording in the next room and she stopped over and said she liked the drum sounds." We got back in the van and I said, "That's really cool that George Jones and Tammy

I.R.S.

INTERNATIONAL RECORD SYNDICATE, INC.

May 21, 1986

To: CARL
Fr: RON
Re: R.E.M. LP label

Michael has asked if it is possible for R.E.M. to have a special 1/color label on the record. How do you feel about this?

Thanks,

Ron

JAY?

No

IRS label only.

Next he'll not want the man on package at all.

LOS ANGELES 100 UNIVERSAL CITY PLAZA, UNIVERSAL CITY, CA 91608 • 818/508-4730
NEW YORK   445 PARK AVENUE, 6TH FLOOR, NEW YORK, NY 10022 • 212/605-0601
CHICAGO   10700 W HIGGINS RD. SUITE 100, ROSEMONT, IL 60018 • 312/298-6600
DALLAS   6311 N. O'CONNOR, SUITE 201, IRVING, TX 75039 • 214/556-2002
         LONDON   **PARIS**   **TORONTO**

THIS CORRESPONDENCE PROBABLY NEVER MADE IT TO STIPE

Wynette were there," and Cline was like, "You idiot, can't you tell when Michael is putting you on?" No, I can't.

BUREN FOWLER: In Nashville, I lived in a room with Curtis. Peter and Michael moved into a house and Bill and Mike moved into a condo and they made the record at the Sound Emporium. The way they write songs is almost unorthodox. Peter will come in with two guitar chords and start strumming them. Mike will play keyboards. Then they would make a tape on a boom box and give Michael the tape.

GEOFF GANS: I worked at IRS around the time *Document* came out. The photo on the cover of is a double exposure polaroid taken by Michael Meister of Michael Stipe in his backyard. The actual photo was stolen at one point while the IRS art department was working on the cover. At least on the first ep it might've been true that Michael Stipe didn't have a lot of creative input on the sleeve, but after that there was definitely strong collaboration from Michael on everything.

Sometimes files and things would get thrown out and eventually I went through some old stuff gathering things up to return to them. I found a lot of the old pieces that Michael had worked on back and forth with the art department at IRS.

BUREN FOWLER: I had just found two really old Lightnin' Hopkins records and one was called *Lightnin' Hopkins' Greatest Country Hits*. It had a picture of a white guy with a flannel shirt on and I brought it to practice. Michael picked up the record and said, "wasn't Lightnin' Hopkins black?" He put that record on the floor and came in and wrote the song "Lightnin' Hopkins" that day.

"I don't mean to sound high and mighty, 'cause it's not a perfect album. It's flawed of course, as is every record that we've ever put out, as is everything I'll ever work on. I'll never achieve my idea of perfection. But who's to say that's an end in itself? Part of what we are and what we represent is that we're just doing what we do and we split ourselves wide open for anyone and everyone to come grow with us or reject us. I would prefer people love us or hate us. It's the ones in between, the ones who can't make up their mind. Purgatory to me or anyone who makes something to give to other people would be to always have people be nonchalant about it: 'Well, it's okay . . .' I would like people to really react to it. That's why I'm doing it."
—Michael Stipe to *Musician*, January 1988

GEOFF GANS: R.E.M. were in LA because they were working on mixing the record. While they were in town, Texas Records sponsored an all-acoustic show at McCabe's. The night before the show we were having dinner and it was a very festive occasion. Natalie Merchant, Downey Mildew and Michael were going to practice. I wasn't going to participate, I was just going to tape the show. The year before I taped a show in Santa Barbara where they played "The One I Love," so I knew the song and as a joke I started to play it on the guitar. Michael was really surprised that I knew the songs. He said, "We just finished recording it. You know, it would be so funny if tomorrow night before the band comes onstage, I say I'm going to have my friend Geoff come on and we play a song." We did it a couple of times but I thought it would never happen because it was such a big deal show and I was going to be busy working there. I thought it would be really cool, but there was a *lot* of stuff talked about that night . . . That next night at McCabe's everyone was waiting upstairs to go on. I think Michael did one song with David Roback [*Opal, Mazzy Star*] and then said, "I'm going to do a song with a friend." Peter starts walking onstage, right by me, and I'm holding a guitar. Michael says, "My friend Geoff is going to come on." We played a really haunting, slow and quiet version of "The One I Love." I came off stage and Peter looked at me like, gasping and Jefferson couldn't believe it.

GINA ARNOLD: The rank and file critics kind of ignored R.E.M. until "The One I Love." Everybody praised that song and then the mainstream was on it.

> *"I've been announcing at shows that I wrote it to myself, because it's such an incredibly violent song, perhaps the most violent song I've ever written. It's very very brutal. I almost didn't want to put it on the record. I thought it was too much. 'Harborcoat' and 'Laughing' were violent and brutal, but they're both so internal and folded in on themselves that no one would ever pick up on that except as a general gut feeling. 'The One I Love' is lyrically very straightforward. It's very clear that it's about using people over and over again. I think that's probably a sentiment everyone has felt at one time or another, so you can apply it to yourself. But it's not an attractive quality."*
> —Michael Stipe to *Musician*,
> January 1988

GEOFF GANS: The whole "The One I Love" scenario was a very Stipe-type thing. "Another prop to occupy my time," using people, meeting

others and moving on. I think that
was the only time Michael came
clean about one of his personality
traits. It was true. People who had
known him in his artist days told
me he stole ideas and then went off
and did his own thing.

WOODY NUSS: I think the "fire"
stuff in "The One I Love" has to do
with the fire at Tyrone's. The song
"Burning Hell," obviously has to
do with fire and that could be about

Tyrone's. But in the video for "The One I Love," the fire starts with a
spark and that's the way it started at Tyrone's.

> *"The whole album is about fire. About everything you think about*
> *fire as being cleansing, something that destroys everything in its*
> *path. It's an element that's everywhere, the metaphorical and alle-*
> *gorical interpretations of 'Fire' are endless."*
> —Michael Stipe to *Musician*, January 1988

BUREN FOWLER: They got done with the record, came home and we
made "The One I Love" video. Curtis was really sick by then. He was
going for chemotherapy once a month and he'd lost all his hair. He
made it into the video [*seated next to Jefferson in courtroom scene*]. In fact,
just about everyone that was anywhere near that video was in it except
for me!

GEOFF GANS: I just recorded the version of "The One I Love" that we
did at McCabe's on cassette and we didn't think anything was going to
come of it. Six months later Michael called me up and asked if he could
use it as a b-side [*to "The One I Love" twelve-inch*] and I said of course.

BUREN FOWLER: Curtis was telling everybody that he was going to be
okay, but I knew he was dying. I was falling apart because he was the
greatest guy that ever lived. I called him "Little Big Man" because all
he cared about was other people. The last thing he did before he was
hospitalized for the last time was the "Its The End of The World . . ."
video, with Michael, Michael Lachowski and Jim Herbert. He was
really weak and getting headaches and taking morphine. I kept asking
him if he was okay but he said he really wanted to make that video.

KATHLEEN O'BRIEN: The way Michael sings certain songs like, "Its The End Of The World (As We Know It)", it's just a bunch of phrases and it describes what he's talking about. It's not like you understand everything that's being said but it tells a little story and it's over. Probably in Michael's heart of hearts he felt like he was selling out when he had to have intelligible and narrative lyrics. But he's gotten around that very well. Some of the best nursery rhymes don't make any sense. It's the sounds and it's the words and how they appeal to the ear. I think Michael always had a grip on that. He's the kind of artist who is an anti-artist. He is so internalized about his art form that he wants to keep it for himself even though it's out there for the world to pick apart.

BUREN FOWLER: R.E.M. went to Europe and did a three-week tour. They took Microwave and this other guy and I ended up getting left at home after I'd done all this work preparing them for it. But Michael told me later that they wanted me to stay home and be with Curtis. When they got back, we went to Knoxville and started rehearsing for the U.S. tour, and Curtis died the day before the first show of the tour in Knoxville.

KEITH ALTOMARE: I will always remember this as long as I'm in the record industry and even after, but I watched a band grow up. The last tour with them wasn't so nice because there were so many people in between me and the band and my heart was broken. I thought I was closer to them and I wasn't. You had to have "x" amount of laminates to get into a room and another number of laminates to get into another room where I used to be able to go, "hey, it's Keith, let me in." But we used to have a great time talking about baseball or women or music or old movies. Anything outside of "gee I really like your new record." I loved them and their music so much, yet I understood my place. Even when my heart was broken, I realized, I was the label and there's that division. You can be loved by someone, but you're still the label.

> *"I realized last year that people were paying $16.50 to see something. There's some songs I can't sing unless I move, I literally can't hit the notes unless I'm moving. I always paint my eyebrows. I'm big on eyebrows. It's vaudeville, it's Dickensian, it's a comedy of errors, it's entertainment."*
> —Michael Stipe to *Musician*,
> January 1988

ROBERT LLOYD: The only thing that changed my feelings about them which have since been revised was on the *Document* tour I thought they were incredibly boring and at a show at the Universal Amphitheatre Michael was unbelievably rude to the audience. He said things like, "Last night we played in Irvine and that audience was *really* lame." He was hostile in a surprising way that I would never expect from the band. Coupled with the fact they weren't playing very well, I ended up writing nearly a whole column about it in the LA Weekly. Michael may have been reacting to the phenomenon that suddenly a whole bunch of people were into the band, but he wouldn't necessarily want to sit down and have dinner with all of them. Anytime you do something in public you run that risk.

VICTOR KRUMMENACHER: After the tour we did with them, we got to Athens and they treated us like it was no big deal. There was all this internal weirdness with us because some people in Camper Van Beethoven felt that every time we went back to Athens, R.E.M. should be at our gigs. I thought it was fair that they didn't show up. As nice as they were to us and to me personally, there was always some wariness from them, maybe because of something that our manager had said to *Musician* magazine. But I think that's the way they conduct themselves around people. They are very reserved.

> "At some of the gigs we made $500 and at some we made $1000. I found out halfway through the show that they were budgeted for $1000 every night, and I got all pissed off and made some accusations. [R.E.M. was] making $10,000 guarantees plus points, they were taking in 30 grand a night. And granted, they had to spend a lot of it, too, but why cut our quarter?"
>
> —Jackson Haring to *Musician*,
> August 1988

> "Of course there was never any attempt to screw CVB out of any money—it's simply preposterous. I think most people who know R.E.M. know that we try real hard to make things go well for our support acts—financially and otherwise. We really enjoyed working with CVB and I'm really bummed out that they remember things this way."
>
> —Jefferson Holt to *Musician*,
> August 1988

JACKSON HARING: Gina Arnold wrote a piece for *Musician* about hardworking-touring bands and she asked me how R.E.M. treated Camper Van Beethoven on the road. I flashed on a moment at one of the shows when one of the promoters said to me, "Hey, Jackson, what's going on here? The budget shows that the support act gets $1,000 but you guys are only getting $500. What's the deal?" And I was like, "uh, I don't know." I was a little freaked out about it because we were worth a grand. We didn't have a label to give us tour support. We had eight people in a van and we were trying to keep pace with R.E.M., with their busses and trucks. But now I understand that they were trying to cut costs and that was one of them. It had nothing to do with the band. They have a firm grasp of their career, but that's just a line item on a budget somewhere. For our stature at the time, $1000 would have been right and in smaller venues $500 would have been appropriate but maybe our agent didn't think we could get that kind of money. So when Gina asked me how it went, I said, "R.E.M. kind of screwed us," not differentiating between band, management, agents and all the other people who represent a band. I know I should have been more explicit about that, but to a certain degree you can't divorce yourself from the people that work for you. I erred, but no one had ever explained things to me at the outset.

Nowadays, no one would care how much they were paid as an opening act. The promotional benefit of getting on a big tour is greater than the amount of money a band is being paid to perform.

BUREN FOWLER: I don't think R.E.M. ever took any tour support from their record company or publishing advances. They were paying me just enough for the job I was doing and then I would have to run to the next job. They earned money at their own speed and were very smart with their money.

GEOFF GANS: A lot of times I'd see Peter in town and he would act like he didn't know me. But sometimes he would. He was very on/off.

KEN FECHTNER: In about '87 I met Peter one time in Pittsburgh so we could shop for records. They have some great singles there. I took him to this great record store that had three rooms filled with great picture sleeve singles like old Byrds and a rare Derek and the Dominoes single. He walked in, stopped a couple of seconds and said, "oh my God, I just forgot the name of every single I'm looking for." We spent about three hours in there.

*"I'm not one of those anal types of collectors though that wants
every different matrix number. I've got about four or five thousand LPs and ten thousand singles but it's not like I keep them in
plastic or anything. I play records at parties when I'm drunk."*
                    —Peter Buck to the *Rocket*, October 1986

SARA BROWN: Some of my best memories are parties at Peter's house
till five or six in the morning and him doing his dj show. He turned me
on to some of the neatest stuff. There was a song called "Terrible Boots"
that I really liked and this really killer gospel song by King Hannibal
about heroin and a steel band doing Jackson Five songs. He always had
the most eclectic taste in music of anyone I've met so far. He'd run over
to the turntable, put a record on, and in the first few strains he'd be
dancing then he'd go sit down, talkin' music then he'd jump up again,
running through forty-fives, spinning discs and dancing. He's thor-
oughly entertaining. I imagine if you lived with him it would get old,
but it was definitely fun for beginners.

GEOFF GANS: When I became friends with Michael, people would
warn me that they remembered when they were friends with him three
or four years ago and that he wouldn't even talk to them now. People
who had worked closely with him as photographers and others . . .
Basically, it didn't concern me at the time.

GINA ARNOLD: R.E.M. was the first band I ever interviewed for a daily
newspaper, the San Jose Mercury News. It went really well, it was a
great interview, I had a great time, I wrote the piece quickly and the
paper loved it. In that way, R.E.M. really helped me in my career. Their
publicist at IRS was really sharp and said to me, "if you can get the story
in a major paper, I'll let you interview them." Five years and five records
later, I'm in Los Angeles working for the LA Times. R.E.M. came to town
and I was so upset because I had to review James Taylor the first night
they were playing. I asked the same publicist who set up the interview
for me if I could go the next night and he said, "You're not reviewing
it, Robert Hilburn is, so I don't want to give you tickets."

I lost my mind. I told him he'd better do something because I
worked for the Times, he couldn't just say "No, I can't have tickets." He
finally relented and gave me one. I was so sad because I couldn't bring
a guest. I drove all the way from Orange County to the Universal
Amphitheatre and I sat alone, with no one in the empty seat next to me.
I loved R.E.M. and I had worked so hard for R.E.M. and the minute this
publicist had any power—perhaps because it was the week "The One I

Love" went into the Top Ten—they started to move away. And I was convinced that's what happens when bands get popular. It made me question a lot of things. Like why did I work so hard to become a critic at the LA Times if I can't even get on the guest list to see R.E.M.? It says nothing about R.E.M. who had no idea what was going on, but more about the record industry and that turning point in 1987 when alternative began to go mainstream. I didn't think R.E.M. owed me anything, but it hurt my feelings. I still love them dearly, but it's the kind of thing that happens when bands get big.

KATE INGRAM: Whenever you see fame you also see this kind of bitterness that goes on around it because not everyone can have it. It's sort of the nature of fame, that's what makes it special.

GEOFF GANS: People I didn't even know would come up to me and ask me stuff about Michael. I could see how that could make a person paranoid. In a way, I felt like myself and others acted as body guards for Michael. After shows we would wait for him to sign autographs and then he would say, "Ok, walk me away from here."

STEVE WYNN: I think if you talk to R.E.M., Soul Asylum, myself or Green on Red or any number of bands that came out of the early Eighties, I think when we saw our first records in the store that was like a dream come true in itself. When any of us had a taste of "this could be the big time," it was kind of scary, and it brought a whole new set of pressures. Everyone was affected by it. It broke us up. It changed bands like Bangles and True West. The Replacements went through it later on, but I think it ultimately broke them up. I'm sure R.E.M. was affected by that pressure but they managed to survive by continuously doing the right thing. They grew just enough and a lot of bands can't do that. Even if you say, "We don't care," like R.E.M. did and Nirvana did, it's still a response to success.

BUREN FOWLER: I was playing a lot more, anywhere from 10-15 songs a night. Part way through that tour, I met Drivin' n' Cryin' in St. Louis. They came to a show and gave Peter a copy of *Whisper Tames The Lion*. On the drive from St. Louis to San Francisco (which took two days), I stayed up all night and learned the songs on that Drivin' n' Cryin' record. At the end of that eight and a half or nine week tour, when we got home, R.E.M. were going to take a break and they weren't going to need me to work. They were going to keep me on a small retainer. The last night of the tour, I was talking to someone about what my plans were and Peter was sitting right behind me. I said, Drivin' n' Cryin' might need a rhythm guitar player and Peter said, "do it, do it, do it." The last R.E.M. show was two days after Thanksgiving and I played my first Drivin' n' Cryin' show December 7. R.E.M. paid me enough money and kept me on health insurance for a year while I played with Drivin' n' Cryin'.

RUSS TOLMAN: The image of R.E.M., and I think it's true, is that they are a democracy. That's so rare for that to work. Most of the time when you *attempt* a democracy, there are four different guys going four different ways.

DON DIXON: The democratic aspects of the band are hard to discount as a reason for success. They are an incredibly sensitive bunch. Their ability to fight through serious differences of opinions and problems and stay together for obviously more than financial reasons is laudable. A lot of bands implode under the power of one individual—not everyone can hold their own—but not them.

GEOFF GANS: I went to Athens before they were mega-stars in '88 and Michael's car had been vandalized a week before by some jocks. There was definitely some "where you going hippie boy," kind of attitude toward Michael. When we were downtown, there were two sides—the friendly people and the not-so-friendly. People would drive by his house and yell shit. I guess that's the point where people started to become bothersome.

DAN WALL: I think they are basically hometown boys. They didn't get big headed when they got famous. Just the fact they stayed and didn't move is to their credit.

GEOFF GANS: The inside of Michael's house was kind of stark. One of the rooms was his bedroom, with a mattress on the floor and stuff around, paintings and sculptures. Mostly weird shit, like two or three of his paintings that I thought were unfinished but he told me they were finished. One room just had a bunch of cassettes piled on the floor. He knew I was into tapes and I told him I would organize his tapes for him. He thought that was really funny and called me the "Tape queen." Another room where I stayed was totally empty. The happening areas were the patio and the kitchen.

LAUREN HALL: The band decided to settle in Athens because they liked it and it was fun. I don't know that it's like that now. I think it's gotten very difficult for them to live there. But it was once a nice little small place to come home to after a gruelling tour. Early on, when they would come home from a tour, we would pile into someone's car and all go to the drive-in movies. Where else can you do that? I don't know of too many places anymore that you can.

GEOFF GANS: One night Michael did this really amazing thing. He invited a bunch of people over and we read his fan mail.

CURTIS CROWE: They actually read all of their fan letters and respond to a huge percentage of them. That's quite a feat. It's hard work keeping up.

GEOFF GANS: Everyone there that night got to open up a fan letter and read it. It was kinda weird. Michael read one from a woman in Europe who had sent a bar of chocolate with the letter and we all split the chocolate and ate it while he read the letter. He wasn't making fun of anybody, but it was a weird thing. I got the feeling he was getting off on it more than anyone.

ROBERT LLOYD: Any band's success is due to a mixture of elements that are totally uncontrollable and unpredictable. That's why you can't make another Beatles. There's been enough history that you'd think you could feed all of the information into a computer and it would tell you all of the elements that are necessary for success but it can't be done. The audience is unpredictable and the spirit of the times moves on in an unpredictable way and at a steady rate. You need the right time, the right people, the right sound.

JACKSON HARING: As a young person getting into the business, you hear all these stories of how fucked the music business is so you expect the worst and you go looking for it and create it. I learned from R.E.M.'s people that you could be professional, courteous and nice and pleasant. That was the biggest lesson I learned. You don't have to be a dick to get stuff done. I was desperately looking for a mentor in Jefferson. At that point I really needed hands-on direction as a manager. I had the vision, but I needed to learn the nuts and bolts of the business. Geoff Trump [*tour accountant and aide-de-camp*] was especially helpful to me as an inexperienced manager. If I wanted to see what the gross receipts for a night were, he'd show them to me. Anything that I wanted to know wasn't held back from me. Everything I wanted to know I learned from those people. I wish I'd learned more.

STEVE WYNN: I saw no evidence of Jefferson's influence at all. I think all four of them understand the underground and the mainstream very well and wanted more or less the same things from them.

KEITH ALTOMARE: Sometimes you see bands that are being aimed at college and you know they don't want to be there, they want to be doing bigger things. But R.E.M. was never like that. It amazed me when they started to hit millions of units in record sales how Peter could say something in print about being a "struggling artist," and people would really go along with it. It is what Peter felt inside. Externally he's got plenty of cash, but the people who grew up with them still related to him as a struggling artist. R.E.M. seemed to be happy and satisfied with being at college radio. It was everyone else who forced them to the next level.

1988-89

1988

Green recording sessions, Ardent Studios, Memphis and Bearsville Studios, Bearsville, NY

October 3 — *Eponymous*: Greatest album tracks

October 13 — Live satellite presentation of the *Green* album to Warner Brothers personnel

November 8 — *Green*, produced by Scott Litt & R.E.M. The first album in a multi-million dollar pact with Warner Brothers, *Green* had fans and critics reading the title as a self-effacing jab at newfound wealth. It was in fact a plea to continue to consider the environment. The album yielded one top ten hit with "Stand."

1989

Seven-inch Singles

February — "Stand"/"Memphis Train Blues"

May — "Pop Song '89"/"Pop Song" (acoustic)

September — "Get Up"/"Funtime"

November — "Dark Globe" *Sassy Magazine* flexi-disc

— Box set, *Singleactiongreen,* including all picture sleeve singles from *Green*

December — "Good King Wenceslas"/"Academy Fight Song" (fan club only)

CD Singles

February — "Stand"/"Memphis Train Blues"

Videos

"Talk About The Passion," directed by Jem Cohen. First project for C-00, Michael Stipe's film company, to coincide with *Eponymous* release.

Green promo video for Warner Brothers

"Orange Crush," directed by Matt Mahurin

"Stand," directed by Katherine Dieckmann

"Pop Song 89," directed by Michael Stipe

"Turn You Inside Out," directed by James Herbert

"Get Up," directed by Eric Darnell

Film and Television Appearances

Greenpeace Promo, *Its The End Of The World As We Know It*

A Time For Action/Agent Orange PSA with "Orange Crush"

Rockumentary, MTV

"Stand" and "Get Up" live performances on *Arsenio Hall Show*

Select Guest Appearances

Peter Buck appears on Robyn Hitchcock's *Queen Elvis*

Nigel and The Crosses (Peter Buck and Robyn Hitchcock) "Wild Mountain Thyme" on *Time Between—A Tribute To The Byrds*

Peter Buck contributes electric dulcimer to *Mystery Road* by Drivin' n' Cryin'

Berry/Buck/Mills/Stipe all appear on *Indigo Girls* debut

Michael Stipe adds vocals to "Little April Shower" on *Stay Awake*, a tribute to Disney film music

Stipe co-writes and performs "Future 40's (String of Pearls)" with Syd Straw on *Surprise* and appears in video

Bill Berry releases "My Bible is the Latest TV Guide"/"Things I'd Like to Say" under the name 13111 on Dog Gone, Jefferson Holt's label

Awards/Recognition

Murmur was 58 in *Rolling Stone* Poll of the 100 Best Albums of The Eighties

Rolling Stone proclaimed R.E.M., "America's Best Rock and Roll Band"

GREEN WORLD TOUR, 1989
(photo © Ebet Roberts 1992)

8

GREEN

GINA ARNOLD: There wasn't a lot of suddenness to R.E.M.'s success. It was a steady rise. They weren't huge till their sixth record. Their rise was more like a 45 degree angle. Bands like the Meat Puppets and the Replacements would play the same small club year after year while R.E.M. very quickly were playing in theatres.

STEVE WYNN: You can rebel against fame or try to deal with it. I don't think they really dealt with it till *Green*.

LANCE SMITH: It's been interesting to watch them capture a whole new audience without losing their core audience.

> *"In our own case, R.E.M. is always trying to figure out where the line between 'commerce' and what we do because it means something to us. We tend to bend over backwards to avoid commercial moves because we're afraid of diluting the essence of the band, but we also realize that we're part of the machine. Like many other bands, we started out doing something we love, learned that it could be something that makes money, and now we have to decide what the difference is between doing it for its own sake and doing it because it's a potentially profitable career."*
> —Peter Buck penned article in the *Record*, October 1984

KEITH ALTOMARE: When they left IRS I wanted to hate them like you wouldn't believe—not because they went to Warners because I think in the back of my mind, it was the right move for them. IRS didn't have the money to take them to the next level. I was hurt that they weren't really talking to me or relating to me and I had put a lot of energy into their careers. I just wanted them to recognize me.

LANCE SMITH: They got out of IRS and that was a great move. They appeared to be pretty happy there, but I heard it was hard for them to get their records distributed throughout Europe so that's why they decided to leave.

KEITH ALTOMARE: I don't think *Eponymous* was intentionally released to deflect attention from *Green's* release, but as I recall, they gave us the opportunity to do that. It may have been a ploy on IRS' part to ride on the coattails of *Green* to schedule it within about a month of *Green's* release, but that would be the policy at most labels and I don't think it detracts from either record.

GEOFF GANS: At the time Jay Boberg at IRS didn't want to put out *Eponymous* with the picture of Michael in high school and the type that said, "they airbrushed my face." But that was totally something Michael wanted on there. It was all his vision, putting the wheatfield and the big ugly thing in front of it [*on the cover*]. Originally it was going to have everybody's childhood photos on it, but no one else was willing to do it.

Somehow the rumor got started that R.E.M. was really mad about the album cover, especially that photo.

GEORGINA FALZARANO: When you are in the public eye as R.E.M. is, the rumors start up. Does this person have too much power? Should we nip it in the bud? That's when the backlash begins. It's a hard job.

GINA ARNOLD: I never felt a backlash against them for moving to a bigger label. I think they lucked out because IRS was such a transitional label. It wasn't like being on Homestead or SST. I always thought it was because of IRS' association with the Police and bands like the English Beat. They were *really* big bands, so R.E.M. going to Warners didn't seem like a big deal or as big a deal as when the Replacements or Hüsker Dü went to Warners.

KEITH ALTOMARE: We were a decent record company at the time, but they needed so much more. They needed two or three singles in the top ten.

BUREN FOWLER: The Drivin' n' Cryin' tour ended in Memphis two days after R.E.M. started recording *Green* there so I got dropped off in

Memphis. Microwave was there and they just didn't need me. I was talking to Michael and he said, "What are your plans?" and I said, "I really should be playing in Drivin' n' Cryin" and he said, "Yea." I went out to eat with Peter one night and we were both drinking a lot because we were both really nervous. We were drinking double screwdrivers at 4:00 on a Sunday in this Cajun restaurant and he was like, "Well, uh . . . well," I had hinted around to his wife that I might want to keep playing with Drivin' n' Cryin' so I thought he knew what I was about to say. I went to the bathroom and looked in the mirror and said to myself, just look him in the eye and say, "I think I really need to be playing with Drivin' n' Cryin' and not working with R.E.M. Y'all don't really need me." I walk out to the table and he says, "Man, we've been talking and on the next tour, we might want you to play a little mandolin or bass and you might have to play a lot more guitar and we might need to buy you a new amp. I don't know if you'll have time to be on the crew." I was like, "Uh, ok." I didn't know what to do. I talked to Michael and Jefferson that night and told them I think I really need to leave. Peter came up to me the next day and said, "Hey man, you really need to be playing with Drivin' n' Cryin'."

ARMISTEAD WELLFORD: One time Love Tractor played in Memphis when R.E.M. was recording there. Michael was out on the floor dancing to our stuff. When we see each other in another town, it's like "It's so good to see you, we're brothers" but then when we're at home, we don't see each other.

KATE INGRAM: I was approached by some movie producers to put together a soundtrack album. They brought in a director who was totally enamored of R.E.M. and I think had an agenda before he even started working on the movie to do something which would include R.E.M. He wanted to make it like *The Graduate* was to Simon and Garfunkel, this movie would be to R.E.M. They were recording *Green* in Woodstock, NY and so the director and I went up there to stay with Kate Pierson. It was more like a social visit, but we went to the studio where R.E.M. was recording one night. They seemed to have a laid back approach to recording at Bearsville Studios. I think Michael liked the idea of the film, but he had some reservations and I think the rest of the band did too.

JARID NEFF: I joined this golf course and the pro found out I worked for a record company. Every Saturday someone would come up to me and go, "I hear you work for a record company. My son's got a band, here's a tape." Of course they all sucked. [*One day*] an older gentleman comes up to me and says, "I hear you work for a record company" and I'm thinking to myself, here we go again. He says, "My son's in a band, you might know him." I'm like, "Uh . . . what band?" and he says, "R.E.M." And I go, "That's nice." I figure someone put him up to it, so I was kind of rude to him and I go, "Nice talking to you. See ya." A few more months go by and we sign R.E.M. There was a party in Athens to celebrate and the Presidents of Warner Brother's, Lenny Waronker and Mo Ostin, were there. We were sitting in this restaurant in an old hotel that the band likes a lot and someone mentioned golf. I ask Mike Mills if his dad played golf and he said, "Yea, he belongs to a country club in Atlanta called Metropolitan." That's the place I play and it *was* his father. The next time I saw him, Mr. Mills senior said, "Thanks a lot. I just want to let you know, you made my son a millionaire."

BRUCE MCGUIRE: There was unbelievable anticipation at Warners before *Green* came out. It was really exciting. I got the impression that the band was keeping a low profile throughout it all because they wanted the music to speak for itself. I loved how they didn't have any comment for about a year. It wasn't important that they had left IRS or come to Warner Brothers. The important thing was that they had a good record.

KATE INGRAM: One of their strengths as a band is that they can sort through what will and what won't be good for their career. A lot of opportunities were being laid out in front of them and at the same time, they were becoming leaders in the movement toward rock and roll bands taking stands on social issues.

LAUREN HALL: As things got more complicated and they got more popular, I think Bertis Downs helped them sort through all of the major career dilemmas. I think he provided a level-headed reality-check for them.

KEITH ALTOMARE: When the deal went down and they had finally left IRS, Warner Brothers did a beautiful job including us at IRS. They invited us to come over and hear *Green* before it came out—they had copies ready for us. It was extremely generous and gracious of them and I still wanted to hate the record. I put it in my car and only listened to it there. But I couldn't hate it, it was too good.

DAVID T. LINDSAY: They claimed they had no control over those billboards that went up before *Green* came out, but if they have control over everything else, why suddenly didn't they have control over something that more people were going to see than anything else.

[*Billboards*] are the best way to contact people. If they were so ugly, maybe they should have said something to someone.

GIL RAY: The night Bush beat Dukakis, we [*Game Theory*] were playing in Athens and Peter came to the gig. He was in a bad way. He was very upset. He might've seen us that night, but I don't know. I was nervous as all get out. "Oh, God, we're playing here." I was really embarrassed. It was the day *Green* was released.

> *"I decided that this had to be a record that was incredibly uplift-ing. Not necessarily happy, but a record that was uplifting to off-set the store-bought cynicism and easy condemnation of the world we're living in now."*
> —Michael Stipe to *Rolling Stone*, April 20th 1989

GEORGINA FALZARANO: It was really evident on *Green* that Michael wanted to get the environmental issue right out front. That's all really conscious on his part. The whole presentation was his—the stage set and lighting design and the video. The power he had available to him is pretty mind-boggling and the fact he chose to use his power in a very positive and carefully chosen way shows his intelligence and his re-sponsibility in his role. Michael told me he really wanted to make a movie, but he knew he could reach so many more people through his music. I respect and admire him for that.

DANNY BEARD: I didn't think *Green* was that great. Now I might like it, but at the time I didn't. I don't think anybody felt they sold out by signing to a big label. I didn't get any feeling that people resented them doing that. It was a step up. From my knowledge of the industry, Warner Brothers is the best company—not that it's great.

LANCE SMITH: In '89 my 10 year old cousin lent me his copy of *Green* and when I returned it he said, "I don't know about this record. I think R.E.M. sold out." What did he think when he was 8, that they really rocked?

JARID NEFF: I saw them rehearse the *Green* Tour. They were getting ready to go and they went song by song through the whole set—ten songs in a row. There was nobody in there except me and a couple of others in a big old rehearsal studio.

WOODY NUSS: Robyn Hitchcock had been asked to tour with R.E.M. repeatedly but it never made sense financially. There was no reason for

R.E.M. to pay an opening band a lot of money. That's why Camper Van Beethoven got in all that trouble when Jackson Haring said that stuff about not getting paid well to *Musician* magazine. But it was true. There is no reason to pay an opening band any money and there was no reason for Robyn to tour the way he does and lose money when his record company isn't going to help him. Finally, A&M said they would give him the money because it would do something for Robyn—because it was an arena tour.

BUREN FOWLER: By the time the *Green* tour came around, things had really changed a lot. They had a production manager and everyone had walkie-talkies and was dressed in black and nobody was allowed on stage. When it was Curtis and me and Microwave, it was really relaxed. We did our jobs, but it was like living in the hippie/punk kingdom. If someone wanted to stand on the side of the stage, they could stand on the side of the stage.

WOODY NUSS: When I was working for Robyn Hitchcock on the *Green* World Tour, Bill and Mike recounted the tale of when I jackknifed the trailer and wrecked the LTD. It was a much smoother tale than I told and the way Bill tells it, I was the impetus for them getting their first van. Because we trashed the LTD, he had to borrow money from his dad to buy the van.

BUREN FOWLER: It worked out pretty well that I didn't go on tour with them because The dB's had just broken up so Peter Holsapple was available and wound up playing with them [*guitar and keyboards*]. I was pretty much in Drivin' n' Cryin' by then and we opened some shows for R.E.M. on that tour.

DAVID T. LINDSAY: I was friends with Liz Hammond. She was R.E.M.'s secretary and ran their fanclub for awhile. During the *Green* tour Liz called and asked if I wanted to see the band at the Omni in Atlanta. I told her I'd seen the band in clubs that seat 500-600 people, why would I want to go to the Omni? She said that she was going to be there and she'd like to see me. She asked couldn't I think of one person that I would want to take? There was one person I could think of. The show was sold out so she probably would really appreciate it. Turned out she was going to be out of town but she knew a sixteen year old girl that would die to go and would I take her? I said, yes, if she understands that I'm going to be hanging out with my friend Liz. I called Liz back and it was all arranged. I said, "I'm bringing a kid with me who has never seen the band and she is really excited." We got there and I went to pick up the tickets. I said I'm David Lindsay, Liz Hammond put two tickets on hold for me. The woman in the booth got a very weird look on her face and said, "Oh my God." I said, "If my name isn't there can you put me in touch with Liz Hammond or Jefferson Holt?" She said, "No. Your name is here, but this is all that is in the package." She handed me a copy of my review of *Green* from *Creative Loafing* [*Atlanta weekly*]. Written at the top with a magic marker was, "No way, not with a review like this. You've got to walk it like you talk it. JMS" I said obviously there was some mistake, Liz had called me and told me the tickets were here and she even told me to bring someone. I went to a phone and tried to get in touch with Liz and couldn't so I finally called my friend Velena's house. I asked if she was going down to the show and could she please tell Jefferson or Liz that my tickets weren't there. I told her what was in the envelope and I said, "Signed, JMS. Who's that?" And she said, "That's Michael Stipe." He could have left *one* ticket there. For a guy who is supposed to have so much compassion and wants to save the world, he devastated this child. She was very upset. I think he made himself more of a valued enemy than I could ever be. I believe in trading value for value and if I ever see him I am going to punch him in the nose. Afterwards, I wrote him a postcard saying, "Thanks for your autograph Michael. I sold it for a large sum of money and gave the money to Operation Rescue in your name." Liz told me Michael took one look at the card and said, "He's got my address now. Who's Operation Rescue anyway?" She tried to explain it to him and he said, "At least he gave it to a cause." That's the real punchline to the story.

MARC WALLACE: Michael behaves toward strangers depending on how they behave toward him. He doesn't like to sign autographs but he always offers people a handshake.

BUREN FOWLER: The only time I ever met Chris Blackwell, President of Island Records [*Drivin' n' Cryin' recorded three records for the label*] we were mixing *Mystery Road* in the Bahamas. He was having a Christmas party and he said, "Aren't you the roadie that plays with R.E.M.?" I said, "Yea." He said, "Aren't you supposed to be on tour right now?" and I said, "No, I quit that job, I'm going to play with Drivin' n' Cryin'." He looked at me and said, "You're kidding."

KATHLEEN O'BRIEN: Around 1989 I had a really rough year. My mom died and I had a tumor in my head that I had to have removed. I went to one of R.E.M.'s shows and I ended up getting real emotional. Jefferson said to me, "Why do you even bother to come here if you're just going to have a bad time?" It was the last show of theirs I went to. Jefferson said I would always be an honorary member of the fanclub but around then it just stopped. And it hurt. It got to the point where I had to stop buying their music.

KEITH ALTOMARE: IRS gave me a triple gold record for the first few records that finally went gold.

GEORGINA FALZARANO: During the *Green* tour, Peter said there were 20 songs that had to be in every set. There's no room for creativity anymore. On the Pageantry tour, every night was different. They never played the same songs in the same order. You don't have the room to do that when you have to play 20 certain songs in your set.

KATE INGRAM: In March of '89 we went to see them in Sacramento and had a fairly awkward meeting about the film I was working on with the band backstage. By this time, I think they'd been offered to do a song for the film, *Born on the 4th of July*, which they also declined. They basically were held to focus by Jefferson and Bert that they needed to make decisions about touring and scheduling and one of the great buffers that was afforded to them was, "You don't have to do something unless you really want to." Any one thing wasn't going to make or break them so it enabled them to make more informed decisions about what to do.

LANCE SMITH: They did a great job at staying true to what they wanted to do and who they originally were even while becoming progressively more mainstream. The only song I ever hated of theirs was "Stand."

GEORGINA FALZARANO: "Stand" was written about a comment I made. I have really bad direction so I make a real conscious effort to know where north is in a town. The left/right thing is very difficult for me. Michael was really intrigued with how I remembered direction and asked me exactly what it was I do. I told him I visualize I'm standing in front of my house because when I'm looking at my house I can tell that's north, then I can tell where east and west and south are in relationship to where I am.

GINA ARNOLD: Two days after the [*San Francisco*] Earthquake in October of '89, they played the Concord Pavilion. I wasn't that into R.E.M. at the time because *Green* is my least favorite record and they'd already played here on that tour. I was still a little shaken from the earthquake experience and found that performance to be very moving. They laid off the sarcasm (which they were using a lot). Just before they did "Stand" Michael said, "I know y'all have had a really rough week and this goes out to the Bay Area," and all of a sudden that song, 'Stand in the place where you live, think about direction, think about why you are living here,' meant so much more that night. That's a goofy little trivial, annoying song, but boy, that night it resonated a lot. It was a very healing kind of performance.

KATE INGRAM: The producers of the film were kind of taking the same attitude that college radio had after R.E.M.'s big commercial success. It was kind of like, "They're ok, but we don't want them as our whole sound." We gave R.E.M. a tape of some of the film cut to the music they'd given us and things strung on for maybe three more months. Finally, Jefferson called me from Europe and said he talked to the band. It wouldn't fit into their schedule in the coming year to finish a song. After looking at the film [*A Matter of Degrees*] when it came out, I think they made a good decision.

VICTOR KRUMMENACHER: As pleased as I was with Michael's early forays into politics, I was chagrined when he started doing things by rote like "Orange Crush."

GEORGINA FALZARANO: Some of the references in "You Are The Everything" were from the trip I made with Michael from Seattle to Boulder back in '86. Looking at the stars, little comments would be made and later they reappeared in the song. The last time I saw R.E.M. play, Michael sang that right to me. It was really, really touching.

GEOFF GANS: My interactions with Michael helped demystify rock and roll. When I was a kid I saw Led Zeppelin at the Forum in LA and I thought the coolest thing in the world would be to stand onstage during a big show at the Forum. I got to do it when R.E.M. played there and it wasn't so cool after all.

KEITH ALTOMARE: I saw the *Green* Tour at the Forum and I went backstage and Michael hugged me and didn't really say anything. It was kind of lonely for me because I knew I was an outsider. But Mills came up and talked to me too. I know deep down inside they still have a warm spot for me. I think the spot's gotten smaller and that's ok. They always remember what we did at IRS for them. In many cases I think they might prefer to still be there.

WOODY NUSS: We planned the Robyn Hitchcock tours around when R.E.M. was available, when Peter was available, when we could go to

Athens and hang out and use their rehearsal rooms. We prepped a whole tour in their basement. A lot of that has to do with Peter. He can't live without per diem. He's got to be on the road, he's got to be on stage. So whether it's with Robyn or Drivin' n' Cryin', he's a road dog.

LANCE SMITH: Pete was the biggest stage jumper in the world. He would play with anybody.

BUREN FOWLER: Peter and Kevn Kinney [*Drivin' n' Cryin'*] are good friends. They did the *MacDougal Blues* record together and we did the Drivin' n' Cryin' acoustic tour with Peter and Nikki Sudden which we subtitled "Six Drunk Rock Stars on Parade.' Peter and Kevn still play together. Mike and Peter named *Scarred But Smarter* by Drivin' n' Cryin' as one of their ten favorite records of the Eighties in *Rolling Stone*.

CURTIS CROWE: Pylon begged on bended knee for R.E.M. to take us on tour. But we didn't have to beg very hard. We really wanted to get out there and play. All of us in Pylon simultaneously hit this point in our lives when what we were doing wasn't all that fun and being in Pylon was a lot of fun. That happened exactly at the same time that R.E.M. was starting to make a really big splash. I think the combination of their enthusiasm and their support lent kind of a credible edge to us and we thought, "why not?' so we reformed.

GEORGINA FALZARANO: I saw R.E.M. twice on the *Green* tour. Once about four weeks in and once toward the end. They were getting really tired and the reason was there wasn't anything for them to look forward to anymore. The audience response was exactly the same every night. The band didn't know what town they were in. It was a long tour and they burnt really bad. But they still managed to put on great shows. When you watch *Tour Film* you really see that. The film is really well done and the audience is certainly getting their money's worth.

GEOFF GANS: I was getting ready to leave IRS, but before I did, I noticed a lot of stuff was getting thrown away like original artwork from record sleeves. I started collecting it all in a file. R.E.M. was on the *Green* Tour. I called Bertis and told him, Jefferson and Michael I was leaving IRS. I was collecting all this stuff of theirs in a file and I would send it on to them. Everyone was really excited I found it because they thought it had been lost. I ended up having it for about a year while they were on tour, and when they came through in '89 Michael knew I had everything. We were making arrangements to get it back to him. Sometime in '90 they were in LA and Jefferson pulled me aside at the

Palomino Club and said, "Michael is really pissed off at you. He thinks you stole all of his artwork." He said since I never sent it back, he thinks I stole it. I didn't understand what the big deal was since we had talked about it and he had been on the road for a year. I faxed him the next day and told him I'd heard he was upset, please get in touch. Jefferson called me the next day and said I had to send the stuff immediately. He said he would call Jay Boberg at IRS if I didn't. I still wanted to clarify things with Michael, but he never called me back. I sent the stuff back, but Michael never called me again after that.

CURTIS CROWE: We played in 10,000-25,000 seat places. We decided to be rock stars and got a motor home with a microwave and a coffee pot. The coolest part about touring was driving up to the venue and hanging out in these cinderblock rooms and being treated like a human being for a little while. Then you got onstage and the whole thing was organized. It was a really beautiful scene. After having to deal with seedy clubs and sleazy club owners and leaky pipes and the roof just about to cave in—firetraps—it's a wonderful thing to play in a basketball arena because everything is clean and organized. The other good thing is we got on early, got off early and could go have dinner. The crowds just endured us for the most part. That wasn't a great memory. We didn't wow 'em or take the stage or anything. There wasn't much of a chance for that. We came in on the last leg of a tour that was about 300 days long.

LANCE SMITH: I read something that Pete said about the band already doing arenas and that he thought they had played those venues about the best the anyone ever had. Pat yourself on the back—Hendrix? The Stones in '72? No, it was R.E.M. in '89.

DIANA J. CROWE: At the end of the *Green* tour in Macon, they had learned to shelter themselves from any unwanted attention. They weren't letting anybody backstage and they were being real protective and choosey about who was coming back. After the show they totally disappeared. They made a quick breezethrough and that was it.

MARC WALLACE: Michael tries not to attract attention but at the same time he also loves the attention. Even though he may say that he doesn't. He's totally out there. He doesn't hide.

CURTIS CROWE: At the very last minute they added a show in Atlanta which was a benefit. For a crew that's been on a road for 300 days without girlfriends and wives and families, that's a long time, and they were all very nice and pleasant people. I thought that in itself is a testament to something. I talked to the backline guy and I said, "Everyone's always in such a great mood." He said, "If you work for a cool band, the road crew are cool. If the road crew are real assholes, then the band are probably assholes."

R.E.M. is just a fair, clear and dedicated band. They are dedicated to a variety of goals and it just makes for a real clear, organized system that everyone can fall right into.

SARA BROWN: The L.E.A.F. Benefit show at the Fox in Atlanta at the end of the Green World Tour was completely neat and really unexpected. They started out with "Radio Free Europe" followed by "Pilgrimage" and "Laughing," and pretty soon people were looking at each other going, are they really doing it? They were playing *Murmur* in order. It was weird but neat. I wondered how seriously they were taking it. They were playing songs they claimed they would never play again and in some cases had never played live at all. They followed *Murmur* with the whole of *Green*, in order.

> *"For me, Green had so many connections to Murmur. It was very much in the back of my head the whole time we were working on it. From the album cover to the topics of the songs and the way the songs were carried out, to me, there's a great connection there."*
> —Michael Stipe to *Rolling Stone*, April 20th 1989

GEORGINA FALZARANO: I don't think they had any choice but to take a break from touring after the *Green* tour. Where do you go from the 20,000 seat venues? I think it was a really wise choice for everyone to sit back for a couple of years.

JACKSON HARING: After the *Green* tour, they were playing to their new audience and the R.E.M.-Heads fell away. You see a whole audience singing along only to the new songs and it's a little disheartening.

DIANA J. CROWE: I was at the R.E.M. office once a couple of years ago and some high school age kids were sitting out on the office doorstep hoping that somebody would come by. They had been sitting there for quite awhile but Michael Stipe *did* come up to the office and invited them in and I remember they were just ecstatic. It was like the biggest thing that had ever happened in their lives. I thought it was really neat that Michael did that.

GEOFF GANS: I had never known Michael to be a fair weather friend, but eventually he would only call me to find out where a mutual friend was and then he would have Jefferson call. It was really around '89 when all of a sudden he wasn't accessible.

MARC WALLACE: Michael is 100 percent loyal and his friends are 100 percent loyal back. He has a tight circle and most of the people in the circle have been around for several years.

GEOFF GANS: There were so many incidents like videos in my mind that stand out where Michael would contradict himself. On one hand he would say he didn't have any friends and as time went on there was a whole different vibe. I was on the inside during that transitional period where he and the band went from public to more private personas but suddenly after the transition I was on the outside.

BRIAN CRANE: Michael is really focused now, the way he presents himself in videos and onstage. He's really into getting people into his hands and taking them from one place to the next. Just jumping around playing rock and roll means that the audience and the band are mixed up together, but he's really built up the "I am here and you are there" thing.

I'd love to see them get up and bang out some rock songs because they haven't done it in so long. The *Green* tour they were still doing some heavier rock and roll stuff, but the last couple of albums, they haven't and to me, that's what they were—a kick ass rock and roll band. I don't think Michael is into doing that kind of thing anymore.

1990

1990

January — July recording continues for *Out of Time* at John Keane Studios, Athens, GA and Bearsville Studios, Bearsville, NY

Video/Film

March — *Pop Screen*: Picks up where *R.E.M. Succumbs* left off and ends with *Green* videos

September — *Tourfilm*: Filmed in November 1989 during the last five nights of the *Green* World Tour

Select Guest Appearances/Compilations

October — Hindu Love Gods album with Warren Zevon released four years after it was recorded

— Roky Erickson's "I Walked With A Zombie" recorded for the tribute album, *When The Pyramid Meets The Eye—A Tribute to Roky Erickson*

MacDougal Blues by Kevn Kinney produced by Peter Buck

Seven-inch Singles

December — "Ghost Reindeer in the Sky"/"Summertime" (fan club only)

1991

March 12 — *Out of Time*, produced by Scott Litt & R.E.M. The album is known as the one that brought R.E.M. mass acceptance chiefly because it contained "Losing My Religion" and "Shiny Happy People." The songs' accompanying videos were played probably more than everything the band had ever released to MTV combined. R.E.M. earned video awards and Grammies. In the wake of success, they elected not to tour in support of an album for the first time since their inception.

Seven-inch Singles

May — "Losing My Religion"/"Rotary Eleven"

September — "Shiny Happy People"/"Forty Second Song"

October — "Radio Song"/"Love is All Around"

December — "Baby,Baby"/"Christmas Griping" (fan club only)

Twelve-inch Singles

November — "Radio Song"(Tower of Luv Bug Mix)/"Love is All Around"
(live)/"Belong" (live)

CD Singles

November — "Radio Song" (Tower of Luv Bug Mix)/"Love is All Around"
(live)/"Belong" (live)

Videos

Time Piece — Warner Brothers promo film

"Losing My Religion," directed by Tarsem

"Radio Song," directed by Peter Care

"Near Wild Heaven," directed by Jeff Preiss

"Shiny Happy People," directed by Katherine Dieckmann

Michael makes a cameo in "Deadbeat Club" by The B-52's

This Film Is On: Compiles all videos from *Out of Time,* live television
performances and directors James Herbert's, Jem Cohen's and Jim
McKay's visions of four other songs from *Out of Time*

Television and Film Appearances

The Adventures of Pete and Pete for Nickelodeon — Michael Stipe plays an
ice cream man in the episode titled "What I Did on My Summer Vacation"

"Stand" used as opening theme for Chris Elliot's Fox show, *Get A Life*

"Stand" and "Orange Crush" featured in an episode of *21 Jump Street*

"Fretless" used in Wim Wender's film and soundtrack, *Until The End of
The World*

MTV *Unplugged*

Saturday Night Live: Live performances of "Losing My Religion" and
"Shiny Happy People" (with Kate Pierson)

MTV *10th Anniversary Special*: Live from Georgia by satellite,
"Losing My Religion"

120 Minutes, MTV: Kevn Kinney and Peter Buck

Select Guest Appearances

Michael Stipe contributes vocals and odd instruments to the
Chickasaw Mudd Puppies' *8 Track Stomp*

Stipe and Indigo Girls contribute "I'll Give You My Skin"
to *In Defense of Animals*

Stipe and Buck appear all over Robyn Hitchcock's *Perspex Island*

Stipe and Buck contribute to Billy Bragg song, "You Woke Up My
Neighborhood," and appear in video

Compilations

R.E.M. under the name Bingo Hand Job contribute their version of "Tom's Diner" to *Tom's Album*

"First We Take Manhattan," is R.E.M.'s entry on the tribute album, *I'm Your Fan—The Songs of Leonard Cohen by . . .*

Touring

Acoustic tour of Europe playing small unannounced gigs

Radio station broadcasts in a handful of select U.S./European cities

Awards/Recognition

September — "Losing My Religion" wins six *MTV Video Music Awards*

March — Grammy Nominations for Record of the Year, "Losing My Religion," Best Rock Vocal Performance, "Radio Song," and Album of the Year, *Out of Time*

      — Grammy Awards for Best Pop Performance by a Group, "Losing My Religion," Best Alternative Album, *Out of Time* and Best Video, "Losing My Religion"

May — *Out of Time* reaches Number One on the *Billboard* chart

"Losing My Religion" voted Best Single in the *Rolling Stone* Readers' and Critics' Polls

1990 GRAMMY AWARDS
(*photo © Ebet Roberts 1992*)

9

OUT OF TIME

JARED BAILEY: You get whole bands moving to Athens because R.E.M. started here. They think since they love R.E.M. so much they will get to see them more and be influenced by them in some way. I'm always amazed at whole bands that move here. This local band Five-Eight moved here en masse from Binghamton, NY. They put all their hopes together in one backpack and it worked out for them. I don't know if they were directly influenced by R.E.M., but they came here.

DAVID ZWART: I was a so-so fan of R.E.M., not a huge fan. I went to their shows in '83 and '84 in Michigan. I moved to Athens on a whim. I'd lived in Michigan my whole life. I had to move somewhere.

JARED BAILEY: We get phone calls and mail and people dropping by from all over the world. We get phone calls from England all the time. People associate the 40 Watt Club with the band, or they don't know where the R.E.M. office is or they don't know there is a P.O. Box. Unless it's really insane here I'll try and take a little time out and talk with them, tell them what they can see around town. In a sense, we've worked as a middleman for them.

LAUREN HALL: I think it's gotten very difficult for them to live in Athens.

STEVE WYNN: Peter says that the first month of every semester, people in Athens come up to him and bother him, but then they get tired of it or realize he's just a guy that lives in the same town where they go to school.

CURTIS CROWE: It blows my mind that kids will drive 48 hours to see the houses that some of these guys live in or look at a derelict nightclub that they aren't even old enough to get into. I don't understand it.

JARED BAILEY: In the 40 Watt, most of the time, R.E.M. can deal with overzealous fans themselves. But if a fan is too drunk or too aggressive or has overstepped a boundary, I've had to step in and diffuse situations and get rid of people. It doesn't happen too often.

> *"Almost all the fans I meet are pretty cool people. They're intelligent and tend to think about things maybe a bit more than your average rock and roll fans: sensible people I wouldn't mind having a drink with. But once you're selling like, nine million records, you're attracting people who aren't really your fans. You start getting the psychos, the people who sit at home and the radio talks to them . . ."*   —Peter Buck to *Q Magazine*,
> October 1992

JOHN KEANE: Every once in a while, someone will call me up and say they are from Australia or England and want to come by and see the

studio and see Peter's house which is right around the corner from my studio. Usually I let them come by and see it. Sometimes I get people calling me up wanting me to give something to the band for them. I usually tell them to call the R.E.M. office.

JARED BAILEY: Most of the people who come to town looking for R.E.M. are just average people. They've heard of Athens and they love the band and they are generally nice and shy about their reason for visiting. It's kind of touching and cute. There have been a share of crazy people. Sometimes they will start hanging around the club and then hanging around the R.E.M. office and we start talking back

ONE OF THE TOWN'S LANDMARKS IS STIPE'S BACKYARD (*photo by Geoff Gans*)

and forth about it. We can spot potential problems. I never tell anyone where the office is or where the members' houses are, but if you hang around town long enough, it's not hard to find out.

SEAN BOURNE: They all go to see the Church where R.E.M. began [*the site is now a condominium complex*]. I didn't even know there was a church till the fans started going there. I thought it was really funny that all these bands moved to Athens after R.E.M. got their band identity. I don't think those bands count.

> "You've got a regular turnover of intelligent people. You're in a town large enough to have a couple of good clubs and record stores, but you can still walk from one side of the town to the other. And the myth perpetuates itself, because you've got interesting people coming in search of what they've read about."
> —Bill Berry to *SPIN*, October 1986

CURTIS CROWE: I stay here because you have to live somewhere. What I like about this town is that there are some people here that are fun to hang out with, it's relatively inexpensive, there's big old houses that I can afford to live in, it's got a nightlife that's comparable to what you can get in a city and there are enough intelligent people so it's not like a hick town. The neighborhood we live in is kind of like your "Norman Rockwell Nineties Rock and Roll Neighborhood." This is one of the last towns in the world with a real neighborhood in it. Where you can walk over to a friends, invite yourself for dinner, get drunk, stay the night then crawl home. You never even need your car.

DAVID ZWART: Michael used to come to Daisy's shows and offered to work with us because he had some available studio time. He was supposed to go to Europe around the time of the Persian Gulf War and ended up canceling his trip because it wasn't such a good time to travel. We went in the studio then and he kind of told me what his favorite songs of ours were and what he wanted to record. We recorded two out of the three he liked. We all shared ideas and he would suggest something and we would or wouldn't use it. He had a lot of suggestions. More so than anybody we'd worked with. He was real enthusiastic about the whole thing. We thought it would be our demo but we decided to put it out as a 45.

MARC WALLACE: Michael doesn't bring his work home to Athens with him. We sit around and watch him on TV and root him on. A few of us have been able to go places with him, so he's really generous in that way. I would never have gotten to go to their *Saturday Night Live* appearance if I had not known his generosity. He seems to include [*his friends*]. He talks to us every day and he knows what's going on with us and we know what's going on with him. At the same time there is a lot going on with him that nobody knows. Each different friend knows a different part of him and the same with the next. But we all get together and compare notes.

LANCE LOUD [freelance writer]: I interviewed R.E.M. in 1991 for the Hardrock Cafe newspaper and at the end of the interview Michael Stipe brought up out of the clear blue sky that he knew I once had a band called the Mumps 12 years ago. I was very flattered and thrilled. In summer of 1993, a record company contacted us and said they wanted to release our tapes and they asked if we knew anybody famous that would like to write about the release. I wrote to people I knew like Fred Schneider and others but no one responded to the faxes except Michael. In my request, I stated that I would love to have a paragraph about what they liked or remembered about the band in relationship to the era or whatever and I stressed that we would not use it for advertising purposes. A week later we got a two and a half page article that he'd written about us and a note saying, "Please, if you want to use this for advertising, do so." I thought that was really great.

GEOFF GANS: Personally, I have to wonder why R.E.M. does certain things. IRS coordinated *The Best Of R.E.M.* package that came out in Europe with Jefferson and Bert. Later they sent a letter to the NME [*New Musical Express*], stating they had nothing to do with it. But they totally had everything to do with it. Behaving like that is a weird paranoia which probably comes from having millions of dollars. It's a very strange thing that they do, and I've heard it from more people than you can imagine.

MARC WALLACE: While the band was recording "Losing My Religion" and putting the song together, Michael and I would go back to my store and put it on the tape player, play it back really loud, lay on the floor in the dark and listen to it. The night came when they finally finished the song and we went for a ride to listen to it in his car. Michael and I were driving through the University of Georgia and got stopped by the police. The police officer came up to the car and hostilely asked for a license and proof of insurance. Michael asked him why he had stopped us and the officer would not tell us. He went back to his car and called the license in on his radio. When he came back to our car his attitude had changed. He became friendly but was almost nervous, telling us that the speed limit had recently been changed. He said he was sorry for stopping us and by the way could he get an autograph. Michael, not being one to sign autographs told the cop he couldn't. The cop apologized again and asked when he'd be hearing more from R.E.M. Michael explained how we were listening to a new song just now and that's why we missed the new sign. From there we went to the International House of Pancakes and sitting across from us were some other cops with walkie-talkies. Not knowing we were there, they proceeded to retell the incident to each other while we listened to the whole conversation.

JOHN KEANE: They started doing b-sides at my place and they come in every year and do a Christmas single. Last year they came in and recorded "Silver Bells" and "The Charlie Brown Christmas Song" on the other side. It's usually a two-day thing, real fast. Sometimes they come in and demo a song and it won't end up on the album but they like it and use it as a b-side or they send it off to someone to use as a soundtrack piece. Once in awhile they'll come in and record a demo and decide not to re-record it. They'll use the demo version on the album. That's what happened with "Country Feedback."

DANNY BEARD: On *Out of Time* they did something more challenging and different. They had more folk oriented things and the added voice of Kate Pierson ["*Shiny Happy People*," "*Me in Honey*"] sounded great. It was better than *Green*. I think they got some younger people listening to them with that record.

KEN FECHTNER: I try not to discuss the band much. Peter talks about their music and I hear things he is working on only if he mentions it. He was really excited about *Out of Time*. That was one time he really raved and said, "I think we've done something really good."

MARK METHE: Mike Richmond from Love Tractor could just have easily been in R.E.M. Same style and everything. Love Tractor was like an instrumental R.E.M.

ARMISTEAD WELLFORD: A lot of people have said that the songs on *Out of Time* sound like Love Tractor. We don't hear it, but we were all influenced by each other for sure.

DANNY BEARD: The song "Belong" on *Out of Time* sounds just like Love Tractor.

ARMISTEAD WELLFORD: Rick "the Printer" [*Athens fixture*] said my new band, the Black Label Orchestra sounded like R.E.M. Or Love Tractor. "But then again," he said, "R.E.M. sounded like Love Tractor." It was only said in the spirit of the early days, not that what we or they are doing now really sounds like anything else.

GIL RAY: R.E.M. are my contemporaries, maybe younger. They are veterans of the Southern circuit. We have a lot of similarities. Mike and Bill came up through top forty bands and I did that for years. To keep plugging and keep the same line-up, I mean the Rolling Stones can't even do that.

> *"I'm more famous now than I'd ever like to be. What I'm really looking for, ideally, is that ten years down the line people will think we did something really incredible. Even if it's overlooked now, we will have done something that's so strong it will cross all boundaries. So that in ten years people will listen to it like I listen to the Velvet Underground or the Doors or Muddy Waters."*
> —Peter Buck to *New Musical Express*,
> July 6, 1985

BRUCE MCGUIRE: Pete's got that Keith Richards quasi-skull ring thing happening which is kind of odd, but come to think of it, it's not so odd. He's a lot like Keith in that he's not a great guitar player and he often has to play foil to Michael's Mick Jagger. When they were in Minneapolis to mix *Out Of Time* at Paisley Park Studios, I saw Pete Buck at First Avenue wearing a cape. It might have only been a jacket over his shoulders but it looked real Supermanesque.

ARMISTEAD WELLFORD: When I see Michael I always say hi to him as the Michael I knew back then. That's how I always see him. All the stages we've been through, the closenesses and the not-so-closenesses. That's why I like him, not because of his records or his success. A lot of times you can catch him working it because people are butterin' up to him and he's doing his thing. Sometimes it's hard to be so regular toward him when he's working the icon.

BRUCE MCGUIRE: I think some people's perceptions of R.E.M. today as caricature rock stars or parodies of themselves are based on the fact they are so popular they've almost gone into hiding. People pick whatever they can and blow it into larger than lifesize and then it gets all weird and distorted.

STEVE WYNN: R.E.M. is at least an unconscious influence for me, though I've only seen them play once since the tour we were on together. *Out of Time* was a big influence for me on my album, *Dazzling Display*.

GINA ARNOLD: One of the great regrets of my career was not going to see them on Mountain Stage. [*One of the band's few live appearances since 1989 was the small radio show,* Mountain Stage, *broadcast from an intimate, old theatre in downtown Charlotte, WV.*]

GEOFF GANS: People asked me if I went to the broadcast at KCRW that they did around the time of *Out of Time* and I was like "No . . . I'm no longer in the circle." I'm really kind of sorry about the loss of our friendship. I communicated to Michael that I thought it was kind of weird and stupid that he wasn't responding to my phone calls and he never got back to me. I've had to deal with Jefferson on a couple of occasions and it's just weird.

STEVE WYNN: I didn't have any of their records till 1991. I heard them everywhere I went and didn't really need the records. But they are a band that keeps getting better and better. Some of the stuff holds up and some of it doesn't. A lot of stuff recorded between '83-'88 by any band sounds a little weird because of what was going on in production techniques. They got really icy drum sounds during that period.

GINA ARNOLD: I heard "Losing My Religion" booming out of the soundtrack to *Class of '96*, a truly terrible TV show. I think when they decided to move into the mainstream, they made a real conscious decision to do it in a big way, and that speaks more of their business decisions than any creative decisions.

STEVE WYNN: Peter and I had been talking about doing something together for years but we never really wrote together till '91. We worked on a lot of stuff at his house in the studio till early one morning, none of which has come out. We had already written "Dazzling Display" together, but that wasn't really like writing together. It was just a matter of him putting down a mandolin part on tape and taking off.

WOODY NUSS: Peter plays guitar with Robyn Hitchcock's band from time to time. He has been introduced as the missing Soft Boy. Robyn loves him. While he's on tour, Peter stays up all night and sleeps all day. We were on tour in Southern California and the bus had to go in for service, but Peter was asleep in his bunk. We all got rooms, and we debated whether to get him out but everyone agreed we should let him sleep. The bus was on a hydraulic lift somewhere in Orange County getting worked on. Peter stayed in the bus all day. Guys with pneumatic drills and wrenches worked on the thing all day and he slept through it. During soundcheck I got worried that Peter might wake up and step out of the door of the bus eight and a half feet down. The bus showed up at the club for soundcheck and Peter was still in his bunk, asleep. He had no idea he had left town.

STEVE WYNN: Between the ages of 24-34 you're going to change quite a bit. If you don't change, you've probably got a problem, so yea, I think Peter has changed over the years I've known him. But it never ceases to amaze me how nonchalantly Peter deals with things. When we were making *Dazzling Display*, I remember one day Donovan was playing a noontime acoustic show at Tower Records and Peter said, "We gotta go down there." We went down at about 1:00 and shopped around a bit and waited for Donovan to come on. It was weird to watch how much more attention Peter was getting than Donovan. I think it was kind of weird for him because we just wanted to shop, see Donovan and go back to work and people were mobbing Peter. But he was completely cool about it. For all of the times I've been with him, he's never dealt with it in a weird way, like being over-friendly or under friendly. He just answers questions like anyone on the street would if they were asked a question. He doesn't go around hoping people won't notice him, but you can see other people definitely being aware of his presence. He just ignores the whole thing. I'm sure his being from Athens rather than a bigger city has something to do with how he deals with it.

JARED BAILEY: Part of the reason R.E.M. like the 40 Watt Club is that when they play here or come here they help support the idea that hole-in-the-wall clubs in every town are the lifeblood of a scene. But it's also really easy for them to play here because we're right next door to their practice space. They just have to roll stuff down. Or after practicing, having a couple of beers and hanging out, they can just jump up and use someone else's equipment to play. After rehearsing they've come over, gotten a twelve pack from us, gotten a little loose and after a while would come back and say, "We want to play." What could I say, but sure, twist my arm.

Most of those shows during '91 and '92 [*at the 40 Watt*] were spur of the moment sloppy affairs, but they were a lot of fun. That was the fun of it. They would tell us, "Please don't tell anyone," and we wouldn't tell anybody but somehow word would get out. Someone would see the equipment being loaded in or they would see Peter getting the twelve pack and overhear him say, "Can we play?"

JOHN WESLEY HARDING: [musician] In May, Peter came and played "If You Have Ghosts" and "Gates of Eden" with me and my band at The Georgia Theatre in Athens. I remember I was a little nervous about asking him to play which was stupid because he loves to. It was the very day that R.E.M. went number one for the first time. I'll never forget him telling me that. He was so excited. And then it was all in *Rolling Stone*: "Peter Buck jamming at the Georgia Theatre with John Wesley Harding while Stipe is seeing Follow For Now at the 40 Watt." I figured that was as good as it got.

GIL RAY: R.E.M. were always non-threatening, meaning they didn't have the kind of arrogance that could put people off. In the early days they were an out and out party band. A lot of people now don't relate to them like that. They just see them as an arena band now.

JARED BAILEY: A lot of times there were fake rumors that they were going to play. If a band who no one has ever heard the name of is going to play, people assume it is R.E.M. playing under a different name. There have been several bands whose first gigs had great crowds and made lots of money because of R.E.M. rumors. An example of that was Catbutt Jr. In one interview Michael said if he ever could name a band again, he'd name it Catbutt. We tried to tell people R.E.M. is not playing. We put signs up and said we didn't want to hear any complaining. They all came in and paid their money. But there were times when R.E.M. played and the word didn't get out and there were 75 people there and it was just friends. It was great, you wouldn't have the drunken idiot frat boys. We did three benefits for a mental health organization here in Athens and the band played two of them. One year Peter was supposed to play and Michael was supposed to play and when Peter was on, the whole band ended up playing.

DANNY BEARD: Peter put the money up to remix some stuff by the Fans. It was the first band I worked with and one of the first bands he liked a whole lot. We remixed it and Alfredo, the main guy in the Fans, wanted the tapes that had been recorded in 1978 to sound like a digital 48 track thing. He has been away from the music business for quite sometime. He didn't like the tapes and we ran out of money. I guess I could have gone back to Pete and got the money. He said he would write the liner notes if it ever does come out.

MIKE GREEN: It's terrible after Peter would put so much time and effort into the project and they would disagree. The Fans were some collection of egos and evidently that's still the case. I'm certainly grateful to him for trying.

KATHLEEN O'BRIEN: The last time I went to Athens was for a wedding. I was so excited I didn't eat all day and I drank champagne. It was hot and by the end of the evening, I was out of it. I ran into all these people I hadn't seen in so long. I could barely walk and I was flagging Michael Stipe down in the road. I thought, great, this is what these people think of me now. I was so embarrassed. Between the last concert I saw and Jefferson making that comment about me always getting emotional at their shows, I thought maybe that's why they don't want to have anything to do with me.

GEOFF GANS: I don't have any bad feelings toward the band, but at the time my feelings were hurt when Michael stopped communicating with me because I thought Michael and I were friends. It was a weird thing that happened between us but I get the feeling he has his own trip and he's lost in what he's doing.

KATHLEEN O'BRIEN: Years ago, I thought I should write a book on R.E.M. I know these people and I used to consider myself a writer. Not only could I do a good job but I could capitalize on something that I should have a long time ago. I don't think I could do it because it would end up being from my perspective, no matter how objective I would try to be.

BRUCE MCGUIRE: All of my encounters with them seem to be so normal. The last time I saw any of them in person I was at Lollapalloza in Atlanta in 1991. That day Pearl Jam and the Red Hot Chili Peppers played—both bands are million sellers now, but it seemed so normal. I walked through a hallway and saw Michael just standing there. He was like, "I know you." In retrospect, maybe we *were* in a privileged area, outside the realm of normal experience, but because Michael can't go out in the crowd and watch a show like that, he almost *has* to hide out. He couldn't have any peace otherwise. He's still a very normal person from what I can tell. The only thing that isn't normal is the way he and the rest of the band have been forced to live.

MILLS/BERRY/BUCK AND REG PRESLEY AT TROGGS SESSION
(*photo by Larry Page from The Jud Cost Collection*)

1992-94

1992

January — Appearance at 40 Watt Club

June — Finally, a tribute album devoted to songs by R.E.M. *Surprise Your Pig*

October — *Automatic For The People*, produced by Scott Litt & R.E.M. R.E.M.'s biggest record to date, with over 14 million copies sold worldwide. Though not immediately accessible, it may be R.E.M.'s best ever album—the classic they always hoped to record. The band elected not to tour again, but made a number of special appearances individually and collectively over a two-year period.

November — Appearance at 40 Watt Club

Seven-inch Singles

October — "Drive"/"Winged Mammal Theme"

December — "Where's Captain Kirk?"/"Toyland" (fan club only)

CD Singles

October — "Drive"/"Winged Mammal Theme"

Videos

"Drive," directed by Peter Care

Select Guest Appearances

Peter Buck co-wrote "A Dazzling Display" with Steve Wynn and contributed guitar and mandolin to Wynn's album, *Dazzling Display*

Buck added mandolin to *Lefty's Deceiver* by The Jody Grind

Berry/Buck/Mills and Peter Holsapple collaborated with The Troggs on *Athens, Andover*

Michael Stipe and KRS-One collaborate on title cut for *H.E.A.L.* (Humans Educating Against Lies)–*Civilization vs. Technology*

Stipe sings with Neneh Cherry on "Trout," from her *Homebrew*

1993

Seven-inch Singles

February — "Man on the Moon"/"New Orleans Instrumental #2"

April — "The Sidewinder Sleeps Tonite"/"The Lion Sleeps Tonight"

December — "Silver Bells"/"Charlie Brown Christmas" (fan club only)

CD Singles

January — "Man on the Moon"/"New Orleans Instrumental #2"

April — "The Sidewinder Sleeps Tonite"/"The Lion Sleeps Tonight"

November — "Everybody Hurts" released as CD digi-packs with "Mandolin Strum"/ "Belong" (live at The Capital Plaza Theatre, Mountain Stage April 28, 1992) and "Orange Crush" (live in Georgia, November 1989) and "Star Me Kitten" (demo), "Losing My Religion" (live at Mountain Stage April 28, 1992) and "Organ Song."

Videos

"Man on the Moon," directed by Peter Care

"Everybody Hurts," directed by Jake Scott

"Find the River," directed by Jodi Wille

"Nightswimming," directed by Jem Cohen

Television and Film Appearances

January — MTV *Rock and Roll Inaugural Ball*: Mike Mills and Michael Stipe perform "One" with Adam Clayton and Larry Mullen Jr. of U2 as the fourpiece, Automatic Baby. Stipe performs "Candy Everybody Wants" with 10,000 Maniacs.

September — MTV *Video Music Awards*: "Drive" and "Everybody Hurts" live performance. Buck performs "Runaway Train" with Soul Asylum and Victoria Williams

Awards and Recognition

September — MTV *Video Music Awards*

Pavement records "Unseen Power of the Picket Fence," a song about R.E.M. for *No Alternative* to benefit AIDS charities

Compilations/Soundtracks

"Photograph" — R.E.M. with Natalie Merchant on *Born to Choose*

"Full Moon" — Michael Stipe and Annie Ross and the Low Note Quintet on *Short Cuts* soundtrack album

"Arms of Love" — performed by Michael Stipe, written by Robyn Hitchcock on *In Defense of Animals*

"Drive" — live from the 40 Watt for *Alternative NRG* compilation to benefit Greenpeace

"It's a Free World Baby" — R.E.M. on *Coneheads* soundtrack album

Select Guest Appearances

Michael Stipe duets with Natalie Merchant on 10,000 Maniacs CD-5; "To Sir With Love" and "Candy Everybody Wants"

Mike Mills contributes piano to "Soma," from Smashing Pumpkins' *Siamese Dream*

Peter Buck plays mandolin on "Slowly Fading Evening Sky" by David Lewis from *No Straight Line*

1994

January 1994 — Grammy Nominations for Album of the Year, *Automatic for the People,* Best Video, "Everybody Hurts" and Best Pop Vocal by a Group, "Man on The Moon"

                    — Recording begins in New Orleans for next album

February 1994 — *Patrick Lippert Award* presented to R.E.M. by Rock the Vote and MTV for inspiring young people to participate in the political process

                    — Michael Stipe sings on "Your Ghost" and appears in video with Kristin Hersh from *Hips and Makers*

June — Stipe is a presenter at the *MTV Movie Awards*, Mills performs with The Backbeat Band

September — R.E.M.'s version of "Wall of Death" included on *Beat the Retreat — The Songs of Richard Thompson*

September 27 — *Monster.* Produced by Scott Litt & R.E.M.

10

AUTOMATIC FOR THE PEOPLE

"We finished the promotional tour for Out of Time *in May last year [1991] and started rehearsing for this record the first week of June. We did the fourth video, went to the Grammys, some of the guys went to the MTV thing [Inaugural Ball], we went to England for the BPI awards, went to Paraguay to look at some land for the Nature Conservancy. Then we started doing this record. We don't work in December. We demoed about 30 instrumental things."*
—Peter Buck to *Pulse!* October 1992

DEXTER WEAVER (aka WEAVER D): Michael Stipe(s) and Bertis Downs came into my restaurant in August of '92. When they came to the register to pay they said, "can we talk to you" and I said, yes. Right then I might not have been as friendly as I normally am because the building had been burglarized two or three times so I'm thinking like these are just some salesmen that want to talk to me. When I sat down at a table with them they introduced themselves. I thought, "Oh, boy, I know you . . . I've been to your mother's home." I catered Michael's sister's wedding rehearsal dinner. They was telling me they were getting ready to release their album in October and they wanted to name it *Automatic For The People,* after my slogan. They asked me how would I like that and I said "Oh yea, I'd be very delighted about it." Maybe if I was depressed before, right then I started being real happy about it. I couldn't believe I was sitting at a table with them and they asked me—it was such an honor.

JARID NEFF: They had a record release party at the 40 Watt catered by Weaver D's to raise money for the food bank in Athens. We drove all the way down there, walked in the place and the line for food had at least 200 people in it. I looked around and it was about 150 degrees in there so we left and ate somewhere else. They played the record over a sound system. Nothing happened.

DEXTER WEAVER: I went on to define "Automatic For The People" for Michael. It means "Ready, Quick and Efficient" and Michael said, "Woo, that's what we are." So they told me to get my lawyer to be in touch with Bertis and it went on from there.

RUSS TOLMAN: I liked *Automatic for the People* a lot. At first I thought there were no hit singles on it but it started growing on me. I think they are really good, really talented, really work hard and they deserve any success they have.

DANNY BEARD: I haven't listened to *Automatic for the People* much. It was kind of like the last one but not as good.

DEXTER WEAVER: "Automatic For The People," the slogan, arrived when I worked at a fast food chain. I used to be a manager and the manager over me stated that if we were ever to report late for duty then we were "Automatic" to work a double shift. Me being a people person, when I started my own business I became "Automatic—For The People." One of my customers once quoted "If Weaver doesn't have it today, he will have it tomorrow," so I have lived up to that being ready, quick and efficient.

> *"Digital [recording] makes me sound like what I've always*
> *wanted to sound like. I think people who were fans of the band*
> *early on might not like the progression my vocals have taken, but*
> *there's not a whole lot I can do about it. I'm 10 years older, I know*
> *what I'm doing now. Maybe I've lost something but maybe I've*
> *gained something else. . ."*
> —Michael Stipe in promotional video, *Time Piece*, 1990

JOHN KEANE: Michael's voice has greatly improved over the years. It just gets better and better. He's really grown into an amazing vocalist. He always had a good voice, but he's really come into his own and is really confident. All of them have really gotten better. You can't make eight albums without getting a lot tighter. I think they play best when they are all together. They are such a unit. The sum of the four of them is a lot greater than any of them by themselves.

DEXTER WEAVER: Warner Brothers came in and did an interview with me and they combined it with me and R.E.M. like a documentary [*Automatic For The People* promotional video]. In that deal with R.E.M., they said my peanuts would go around the world with the album—that's what Michael told me. I think we did over 9000 bags. They are for sale in a lot of different places now. I hear they are going for $10 a bag. Someone from Massachusetts told me they went for $20 at an auction block. And I'm still getting calls and letters for peanuts.

DAN WALL: Kids from out of town come in and ask directions to Weaver D's or directions to band member's houses which we would never give out. The whole reason we are a tourist town is more than R.E.M.—it's a neat little town.

Weaver D's "Automatic for the People" ℠

1016 E. Broad ST. • ATHENS, GA 30601

DEXTER WEAVER: We've had high school students, folk from England and Germany and all over the United Kingdom come here in hopes they could get a glimpse of R.E.M. and eat at the place where they named the album from. They take pictures and video the building all the time and it has now become a tourist attraction.

GIL RAY: I get every record R.E.M. does. Maybe it's because I'm from the South and part of me wants to go back there.

DIANA J. CROWE: Whenever I hear the song "Nightswimming" I recall those old days here. But I've never discussed it with other people so I don't know if that's what the song is about. That's pretty much how I got to meet my husband, Curtis—swimming after dancing at one of those Pylon or R.E.M. shows.

JOHN KEANE: I'm not sure which songs are demos and which were re-recorded on *Automatic For The People*. I think maybe "Fretless" [*Until*

The End of The World soundtrack] wasn't re-recorded. They came in and recorded 26 songs, most of them incomplete without lyrics. Then they took the tapes somewhere else and worked on them. By the time I heard the finished product, I didn't know if I was hearing the demo or if they'd redone it or what. I wasn't really involved with the recording of the album and Scott Litt usually isn't there for the pre-production sessions.

GINA ARNOLD: *Automatic For The People* is a great album. If they can make an album like that, they are doing everything right, whatever tensions are going on around them.

JOHN KEANE: Mike Mills is probably the most consummate musician. He studied, he can read it, he knows a lot of composition stuff, music theory and plays a lot of different instruments. He's probably mainly responsible for the extra touches that are added to their albums like keyboards and strings and stuff like that. They bought a mellotron which actually plays a tape of a sound. They'll bring that in and mess around with string ideas. Mike will work with whoever does the actual arranging. When they are in the studio mixing the stuff down, he is the one there front and center focusing in on the mix. He and Michael are the hardest workers when it comes to getting all the details right.

> *"That is why the mixing is so hard. The trick to mixing is that you have to know when to back down. If you have two or three people hearing things in different ways . . . well, obviously you can't please everybody, so you have to be willing to compromise."*
> —Mike Mills to *Flagpole*, Sept. 8, 1993

GIL RAY: *Automatic for the People* was phenomenal, but it means a whole different thing to me than the early records. Music was really sucking bad before R.E.M. came along in 1981. Those were magical days. I'm sure every generation has their own magical days but mine were during the beginnings of R.E.M. and that was fortunate for me.

SEAN BOURNE: Alternative music today totally rides on R.E.M's coat-tails. A lot of bands wouldn't have a scene if it wasn't for them. All the neo-hippie bands want to be like R.E.M.

GINA ARNOLD: Eddie Vedder of Pearl Jam is a Stipey character. Pearl Jam's music isn't R.E.Mish but Eddie is. He has that Stipe thing going on. Kurt Cobain of Nirvana wasn't a Stipey character, but people always call their music R.E.M. with a fuzzbox. The music is very R.E.Mish.

SEAN BOURNE: When rock journalists talk, or people say, "who does it sound like," often R.E.M. is used as a defining factor—"oh it sounds R.E.Mish."

STEVE WYNN: I hate it when musicians say they don't listen to other music because it will taint their ideas. All of the cool musicians are always listening to new things. R.E.M. is definitely up on new things happening and new bands. To anybody under 25 who thinks that R.E.M. was not an important part of the underground—they were! You can hear that a lot of these bands that are around today were affected by R.E.M. in some way. You can hear that Nirvana listened to R.E.M. during the Eighties. You can hear R.E.M. in Sugar's record. These people might not admit it , but they couldn't avoid it because R.E.M. was everywhere if you were part of the underground. I can hear it in stuff I did, for better or for worse.

KURT COBAIN: I know we're gonna put out one more record, at least, and I have a pretty good idea what it's going to sound like: pretty ethereal, acoustic, like R.E.M.'s last album [*Automatic For The People*]. If I could write just a couple of songs as good as what they've written . . . I don't know how that band does what they do. God, they're the greatest. They've dealt with their success like saints, and they keep delivering great music. (To *Rolling Stone*, January 27, 1994.)

GINA ARNOLD: I see parallels between R.E.M.'s career and Nirvana and Pearl Jam today. There is always going to be the rock insider factor that will say, "ohmigod, keep them away, what brats, they ruined rock . . ." That happened when R.E.M. started to make their impact.

STEVE WYNN: When there was the backlash against R.E.M. I got pissed off and wanted to defend them because they are the absolute coolest band that's come along, whether or not you like their music. They invented a whole new ballgame for all of the other bands to follow whether it was Sonic Youth or the Replacements or Nirvana or Butthole Surfers. R.E.M. staked the claim. Musically, the bands did different things, but R.E.M. was first to show us you can be big and still be cool. No other band had done that since the punk rock days. The Clash changed—they became the mainstream. U2 changed—once they got bigger, they behaved as big bands did. But R.E.M. continued to do things their way. They took bands on tour that they liked. They rebelled against videos for so long by not lip-synching. Ironically, they've ended up being one of the best video bands. It was inspirational for a lot of bands that R.E.M. did not change line-ups and did not do the inevitable, firing one guy because he doesn't play as well as the others. R.E.M. did not take on session players because they wanted to make more pro-records and they did not routinely bring in a fancy remix guy. All those moves *had* to be inspiration for other bands.

GINA ARNOLD: I think that guy in the Stone Temple Pilots is a total Stipe clone. They always say he's like Eddie Vedder, but he's not; he's like Stipe. He dresses in exactly the same outfits, he dances like him, he uses a bullhorn, his show is an exact clone of an R.E.M. show.

BRUCE MCGUIRE: There's no sense of a frontier or the unknown anymore. It's all been done. Even though people could have said that 10 years ago about the music we were listening to, we were too innocent to realize it so we could still get excited about new things. I'm sure there are some kids who feel that way about things that belong to their generation, but it's not about their music.

STEVE WYNN: You can draw a line from R.E.M. to anything that is counterculture in music now. R.E.M. have always played by the rules of the underground though they haven't remained underground themselves. That's why I say they've never taken a bad step. It's a really tricky thing not to screw up and look back and say, "we shouldn't have done that."

ROBERT LLOYD: R.E.M.'s sound is very romantic and it may repeatedly appeal to people of a certain age. There are bands that are coming of age bands.

SEAN BOURNE: I think R.E.M. is a college rite of passage band. When we did the midnight sale at Wax 'n' Facts the day *Automatic For The People* was released, we had pretty good sales and it was all college students. R.E.M. is definitely an older generation band. They don't speak to the kids. I think the kids come to appreciate it, when they come of age.

STEVE WYNN: I'd feel old if I said there hasn't been a time like [*the early eighties*] since then. I think there has been, I just don't know what it was. Do you think young people who are buying *Automatic For The People* are turning around and buying *Murmur* and *Reckoning?*

DANNY BEARD: I'd say kids are looking for new things. They are on to Pearl Jam or something else. R.E.M. is old hat. Certainly respectable old hat. They aren't looked at by kids as being awful or anything.

ROBERT LLOYD: For boys growing up, the idea of bands as gangs is very appealing. In old war movies and Bowery Boys movies you had these groups of guys who had their distinct personalities but worked really well together. I think R.E.M. has that in a way. But the vision of the band operating as a unit is in the eye of the beholder.

> *"On every record there's one of us who has less of an involvement than maybe the next record, but nobody needs to know that. By the time we write the bridges and intros and rewrite stuff, it's all of ours anyway. Since we split the money equally, there's no real reason to get egotistical about it. Saying who wrote what is counterproductive, like family business. I like the idea of the four of us indivisible; you can't drive a wedge between us. That's how we stay together."*
> —Peter Buck to Q *Magazine*, October 1992

JOHN KEANE: Now Bill, Mike and Peter tend to come in and run through a bunch of not-quite-complete musical ideas they've been working on in their practice studio. I'll give the tape to Michael and the band won't work on it again until they go into the studio to actually record it. Sometimes they'll book a few days and Michael will come in and put some vocal ideas down. So the songs the way that I'm hearing them are in the incomplete stage.

DON DIXON: This is the way bands have been writing songs for years. The band songwriting process that R.E.M. went through was almost identical to the band songwriting process that Black Oak Arkansas went through. There's not much difference. I spent two weeks recording Black Oak Arkansas in the early Seventies while the band was writing songs and Jim Dandy would pull out his notebook and sing from his notebook till he had something he liked. It's the way R.E.M. does it. I found it very refreshing.

JOHN WESLEY HARDING: Peter's a very generous and relaxed person in the studio, which is obviously because he loves to play. In May of '93, I was producing a record for my best friend who's a folksinger called David Lewis in San Francisco and Peter happened to call to say he was visiting from Seattle with his girlfriend. He's the kind of guy who you don't feel at all bad about asking to play on his supposed "holiday," even on a record that has no label that you're just making for the hell of it. I knew it would blow David's mind because to start with, this was his first studio experience and also he's a big R.E.M. fan. So, late at night, there we all are in the studio playing a song called "Slowly Fading Evening Sky" with Peter on mandolin, Scott Mathews on percussion, David singing and playing guitar, me on pump organ and Robert Lloyd playing accordion. There were so many people playing we had to get Ken Fechtner to turn the machine on and off. And all the time Peter's just playing these great parts and says he needs the practice anyway! Peter just gave us his time and his talent freely. He's remarkable. David said to me just this morning that he wasn't 100 percent happy with the vocal on that song. I said, "I think we may be keeping that one the way it is!"

> *"I'm in the process of depoliticizing myself. I'm glad that people look at the band as politically active. I think that's healthy. But it's a lot to carry, and to quote myself, not everyone can carry the weight of the world. It's enough that people know that R.E.M. are thinking, compassionate people—human beings who support a number of causes, publicly and privately. I don't have to jump on top of a building and scream. I'm not a very good speaker—that's the end—all of it."*
> —Michael Stipe to *Rolling Stone*, June 27th, 1991

GEORGINA FALZARANO: I think Michael pulled back from the political statements on *Automatic for the People* and realized he would be flogging a dead horse if he said too much more.

VICTOR KRUMMENACHER: The reason I liked *Automatic for the People* is that it veered away from sloganeering. It was getting to be like blind semantics. I think Michael was trying to parody the system, but for me it didn't work.

DAN WALL: R.E.M. have even had a hand in national presidential politics.

DEXTER WEAVER: After the album came out, I did an interview saying my goal was that the President would use my slogan. Then Vice President Al Gore was here in Athens campaigning at the Tate Center over the University of Georgia and Michael Stipe introduced him at the rally. Gore said Bush and Quayle was "Out of Time" but him and Bill Clinton was going to be "Automatic For The People." I wasn't there, but everywhere I went that night in town people were telling me that Al Gore used my slogan. That's great because we need a president who is going to be "For The People."

VICTOR KRUMMENACHER: It bugged the shit out of me when I saw Michael on TV onstage with Al Gore. It was too much for me. I understand his arguments, but I can't embrace Al Gore at all. Michael works within the politics of moderation because he understands it's the most effective thing to do. He is aware of and has been exposed to some solid political views that warrant standing up for. The Democrats are just business as usual, and there are statements to be made from the radical left-wing that are very human and very real and under-represented when he goes and embraces MTV politics. I think the power he wields as a "rock star" has gone to his head.

> *"Like it or not, I'm a media figure now. People will listen to me if I speak. Three albums ago that kind of wasn't the case. What I had to say I put on the record. I feel like I've said it. Now I can hold a press conference to bring out the horrors of toxic waste and to introduce Citizens Clearing House or some great group that's doing something, it doesn't necessarily have to go into the songs. I'm not saying that I will never write another political song—in fact I think even though thematically this record is love songs, there's a great deal of politics involved and they're not just personal politics."*
> —Michael Stipe in promotional video, *Time Piece*, 1990

KEN FECHTNER: They are just a rock band. They may have some political viewpoints and participate in some activities, but anybody who takes political advice from a rock band is probably an idiot. The idea that someone who sings or plays guitar should have some control over your thinking is not valid.

STEPHANIE CHERNIKOWSKI: I love their politics and I'm glad they've been as active as they have. I attribute my Clinton conversion to Michael. If he hadn't been as passionate as he was, I don't know that I would have stopped to pay attention to Clinton.

DAVID ZWART: Back when I was watching R.E.M. they were more into a punk rock thing. Back then our parents tried to keep us away from seeing R.E.M. and now I think our parents are coming to see them. It's not as much fun. It's kind of a thrill to my mom and dad that we worked with Michael Stipe of R.E.M. Different types of people come to see them now. It used to be the kind of thing that you weren't supposed to do and now it is a very accepted thing.

JARED BAILEY: They actually invited people in advance to the Greenpeace benefit here at the 40 Watt in November of '92. There was pretty strict security on that. The place can hold 1000 and only 600 people showed up, so it was very comfortable. It was one of the best club performances I've ever seen them do because they spent a lot of time rehearsing.

SEAN BOURNE: I got an invitation in the mail because I'm a member of the fan club forever. Todd Ploharski told me 1999 is the last year R.E.M. will exist so I guess I'm a member till then. I called Todd and asked him what the invitation meant. Is the band playing? Is it the record being played or what? He told me R.E.M. was going to be playing a benefit for Greenpeace and they are going to record a song and do a set. So I called the R.E.M. office and got my name on the list. They sent out a certain number of invitations to fan club members in the area. I was really excited, but I thought it was going to be an out of hand nightmare.

JARED BAILEY: There was a record store in town that made a map of the R.E.M.'s homes and gave out Peter's home number. People were calling Peter's house about when the Greenpeace show was going to start.

SEAN BOURNE: The big day came and we all piled into the car and drove over there. We got there, and we were hanging out waiting for the band to come on and we figured there'd be a line a mile long of people wrapped around the block. We get to the 40 Watt and there's maybe 20-30 people outside. We went into the little store next to the club and looked around for a while, got something to eat, came back and got in with no problem. It wasn't even near packed. The band came on without a lot of fanfare. There was no jostling in the crowd and it wasn't smoky and crappy. We managed to get up right in front of the stage and they started off and everything sounded amazing. There were no mistakes. Obviously they had been rehearsing, but there was this incredible feeling about the show. They were really happy to be there, they were really into what they were doing. It was one of those great shows. Seeing them at the 40 Watt was like seeing the club shows I missed. They had all of their youthful enthusiasm but they had their mature chops. You could reach up and touch the band if you wanted to. It was fabulous. It was a lot of fun.

JOHN KEANE: I played with them at that show. I played steel guitar and bass and some acoustic guitar. I had never played with them before. It was real exciting, but it was also kind of nerve wracking because I didn't know what songs they were going to do till three days before the show and it was being recorded and I knew every mistake I made would be etched in stone for all eternity and would probably end up on countless bootleg CDs.

SEAN BOURNE: I didn't want to hear the bootleg of that show because I had a pretty good idea of what it was like for me and I didn't need to have something on record.

JARED BAILEY: I think they had fun. There didn't seem to be any apprehension. Most everyone there wanted to be there and it was a family and friends situation.

JOHN KEANE: We rehearsed like crazy for three days. They hadn't played in years really. They were really looking forward to it because they love to play. I was really nervous because I just barely knew the material and I had to switch between instruments. I think it came out pretty good.

It's hard for R.E.M. to just go play for fun because it ends up being a really big deal. The only way they can do it is unannounced—go in, do it and get the hell out before the mob arrives. They could end up getting hurt.

> *"Among other things, R.E.M. can't last forever; you get too old for that kind of thing. Between things like writing songs for other people, producing other bands, doing things for movies—sure, that would be the rest of a musician's career, post-band—unless you want to just retire on your ass and do nothing. The money will run out sooner or later."*
> —Mike Mills to *Flagpole*, September 8, 1993

MARC WALLACE: Every Sunday night that Michael is home we watch 120 Minutes on MTV. We have this gathering at my house with Michael, the Magnapop girls and a couple of other friends. We critique everything that comes on.

VICTOR KRUMMENACHER: MTV is going to play them no matter what they do.

> *"It's just a video, not the elucidation of R.E.M. They have to be fairly true to what we are—there won't be many, you know, video babes and exploding mirrors—but other than that, each one is not a peephole into what R.E.M. is."*
> —Mike Mills to *Details*, February 1993

GIL RAY: Their videos aren't going to push them into superstardom. Are they thinking, "how obscure can we make them?" As long as Stipe keeps taking his shirt off, I'm sure they'll keep gaining fans.

LAUREN HALL: At first when I saw the video for "Everybody Hurts" I thought it was kind of dorky and then I thought it was really cool. All of the thoughts of the people sitting in the traffic is kind of what

[*R.E.M.*] are all about. For every single person, it means something different and I think that's how their music works.

GINA ARNOLD: I was with this guy at the MTV Awards and we were standing right below the backstage area. They were interviewing R.E.M. on the Music News and we were right below them under the stage. I looked up and went, "Ohmigod, R.E.M." The guy I was with looked up and said, "Ohmigod, I've never been so close to them." And I said, "I haven't been so close to them since 1984," and he looked and me and went, "You were that close to them then?" I suddenly realized I was showing my age so I kind of shut up about it.

> *"Virtually every video I've seen is just horrible. We make them.*
> *But they're just commercials. We try to make them tastefully in a*
> *way that reflects the band. But I mean it's just like a McDonalds*
> *or Burger King commercial, it means absolutely nothing. By and*
> *large, I think it's a complete and utter waste of time. Especially*
> *the ones that have the story lines and the plot. Ours are collec-*
> *tions of weird images and things. But then again, I don't think*
> *video means anything at all. Anyone who talks about the art of*
> *video is just blowing smoke rings."*
> —Peter Buck to the *Gavin Report*, July 19, 1985

KATHLEEN O'BRIEN: I still think the band is so good. I just got cable and started seeing some of their videos. They are great. I miss them I guess, ultimately. Bill and I couldn't continue to be friends after our relationship ended. Bill is the great love of my life that I lost.

GINA ARNOLD: I thought their performance on the 1993 MTV Video Music Awards was great. It was beautiful. I can't imagine them being bad. They've never been bad. They just don't play bad, ever. That's why it's such a loss that they don't tour. How bad can it be? Can't they do something like Simon and Garfunkel and play for three weeks at Madison Square Garden?

RUSS TOLMAN: When I was in Denmark recently, I was watching TV and there are only two channels there. They had an hour and a half special on R.E.M. in the middle of prime time!

GINA ARNOLD: R.E.M. have become so detached because they don't tour. Their basic contact with fans is through their videos and that's weird. That's as weird as it gets. That makes Madonna look person-friendly.

JARED BAILEY: A lot of people on the E-mail network are pretty weirded out. They spend all their time just gossiping about R.E.M. That really concerns people in the band. A lot of bad rumors have gotten started that way. Some of those people showed up at the last show Michael played with Vic Chestnutt here. Michael was a little concerned about those people, but there weren't any problems.

BRUCE MCGUIRE: You always hear these rumors about Michael having AIDS. Who cares? I don't even think the band goes, "yea whatever," I'm sure they just don't even care what people say.

GINA ARNOLD: All this stuff about Michael being ill . . . when he was on the MTV Awards he looked fine. They've got to play *sometimes*. They can't hate each other that bad. But they must. There must be something they're guarding. My feeling is that it's probably the usual band hatred. They just don't like each other and don't want to be around each other. That's the only explanation and it's ugly and it makes me sad. It seems to be something that happens within all bands.

DON DIXON: I think [*any lack of camaraderie*] is more to do with something like difference between siblings. There's a big difference between hating each other and just being bored with or not liking people you have to work with everyday. Their lives are interlocked much more than any marriage. It's a delicate thing.

JACKSON HARING: They don't need to go on the road to promote their records, but I'd like to see them do it because people enjoy them so much. I think they stopped the Deadhead/R.E.M.-head phenomenon by not touring.

KEITH ALTOMARE: I would go see them again, but I wouldn't pay for a ticket. I don't like stadiums or arenas and part of me feels, and I'm not saying this is right, but I deserve a free ticket to their show!

STEVE WYNN: For a period of time from the mid-Eighties till a couple of years ago, it was cool and hip and common for people to knock them. Lately, it's almost like they've become hip again. Maybe by not touring and going more against the grain is what did it.

KEITH ALTOMARE: If they did a tour where they did three days at the Wiltern Theatre in Los Angeles, they might lose money, but the good will that would be generated and the publicity and the catalog sales would be really cool. Plus, their T-shirt sales would make up for any financial loss.

*"I guess sometime we have to sit down and decide when or if
we're ever going to tour again. I think that the general opinion is
that we will tour again sometime and I think also the general
opinion is we're never going to play those big places again. We
did that as well as we could do it. And if I was going to make a
guess I'd say that we'll probably do something a little bit more
like the acoustic shows we've been doing with maybe a slightly
larger cast of people in three to four thousand seat places. I'm not
saying when, but that would be my goal."*
—Peter Buck to the *Flagpole*, January 8, 1992

DANNY BEARD: I think their absence from the live arena has de-
tracted from their status as a big act. There are several ways to look
at it. Obviously they don't want to do it so more power to them. If
they played live, their new material might change for the better.
That's one negative that might come from not working things out
live.

GEORGINA FALZARANO: They got really caught up in the kind of
music you can't play live. I don't know how much from *Automatic For
The People* could be pulled off live.

KEITH ALTOMARE: I think they are unique in not touring and still
being able to sustain their career, but I think it will end. I don't think
they are the Beatles in that they can sit in the studio and people will just
gobble it up. I don't think that will happen. There will be a point that if
they don't tour, people will go on to something else.

GINA ARNOLD: It's one thing to not tour, but to not ever play is weird.
It shows there's a huge rift. There's something weird going on.

WOODY NUSS: I don't know how Michael has changed or hasn't. He
is an exception to every rule. Mills became more confident. I don't think
Peter has changed since the band started. I hear he is changing since he
moved out of Athens. Bill has not changed. The first thing he did when
they got money was buy a trailer and a fishing boat. Bill still drinks Bud
out of a can, first choice.

DANNY BEARD: Mike Mills is always real nice. I see Stipe every once
in a while. Most recently I saw him at a 10,000 Maniacs show. He was
in the front row at the show and he climbed up on stage to sing with
Natalie Merchant and the crowd went nuts. Not just applause, but it
was like electricity when they recognized who it was.

MITCH EASTER: I haven't followed R.E.M. real closely because I guess they are part of the big wide world now. It's not quite the same as it was. They used to be a little band and the only way you knew about them was if you were a buddy. Now everybody knows about them. Having said that, I do run into them every now and then and it's fine. Being around them now is just like it was years ago.

MARC WALLACE: Michael has his film company [C-00, *pronounced "see-hundred"*]. They've been trying to get the same project [Desperation Angels, *directed by Jim McKay and starring Tom Gilroy; the story of an HIV positive man who drives cross country*] off the ground for awhile.

GEORGINA FALZARANO: Michael got the chance to work on the movie project with Oliver Stone's production company, Peter got off and did some travelling which he's always wanted to do. Bill and Mari do the cocoon thing well and Mike does whatever Mike does—there's no holding him down either. I think it was a good cooling off period for them to be apart a little bit. You can't make creativity happen, so sometimes you have to pull back and let everyone do their own thing. [*The film* Desperation Angels *is still in development.*]

JOHN KEANE: Michael brought the Chickasaw Mudd Puppies into my studio. Michael also brought in the Daisy Group, Opal Foxx Quartet

THE AUTEUR AT WORK
(photo by Geoff Gans)

and of course Vic Chestnutt. Mike Mills most recently worked with Green House and did an ep for his brother Mitch's band, Three Walls Down. It was originally going to be a demo and they put it out. Peter has brought in countless bands. He did Dashboard Saviours, Run Westy Run, Kevn Kinney, Uncle Tupelo and Robyn Hitchcock. Those guys have all pretty much kept me in business.

> *"Probably the most important thing to me as a media figure and as a name producer is that there not be any misunderstanding about my motive or why I am doing this. I think that obviously I am thrilled to be anyway connected to Vic Chestnutt. I think he is an amazing performer and artist, and that applies to all the bands. I just hope that, and I think that this is the case, on hearing the music and hearing all the different bands, 'Produced by Michael Stipe' will step into the background and the music will just take over. I think that makes me serve as more of an inter-agent between the unheard and the now aware of."*
> —Michael Stipe to *Flagpole*, March 20, 1991

MARC WALLACE: A day off for Michael might include driving out to his family's because they are number one on his list. He never really has a day free though. He always has things going on. He likes to go shopping and go drink coffee and do the simple things.

DEXTER WEAVER: One day Michael's mother and grandmother and sister and some friends were here all seated at one table. The next thing I knew, Michael eased through the door with a hat down like over his eyes and just slid in and sat next to his mother. They all bought mugs and glasses and auto tags. Most of them are vegetarians except for the grandmother. Michael Stipe's grandmother is the only one that ate meat so she got the fried chicken—white meat. But he and his mother both love my squash casserole, field peas and fried okra. Radio stations from around the world ask me if I will change the names on my menu to Buck's Barbecue or Stipe Squash Casserole, but I told them no.

MARC WALLACE: Michael stays on top of everything. Some of his favorites right now are Grant Lee Buffalo, Utah Saints, Massive Attack. Right now he's very into hi-NRG dance music. He's a big fan of Peter Gabriel and The Smiths. He also likes live bands.

NEIL FEINEMAN [freelance editor/writer]: Rhino Records in LA did an in-store with Grant Lee Buffalo. It was your typical 40-person California assortment of surfer types and record company hangers-on. There was this very strange looking man there. He was so surprising looking that I thought it couldn't be Michael Stipe. [*Some mutual friends*] had been wanting to introduce us for some time and said, "Oh good, you can finally meet Michael." He didn't seem approachable. He was dressed in a costumey way. As he started walking toward us, I just bolted. I literally ran out of the room. My instinct was to bail.

DAVID ZWART: Michael is still supportive of our band [*the Daisy Group*] and definitely more supportive than most people in his position might be.

HOWARD FINSTER: In New York they are doing a Howard Finster Foundation and Michael is one of the board members of it. They are trying to get artists grants.

MARC WALLACE: Michael likes the work of Todd Murphy, an artist from Atlanta and the photographer Sally Mann. He's into photography himself right now. That's his big thing. He's apprenticing with local photographers and getting it down. He does a great job. Sometimes Michael will pull out a home movie camera and experiment with old cameras.

NEIL FEINEMAN: Michael's photographs are equally interesting as any number of photographers' who have a small chance of getting retrospectives of their work published in magazines. When he approached me at Ray Gun [*Stipe is a contributing photographer to the magazine*], I said I would love to run his photos, though I hadn't seen them. I figured he would want to be represented as a photographer rather than as a rock star whose photographs were placed in an arty magazine. But he was clearly trading off his name. He wanted to build up a portfolio of published photographs. I heard from people he was anxious to get a book publisher for them.

HOWARD FINSTER: R.E.M. are under about a 10 million dollar contract the last I heard from them. MTV, the biggest network in the United States called on me to do a painting for them for $15,000. They got ahold of my agent and they wanted me and Stipe(s) to do another tape together and Michael called me from California and told me, "Howard, I've got to see you soon." I figured that his manager probably wouldn't let him do it because I didn't hear any more about it. This was about a year ago.

MARC WALLACE: Michael is a good laugh. The great thing about being here in Athens is that we don't have to see him live the rock star life and we always feel equal no matter what. Although we know what he does and we know who he is, unless we go to a big city and hang out with him for a while, he doesn't subject us to the rock star thing and that's good. He has a great sense of humor and he's a really good person, but people don't see it. The people that are close to him know, but other people don't see it.

JARED BAILEY: We had a benefit for our soundman Bruce Neese who needed an operation in August of 93. We asked Michael if he would play, and he said yes, as long as he could play with Vic Chestnutt. Michael came out in a cowboy hat with a boombox playing "Rhinestone Cowboy." He danced and lip synched to it then he played five or six songs with Vic and David Barbe from Sugar. Then Kevn Kinney came out and Mike Mills played bass and they did "Rockville." The final encore, Michael came out and did "The One I Love" with them.

MARC WALLACE: Michael socializes every night. I think he was away so much [*on tour*], no one ever saw him. Now that he's here, he likes to go out.

ARMISTEAD WELLFORD: Michael and I were friends (thank God) before he was ever in a band. He used to be real self-conscious, even though everyone liked him. Now so many people want to be his friend because of the music he's given them. There are so many people he has access to that will tell him what he wants to hear. I don't think he really likes to hear that all the time.

SEAN BOURNE: Peter is a real nice guy and has even bought some of my artwork, but I'm not pals with any of those guys.

KEN FECHTNER: Peter doesn't seem to know whether what they do will be successful. He knows what he likes. As big as they are, I think he still does it because he likes music. Every time you see him he's dragging out singles to play for you.

STEVE WYNN: I think the main difference between Peter then and now is that when he goes to a bookstore or a record store now, he can walk through and pick up everything he wants, no problem.

DANNY BEARD: Pete never seems real comfortable out in public or maybe that's how he is all the time. I don't think he's real comfortable with being famous, which is understandable.

DON DIXON: The amazing thing to me is how *little* they've changed, not how much. These guys have forged an incredible career with incredible amount of integrity. I think a lot of it has to do with being protected from the bone-crushing and jarring crap by Bert and Jefferson. They babied the band in a way that allowed them to maintain a naive approach. They are still protected, but in a really wonderful way. I have a huge amount of respect for Jefferson because I don't think people realize what a hard job he has and how dedicated to them he is.

DIANA J. CROWE: In my opinion, Mike really hasn't changed that much. He is almost exactly the way he was in high school. Bill has gotten a lot quieter. I think the fame and the money—he didn't really quite know what to do with it. Once they reached a certain level, he kind of quieted down. He kind of faded into the background and wanted to watch the other people make things happen for a while. I know that being recognized everywhere he goes bothers him and he didn't go anywhere for a long, long time. He still has a pretty low profile.

DAVID ZWART: I think at some point the Daisy Group will probably work with Mike Mills because we've talked about it and he's real supportive of local bands.

JOHN KEANE: I think there are a lot bands that want to sound like R.E.M. For a while there was a lot of R.E.M.-clones in Athens. After a while, it wasn't the hip thing to do anymore. They are sort of a musicians' band. A lot of musicians really like those records and the way they are produced, so I get a lot of business like that.

DAVID ZWART: Everybody in Athens hates you if you are associated with R.E.M. at all. It couldn't be more than a hundred people, so it doesn't really matter, but I don't see how they can condemn R.E.M. If anyone could carry themselves the way Peter or Michael do if they were in their shoes . . . Most people couldn't function the way R.E.M. does and not let it affect them. They are really a couple of classy guys.

BRUCE MCGUIRE: The fact they still have any connection to Athens is pretty amazing. They could have abandoned it a long time ago, but they don't even play off that fact. They never have. I have no idea how much time they even spend there. Seems like any time I run into Michael he's in New York.

ARMISTEAD WELLFORD: There has always been huge support from people in Athens wishing them well. They've built up a good energy. They are the kings of the town, that's for sure.

BRIAN CRANE: Every single one of them has sunk money into local businesses or started businesses of their own. Michael's into buying old buildings and saving them from the wrecking ball and putting up nice independent locally owned businesses like the Grit and the

Daily Grocery. They've been real supportive of local music by producing different bands and talking to record labels for them. They've showed the bands the ropes because they've been through it all and know what the hell is going on.

DAILY SPECIALS SERVED UP AT THE GRIT
(*photo by Geoff Gans*)

LANCE SMITH: The last time I was in Athens I realized the only thing to do is to decide where to go eat and whose porch to sit on. I only get back there at Christmas and I don't like to go in summer because it's too hot.

ARMISTEAD WELLFORD: One night in the Fall of 1993, Alejandro Escovedo played in town and Jefferson, Michael, Vic Chestnutt, Kevn Kinney, Syd Straw and some other people and I all went over to Jerry Ayers' (who wrote "52 Girls" for the B-52's) house afterwards. It was just like the old days. Alejandro was singin' and Kevn did a song and Vic did a song and Syd did some songs. Michael didn't do any songs. But it was just like the old days. Michael said to me, "Hey it's good to see you. I haven't seen you in a long time," and I said, "I see you all over the place. I see you on TV or read your name." He said, "Ah, you've been seeing the two-dimensional me."

BRIAN CRANE: If R.E.M. got together anywhere else, I think the same thing would have happened for them. They have a real exact idea of what they don't want to do, and not so much of an idea of what they want to do. That's rare in this world. They've been great about staying here when at the point they are at in their careers, it's more problematic to be here than it is to be somewhere else. There aren't the giant lines of communication here, that's why when they want to work on their next record they have to pick a city in America and go there. They really can't do it here.

> *"We just want to make the albums we want to make. To be in complete control of what we do. We don't have any commercial goals at all. You hope your records sell, but if this album didn't sell absolutely one copy I wouldn't feel like it's a bad record. I won't feel that we've made a mistake. Commercially, we just assume if we make good records, eventually we're going to sell a fair amount of them. But I don't get up in the morning and think about how to sell records. I get up in the morning and think about how to write songs and how to differ what we're doing, how to push on to a new way of writing songs."*
>   —Peter Buck to the *Gavin Report,* July 19, 1985

JOHN KEANE: I think they are getting back together in the early part of '94 to begin working on material for the next album. Peter called me up the other day. He wants to bring in Nanci Griffith and do some stuff with her. An acoustic thing similar to what he did with Uncle Tupelo.

ROBERT LLOYD: A band can keep going as long as it wants. A band never has to make a record or play to more than four people and it can still last for twenty years if the people that are in the band still want to keep doing it. Another band might have been discouraged to continue when R.E.M. wasn't, so they've sustained.

GEORGINA FALZARANO: I think what keeps them from falling into a creative rut is that they keep switching styles a bit on each record. Apparently the next album is going to sound very much like the Rolling Stones' *Let It Bleed.* I think they need a good rock album and I think they all realize that it's okay to put out a good rock album. There's nothing wrong with that. People really want to hear them rock again.

BRUCE MCGUIRE: I still seem to be interested in what R.E.M. is doing. It's very weird. It's always amazed me how I've continued to love them. All the other bands I got into at that time I've gotten so damn sick of.

KATHLEEN O'BRIEN: If I get married I'm going to send these guys an invitation even if I haven't seen them in all these years because they were a big part of my life.

ROBERT LLOYD: At a certain point, being R.E.M. may not be important to its members anymore. They talk about having a set date when they are going to break up [*New Year's Eve, 1999*]. They spend so little time being R.E.M. these days it could easily be an option not to be R.E.M. at all. It's gotta be different than it was. At one point they were touring all of the time, riding in a van and living in hotels with each other. It was all about conquering new areas together. At this point, where is there to go?

"Every time you make a record, you think, why am I doing this?
When we get to the point where we don't have anything to say to
each other musically, you couldn't pay me to do it. If we start
making bad records, I'll quit, but I'm still learning things. We do
what we do. Eventually there'll be a time when we're not needed
in the scheme of things. I'd like to think we'll figure it out before
everyone else does."

　　　　　　　　　　　　　　　　—Peter Buck to *Pulse!*, October 1992

DON DIXON: We have very few legitimate bands—guys that have known each other for a long time, gotten into one car and driven all over the country together. It makes them different—the way they play together when you finally turn that tape recorder on.

BRUCE MCGUIRE: They never seem to follow anyone, but they also seem to be the kind of people that don't consciously try to do something different.

ROBERT LLOYD: I don't think they've made any dishonest records, because they don't want to live with bullshit. The fact that they all have veto power is going to keep the music honest. As established artists, their job now is to find ways to keep their art honest.

JACKSON HARING: R.E.M. makes music of great enduring strength and beauty.

In July of 1994 R.E.M. completed work on their ninth
studio album, Monster, *after spending the early part of the*
year recording in New Orleans and Los Angeles. They will
begin touring again in January of 1995. It is their first
time on the road since 1989's Green World Tour. R.E.M.
has stated on numerous occasions the band will cease to
exist at midnight, December 31, 1999.

DISCOGRAPHY

The following releases were commercially available in the U.S. and U.K. at the time of release. IRS/WB prefixes are U.S. releases. All other prefixes are U.K. releases. Most seven and twelve-inch titles are out-of-print and command high prices on the collector's market. For more complete promotional item and international discography information, please consult *Remnants, The R.E.M. Collector's Handbook and Price Guide*.

ALBUMS/EPS

1982
    Chronic Town (IRS SP70502)

1983
    Murmur (IRS 70014)

1984
    Reckoning (IRS 70044, IRSA 7045)

1985
    Fables of the Reconstruction (IRS 5592, MIRF 1003)

1986
    Lifes Rich Pageant (IRS 5783, MIRG 1014)

1987
    Dead Letter Office (IRS 70054) Collected b-sides
    Document (IRS 42059, MIRG 1025)

1988
    Eponymous (IRS 6262) Collected album tracks
    Green (Warner Brothers 9 25795, WX234)

1991

   Out of Time (Warner Brothers 9 26496, WX404)

1992

   Automatic For The People (Warner Brothers 9 45055, WX404)

SEVEN-INCH SINGLES

1981

   "Radio Free Europe"/"Sitting Still" Hib-Tone (HT 0001)

1983

   "Radio Free Europe"/"There She Goes
      Again" (IR9916, PFP 1017)

1984

   "So. Central Rain (I'm Sorry)"/"King of the
      Road" (IR 9927, IRS 105)

   "Don't Go Back to Rockville"/"Catapult"
      (live) (IR9931)

   "Don't Go Back To Rockville"/ "Wolves,
      Lower" (IRS 107)

1985

   "Can't Get There From Here"/"Bandwagon"(IRS 52642, IRM 102)

   "Driver 8"/"Crazy" (IRS 52678, IRM 105)

   "Wendell Gee"/"Crazy"/"Ages of You"/"Burning Down" (IRMD 105)

1986

   "Fall on Me"/"Rotary 10" (IRS 52883, IRM 121)

   "Superman"/"White Tornado" (IRS 52971, IRM 128)

1987

   "The One I Love"/"Maps and Legends"
      (live at McCabe's) (IRS 53171)

   "Its the End of the World As We Know
      It"/"This One Goes Out" (live) (IRM 145)

   "The One I Love"/"Last Date" (IRM 146)

1988

   "Its the End of the World As We Know It
      (And I Feel Fine)" (edit)/"Last Date" (IRS
      53220)

   "Finest Worksong"/"Time After Time" etc. (live) (IRM161)

   "The One I Love"/"Fall On Me" (IRM 173)

1989

"Stand"/"Memphis Train Blues" (WB 7-27688, W7577)

"Orange Crush"/"Ghost Riders" (W2960,W2960X,W2960B)

"Pop Song '89"/"Pop Song '89" (acoustic) (WB 7-27640)

"Stand"/"Pop Song '89" (acoustic) (W2833, W2833W)

"Get Up"/"Funtime" (WB 7-22791)

1991

"Losing My Religion"/"Rotary Eleven" (WB 7-19392, W0015)

"Shiny Happy People"/"Forty Second Song" (WB 7-19242, W0027)

"Radio Song"/"Love is All Around" (WB 7-19246, W0072)

"Near Wild Heaven"/"Pop Song '89" (live) (W0055)

"The One I Love"/"Crazy" (IRM 178)

1992

"Drive"/"Winged Mammal Theme"
   (WB 7-18729)

"Drive"/"World Leader Pretend" (W0136)

"Man on the Moon"/"Turn You Inside-Out"
   (W0143)

1993

"Man on the Moon"/"New Orleans
   Instrumental #2" (WB 7-18642)

"The Sidewinder Sleeps Tonite"/"The Lion Sleeps Tonight"
   (WB 7-18523)

"The Sidewinder Sleeps Tonite"/"Get Up" (W0152)

"Everybody Hurts"/"Pop Song '89" (W0169)

"Find The River"/"Everybody Hurts" (live from MTV Video Music
   Awards) (WO211)

TWELVE-INCH SINGLES

1983

"Talk about The Passion"/"Shaking Through"/"Carnival of
   Sorts"/"1,000,000" (IRS PFSX 1026)

1984

"South Central Rain"/"Voice of Harold"/"Pale Blue Eyes" (IRSX105)

"Don't Go Back To Rockville"/"Wolves, Lower"/"9-9"
   (live)/"Gardening at Night" (live) (IRSX107)

1985

"Can't Get There From Here"/"Bandwagon"/"Burning Hell" (IRT102)

"Wendell Gee"/"Crazy"/"Driver 8" (IRT 105)

1986

"Fall On Me"/"Rotary 10"/"Toys in the Attic" (IRMT 121)

1987

"The One I Love"/"The One I Love" (live at McCabe's 1987)/"Maps and Legends" (live at McCabe's) (IRS 23792)

"Superman"/"White Tornado"/"Femme Fatale" (IRMT128)

"Its The End of the World..."/"This One Goes Out"(live)/"Maps and Legends" (live) (IRMT 145)

"The One I Love"/"Last Date"/"Disturbance at the Heron House" (IRMT 146)

1988

"Finest Worksong" (Lengthy Club Mix)/"Finest Worksong" (other mix)/"Time After Time" etc. (live) (IRS 23850, IRMT 161)

"The One I Love"/"Fall On Me"/"So. Central Rain" (IRMT 173)

1989

"Stand"/"Memphis Train Blues"/"Untitled" (instrumental remix) (W7577T)

"Orange Crush"/"Ghost Riders"/"Dark Globe" (W2960T)

"Stand"/"Pop Song '89" (acoustic)/"Skin Tight" (live) (W2833T)

1991

"Radio Song" (Tower of Luv Bug Mix/"Love is All Around" (live on Rockline 1991)/"Belong" (live from Green World Tour, Greensboro,NC 1989) (WB 9 40229-0)

"Losing My Religion"/"Rotary Eleven"/"After Hours" (live) (W0015T)

"Shiny Happy People"/"Forty Second Song"/"Losing My Religion" (acoustic) (W0027T)

"Near Wild Heaven"/"Pop Song '89" (live)/"Half a World Away" (live) (W0055T)

"Radio Song"/"Love Is All Around"/"Shiny Happy People" (Music Mix) (W0072T)

1993

"Nightswimming/"World Leader Pretend"(live)/"Belong
(live)/"Low"(live) (W0184TP)

"Everybody Hurts" (WB 9 40992) with
"Mandolin Strum"/"Belong" (live on
Mountain Stage 1992)/"Orange Crush"
(live Green World Tour 1989) and
(40989) "Star Me Kitten" (demo)/
"Losing My Religion" (live on Mountain
Stage 1992)/"Organ Song"

CD SINGLES

1987

"The One I Love"/"Last Date"/"Disturbance at the Heron House"
(DIRM 146)

1988

"Finest Worksong"/"Time After Time" etc. (live)/"Its the End of the
World..." (DIRM 161)

"The One I Love"/"Fall On Me"/"So. Central Rain" (DIRM 173)

1989

"Stand"/"Memphis Train Blues" (WB2-27688)

1991

"The One I Love"/"This One Goes Out"(live)/"Maps and Legends"
(live) (DIRMT 178)

"The One I Love"/"Driver 8" (live)/"Disturbance at the Heron
House"(live)/"Crazy" (IRMX 178)

"Its the End of the World..."/"Radio Free Europe"/"Time After Time"
etc. (live) (DIRMT 180)

"Radio Song" (Tower of Luv Bug Mix)/"Love is All Around" (live on
Rockline 1991)/"Belong" (live on Green World Tour, Greensboro,
NC 1989) (WB 9 40229-2)

1992

"Drive"/"Winged Mammal Theme" (WB 9 18729-2)

"Its the End of the World..."/"Last Date"/"White Tornado"/"Radio
Free Europe" (Hib-Tone mix) (DIRMX 180)

1993

"Man on the Moon"/"New Orleans Instrumental #2"
(WB 9-18642-2)

"The Sidewinder Sleeps Tonite"/"The Lion Sleeps Tonight"
(WB 9 18523-2)

"Everybody Hurts" (WB 9 40989-22) released as CD digi-packs with
"Mandolin Strum"/ "Belong" (live on Mountain Stage
1992)/"Orange Crush" (live Green World Tour 1989) and
(40992-2) "Star Me Kitten" (demo)/"Losing My Religion" (live on
Mountain Stage 1992)/"Organ Song"

FLEXI-DISCS

December 1982
Trouser Press, "Wolves, Lower"

February 1985
Bucketfull of Brains, "Tighten Up"

May 1986
The Bob #27, "Femme Fatale"

November 1989
Sassy, "Dark Globe"

March 1992
Bucketfull of Brains, "Academy Fight Song" (live, Green World Tour
1989, black vinyl)

FAN CLUB CHRISTMAS SINGLES

December 1988
"Parade of the Wooden Soldiers"/"See No Evil"

December 1989
"Good King Wenceslas"/"Academy Fight
Song"

December 1990
"Ghost Reindeer in the Sky"/"Summertime"

December 1991
"Baby,Baby"/"Christmas Griping"

December 1992
"Where's Captain Kirk?"/"Toyland"

December 1993
"Silver Bells"/"Charlie Brown Christmas"

COMPILATIONS AND SOUNDTRACKS
(non-LP tracks, U.S. release)

1984

"Windout," *Bachelor Party* soundtrack (IRS SP 70047)

1986

"Ages of You," *Live For Life* (IRS IRS5731)

1987

"Romance," *Made in Heaven* soundtrack (Elektra 9 60729-1)

"(All I've Got To Do Is) Dream"/"Swan Swan H," *Athens GA.-Inside/Out* soundtrack (IRS IRS6185)

1990

"I Walked With A Zombie," *Where The Pyramid Meets The Eye—A Tribute to Roky Erickson* (Warner Brothers 9 26442-2)

1991

"First We Take Manhattan," *I'm Your Fan—The Songs of Leonard Cohen by...* (Atlantic 82349-2)

"Tom's ?" by Bingo Hand Job, *Tom's Album* (A&M 75021 5363-2)

"Fretless," *Until The End Of The World* soundtrack (WB 2-26707)

1993

"It's A Free World Baby," *Coneheads* soundtrack (WB 45345)

"Drive" (live at the 40 Watt '92), *Alternative NRG* compilation (Hollywood 614492)

"Photograph," with Natalie Merchant, *Born to Choose* (Rykodisc 10256)

1994

"Wall of Death," *Beat the Retreat—The Songs of Richard Thompson* (Capitol 79404)

SELECT GUEST APPEARANCES/SIDE PROJECTS

Michael Stipe—vocals

1984

"Hot Nights in Georgia," Jason and the Scorchers *Fervor* (EMI 19008)

1985

"Clustering Train," "Omaha," "Boy (Go)," Golden Palominos *Visions of Excess* (Celluloid 6118)

1987

"A Campfire Song," 10,000 Maniacs *In My Tribe* (Elektra 60738, Elektra EKT41)

"Eureka" and "Grow Wild," Hugo Largo *Drum* (Relativity 88561, reissued on Opal 25768, Land 002)

1989

"Kid Fears," *Indigo Girls* (Epic 45044, CBS 4634911)

"Little April Shower," *Stay Awake* (A&M 3918)

"Future 40's (String of Pearls)," Syd Straw *Surprise* (Virgin 91266, Virgin VUS6)

1991

"I'll Give You My Skin," with the Indigo Girls, *Tame Yourself* compilation (R.N.A./Rhino 70772)

"She Doesn't Exist," Robyn Hitchcock and the Egyptians *Perspex Island* (A&M 75021 5368)

"You Woke Up My Neighborhood," Billy Bragg *Don't Try This At Home* (Elektra 61121, Go! Discs 828279)

1992

"Trout," Neneh Cherry *Homebrew* (Virgin 86516, Circa 25)

"Civilization Vs. Technology," with KRS-One, *H.E.A.L. Civilization Vs. Technology* (Elektra 61141)

1993

"Candy Everybody Wants" and "To Sir With Love," 10,000 Maniacs "Few And Far Between" CD single (Elektra 66296)

"Arms of Love," *In Defense of Animals* (Restless 772747)

"Full Moon," with Annie Ross and the Low Note Quintet, *Short Cuts* soundtrack (Imago 72787-21014)

1994

"Your Ghost," Kristin Hersh, *Hips and Makers* (Sire/Reprise 45413)

Peter Buck—guitar, mandolin, dulcimer

1984

"I Will Dare," The Replacements *Let It Be* (Twin Tone 8441, Zippo 002)

1985

"The Party," *The Dream Academy* (Warner Brothers 25265, Blanco Y Negro 6)

"Wind Out," The Fleshtones *Speed Connection II* (IRS 26412)

1988

"Balloon Man," "Chinese Bones," "Flesh Number One," Robyn Hitchcock and the Egyptians *Globe of Frogs* (A&M 5182)

1989

Drivin' n' Cryin' *Mystery Road* (Island 91226)

"Wild Mountain Thyme," with Robyn Hitchcock as Nigel and The Crosses, *Time Between—A Tribute to The Byrds* (Imaginary III 400)

"Madonna of the Wasps," "Wax Doll," "Swirling," "Freeze," Robyn Hitchcock and the Egyptians *Queen Elvis* (A&M 5241)

Kevn Kinney *MacDougal Blues* (Island 91331)

1991

Robyn Hitchcock and the Egyptians *Perspex Island* (A&M 75021 5368)

"You Woke Up My Neighborhood" and "Everywhere," Billy Bragg *Don't Try This At Home* (Elektra 61121, Go! Discs 828279)

1992

"Third of July," The Jody Grind *Lefty's Deceiver* (DB 155)

"A Dazzling Display," Steve Wynn *Dazzling Display* (Rhino 70283)

1995

"Slowly Fading Evening Sky," David Lewis *No Straight Line* (DejaDisc 3215)

Bill Berry—drums, solo project

1988

Michelle Malone *New Experience* (Aluminum Jane 01)

1989

13111 *My Bible is the Latest TV Guide* (Dog Gone 13111)

Mike Mills—bass, keyboards, vocals

1987

"Return," Waxing Poetics *Hermitage* (Emergo 9610)

1989

Vibrating Egg *Come On In Here If You Want To* (Dog Gone 333)

1991

"Shake This Town," Robbie Robertson *Storyville* (Geffen 24303)

1993

"Soma," Smashing Pumpkins *Siamese Dream* (Virgin 88267)

1994

Backbeat soundtrack (Virgin 39386)

Berry/Buck/Mills—backing band

1985

> Hindu Love Gods "Gonna Have A Good Time Tonight"/"Narrator" (IRS 52867)

1987

> Warren Zevon *Sentimental Hygiene* (Virgin 90603-1, Virgin V2433) Stipe adds vocal to "Bad Karma"

1989

> "Tried to Be True," *Indigo Girls* (Epic 45044, CBS 4634911)

1990

> *Hindu Love Gods* (Giant 24406)

1992

> The Troggs *Athens, Andover* (Castle ESS 180)

VIDEOS/LASERDISCS (U.S. release)

1987

> *R.E.M. Succumbs* (A&M Video 089873, LV38403)
>
> *Athens, GA-Inside/Out* (Polygram 041650-3)

1990

> *Pop Screen* (Warner Reprise Video 38156-3, 38156-6)
>
> *Tourfilm* (Warner Reprise Video 38184-3, 38184-6)

1991

> *This Film is On* (Warner Reprise Video 38254-3, 38254-6)

BOX SET

1989

> *Singleactiongreen* (WB7-22780) four picture sleeve singles from *Green*

RECOMMENDED BOOTLEG RECORDINGS

> * Indicates top sound quality and + indicates historical value or performances specifically referred to in the main text.

1980

> *Bodycount at Tyrone's* (LP,Brigand Records BRIG007) Recorded live at Tyrone's on October 4, 1980, this is the earliest gig released as a bootleg.+
>
> *That Beat in Time* (OMK Records OMK CD001)Recorded at Tyrone's sometime during '80-'81, it is the earliest gig released as a CD bootleg.+

1982

Carnival of Sorts (Great Dane GDRCD9020) Recorded April 24, 1982 at Merlin's, Madison, WI during the first tour. Essential early recordings, ("Ages of You," "Romance").*

1980-83

Chronic Murmurings (2 LP, Toasted Record Works 1905) Studio outtakes from Tyrone's session, Drive-In, RCA demos and Reflection. ("Dangerous Times," "Permanent Vacation").+

1983

L.I.V.E. (LP, Bandido, B006), April 8, 1983, University of Rochester, NY. This was the first R.E.M. bootleg.+

1984

Old Man Kensey (Hallmark MN 004CD) November 21, 1984, Rock City, Nottingham, U.K. Live set includes as yet unrecorded "Old Man Kensey," "Hyena," "Auctioneer" and "Driver 8."*

Unreleased Live LP (Unbelievable Music UM029) September 26, 1984, Duke University Durham, NC. The rumor at the time was that this is the live album IRS planned to release till R.E.M. vetoed the idea.+

Rock and Roll Stars (Howdy CD55519) June 27,1984 Music Hall Seattle. A typical set on the Little America Tour.*

1985

Stab It and Steer It (Adobe CD RAIN 1) Includes "Theme From Two Steps Onwards" recorded at the legendary Stock Pavillion show, May 15, 1985, Madison, WI; "I Believe" recorded at Brown University, Providence RI, April 27, 1985 plus Reflection and Rhythmic studio outtakes.+

These Days (Why Not WOT 1008) October 29, 1985. Hammersmith Palais, London plus *Lifes Rich Pageant* demos.*

1987

Acoustic '87 (Nu Noise Nun 004) May 24, 1987 McCabe's Guitar Shop, Santa Monica, CA+

Standing Room Only (Swingin' Pig) Sept. 9, 1987 Muzieckcentrum, Utrecht. The first R.E.M. CD bootleg.+

1989

Love and Squalor (Howdy CD 555-07) April 30, 1989, Orlando Arena, Green World Tour. Much bootlegged performance from a Westwood One radio show.*

1990

> *R.E.M. The Complete Unplugged Show* (RCCD 4742) MTV session.
>
> *Outtakes of Time* (R 01) demos and outtakes from *Out of Time* sessions.*
>
> *No. 8, Demos and Outtakes* (Indian IN02) Demos and outtakes from *Document, Green* and *Out of Time*.*

1991

> *From the Boderline* (Red Phantom RPCD 2038/2039) March 15, 1991, and from the Shocking Club, Milan, Italy, March 22. Excellent quality two disc set from two rare club dates. The band performed both nights as Bingo Hand Job.*
>
> *R.E.M. Acoustic Tour '91* (Real Live RLCD04) East Sound Studio 1, Toronto, May 9, 1991, Mountain Stage, Charleston, W.VA, April 28, 1991 and KCRW "Snap" Show, April 3, 1991.+

1992

> *This is It* (Red Phantom RPCD 1117) Recorded live on November 19, 1992 at the 40 Watt Club, Athens, GA. Benefit for Greenpeace. Includes two tracks from MTV Inaugural ball—"One" performed by Stipe, Mills, Larry Mullen Jr. and Adam Clayton [U2] and "Candy Everybody Wants" performed by Stipe and 10,000 Maniacs. The disc incorrectly lists "Candy" as "Hello in There" by John Prine.*

Name: michael stipe

Born: yes

Age: born in sixties

Influences: patti smith velvet underground bad jazz (pre '58)

Hobbies: token art student

Favorites:
    Color black
    Food
    Drink
    Dessert
    Clothes
    Male Singer
    Female Singer
    Group(s)

    Actor
    Actress
    Car
    City none i despise motor vehicles mass transit

Personal Ambition(s):

Professional Ambition(s):

Important Moments In Life: this bio

Important Books:

Fetishes:
    none

Comments:
    sorry i cant be more helpful here. also sorry about my typing. this is
a 1954 royal that my mother got when shen graduated from high school. same
ribbon.

we are not popsters or pop stars and try to keep the music and image as untainted as possible. not that were completely innocent or niave either... the direction well take musically depends on nothing but how the combo grows... the
change from our first song tod our last one (still unfinished) are remarkable
as far as how we went about finishing them what they hold as songs etc. the
influences are the same as when we wrote the first but perhaps are becoming
more obvious than before. we do not consider ourselves serious musicians or
god forbid artists   both of those titles carry too much connotation that im
afraid we couldnt explain... i doubt any of us could talk our way out of a
paper bag. i suppose i like the title 'folk band' who in this time would
call themselves that? folk doesnt really say much anyway but it beats the
hell out of art-rockers, dance band, pop band, rock band, political etc etc.
i hope this helps.

Denise Sullivan started out as a Bay Area freelance journalist and dj specializing in alternative rock music 11 years ago, when she was diverted by a career in the record industry. As director of publicity for independent label 415 Records, she gained press attention for such groups as Romeo Void, Translator and Wire Train. She subsequently owned a retail record store in the mid-eighties where she pioneered the idea of acoustic in-store performances from artists diverse as Peter Case and Eugene Chadbourne. After working as a regional alternative marketing manager for Warner Brothers Records in Atlanta, GA and Burbank, CA for two years, she resumed work as a journalist and has since contributed to *Ray Gun, The San Francisco Chronicle, The Nose, East Bay Express* and *Q,* among others. She is married and lives in San Francisco and *R.E.M. — Talk About The Passion: An Oral History* is her first book.